“Kindly Call M

The misadventures of
‘Fielding of the FO’,
Eurocrat Extraordinaire
and Vice-Chancellor Semipotentiary

Leslie Fielding read History at Cambridge, where he is an Honorary Fellow of Emmanuel College, and Persian at the School of Oriental and African Studies, London. He joined the then Foreign Service in 1956, working initially in Tehran and (briefly) Singapore, before being put in charge of the British Embassy in Phnom Penh, Cambodia. His subsequent diplomatic career took him to Paris, in the political section; Brussels, as a director in the European Commission; Tokyo, as EU Ambassador; and back to Brussels, as Director-General for External Relations. He has been a Visiting Fellow at St Antony's College, Oxford, and Vice-Chancellor of the University of Sussex. His *Before the Killing Fields: Witness to Cambodia and the Vietnam War* was published by I.B. Tauris in 2008. Previously, he had written *Europe as a Global Partner* in 1991, and contributed to two travel anthologies: *Travellers' Tales*, in 1999 and *More Travellers' Tales*, in 2005. He is married to the medievalist, Sally Harvey; they have two children. Sir Leslie was made KCMG (the 'Kindly Call Me God' of the title) in 1988.

“Kindly Call Me God”

The misadventures of
‘Fielding of the FO’,
Eurocrat Extraordinaire
and Vice-Chancellor Semipotentiary

Leslie Fielding

BOERMANS
BOOKS

ISBN 978-0-9562167-0-0

A full CIP record for this book is available from the British Library
A full CIP record is available from the Library of Congress
Library of Congress Catalog Card Number: available
Front cover image of Sir Leslie as Vice-Chancellor of Sussex University from a portrait by Mr Zhu Guang, 1992.
Back cover photograph of author, posturing in Phnom Penh, 1966
Published 2009 by Boermans Books.
Printed in Times New Roman 12
Printed and bound in Great Britain by
CPI Antony Rowe, Chippenham and Eastbourne

'Sir Leslie Fielding reminds us that a sense of humour remains as indispensable as ever. If readers of this book come to realise that diplomacy is fun, then he will have done a great service to a profession which is often misunderstood and misrepresented'. Lord Hannay

This engaging and unusual book does not set out to be a work of scholarly analysis in the field of international relations, nor a history of British diplomacy. Instead, the author gives us relaxation in the form of a series of, at times, extremely funny true-life anecdotes and adventures.

It is hard to read 'Dracula, Prince of Darkness' or 'The Year of the Cat in Harry Honkers' without a giggle. There is also pure adventure at the diplomatic 'sharp end' ('From Monte with Farsi' or 'Uncle Sam and the Norwegian Mariners'). And the author brings alive some remote and mysterious places ('Ise-Jingu Out of Season' and 'The Crocodile Princess').

Deliciously, Leslie Fielding's stories consistently poke fun at the writer and puncture his occasional (and clearly intentional) pomposities – beginning with his first day at the Foreign Office ('Out of the door and onto the Street in Carlton House Terrace') and continuing through his career ('Alburz Ambush' and 'Pacific Pidgin'). There is warmth and humanity, too. The Vice-Chancellor clearly liked his revolting students ('Welcome, Lord Les') fully as much as the people he worked with and led in Brussels.

In addition to the exotic and absurd, a vein of seriousness runs through the author's reflections on the European Commission; and through his all-too-credible, on the spot accounts of highly charged international negotiations, as the protagonists come up to the wire. In 'Death Squad in Belgrade' and 'Eyeball-to-Eyeball Across the Atlantic', we are reading about life in the front line.

Moving from the anecdotal to the analytical, as befits an academic observer as well as a diplomatic practitioner, the author asks (tongue in cheek?) whether diplomats are immoral, whether they are unnecessary and whether they can be prone to hubris, complacency and misplaced nationalism.

Sir Leslie comes across as an all-rounder, at home in any setting, from embassy to university, from darkest Dartmoor to deepest Cambodian jungle – and apparently in almost any language. But he writes to entertain as well as to inform.

Also by Leslie Fielding

BEFORE THE KILLING FIELDS: WITNESS TO CAMBODIA AND THE VIETNAM WAR

A wonderfully entertaining read and hugely germane to many of our present preoccupations in international relations.

Christopher Patten

A vivid picture of the life of a diplomat abroad; usually arduous, sometimes uncomfortable and dangerous; pompous routine varied by passages of the comical and wildly unexpected.

Philip Zeigler

Matches that other outstanding account of duty done on a far frontier – John Master's 'Bugles and Tiger'.

Milton Osborne

Leslie Fielding was one of Britain's more unorthodox and original diplomats… For all students of diplomacy and of Cambodia, this book provides a vivid and colourful picture of life at the sharp end.

International Affairs

Written with panache and verve… a joy to read… reminds us of a seemingly lost world of good fun but also serious thought and action.

Asian Affairs

Fielding gives a gripping account of Cambodia under the mercurial Sihanouk, as the shadows closed in.

Literary Review

Fielding… cuts a dash in the drawing rooms and opium dens of Phnom Penh… As 'Number One Twister', he developed a better relationship with Sihanouk than his US counterparts… He is proud of a time when Britain stood up to America and did not go to war.

Daily Telegraph

Dedication

For my wife Sally
(who gave up her career, that I might continue mine)
and for our two children (Emma and Leo).
Also, for my friends (who will not be disappointed)
and for my enemies (who will not be surprised).

Contents

Part Two: The European Commission

Part Three: Homecoming

Part Four: To Be Serious

Part Five: In Conclusion

FOREWORD

The Rt Hon. The Lord Hannay of Chiswick GCMG, CH

This book is a diplomatic miscellany, not in any way a classical diplomatic memoir – and all the better for that. The second oldest profession in the world has made its contributions to literature but many of them have tended to be works either of self-importance or self-justification. Leslie Fielding's collection of picaresque and tongue-in-cheek stories falls into neither of those traps, being willing to poke fun at himself and to admit mistakes of analysis or judgement.

The light-heartedness of the tone partly masks some important trends in the conduct of diplomacy over the last half century.

It is hard to exaggerate the changes that have taken place over the period of some fifty years since Leslie Fielding (and I) first joined the Foreign Office in the 1950s. Then, newly-joined desk officers arrived at the gentlemanly hour of 10 o'clock to work in offices still heated (perhaps warmed gets it better) by open coke fires. Telegrams arrived intermittently by a system of vacuum-driven tubes, then were carried along the corridors by elderly messengers on massive trolleys which clattered and banged incessantly. A pervasive smell of boiled cabbage percolated round the Palmerstonian building from the canteen far below. Every paper that entered the Foreign Office was carefully registered by an army of clerks and then, resplendently covered by a separate folder, began to make its way up through the hierarchy gathering comments – often long, copious and self-indulgent comments – appended in manuscript at each stage. No fax machines, no photocopiers, no e-mails. Now, several communications revolutions later, that pattern of work would be unrecognisable to today's officials, hard-driven by the demand for instant reactions to fast-moving events around the world and the requirements of the 24-hour, seven-days-a-week media scene. Not much of that great diplomat Talleyrand's *douceur de vivre* left now.

And then there has been the massive switch away from diplomacy focussed on bilateral relations between individual countries towards the conduct of an ever-greater amount of international negotiation through multilateral organisations, the United Nations, the European Union and many others. In parallel, those negotiations have come to encompass a whole range of subjects that would previously have been considered purely domestic matters. The great waves of interdependence and globalisation have washed onto the beaches of individual countries and transformed their diplomacy. Leslie Fielding's surfboard has carried him from one wave to the other with effortless aplomb and, as ever, with a sharp eye for the ridiculous and pretentious.

The qualities required of a successful diplomat have probably changed rather less than the milieu in which he or she applies them. Integrity and adaptability remain high amongst them. But Leslie Fielding reminds us that a sense of humour remains as indispensable as ever. If readers of this book come to realise that diplomacy is fun, then he will have done a great service to a profession which is often misunderstood and misrepresented.

AUTHOR'S INTRODUCTION

The elegant court sword that I used to wear with my diplomatic uniform was a glittering object of display. With its gilded hilt and golden pommel, it was carried in a shiny black scabbard. But the chased and ciphered blade, so discreetly concealed in lacquered leather, was long and thin and endowed with a wickedly sharp point. Beneath the urbanities and apparently civilised conventions, diplomacy – and the promotion of the nation's interests overseas – can be a fierce affair.

The fact is that the profession is, like rugby football, a contact sport; and a diplomatic career today is not for the faint-hearted. As The Times put it, recently: 'A modern diplomat can expect to spend more time in posts wearing dusty boots and flak jackets than sipping cocktails and munching canapés at embassy receptions'. I admit that I had been under the vague impression, on joining the Diplomatic Service, that I was signing up for a civilised career of elegance and ease, waltzing under the chandeliers with beautiful Contessas, and consorting with Monarchs, Presidents, Prime Ministers and the like, in the Chancelleries of the Great Powers. But I was soon to be disabused.

In my day, as a British diplomat, I have been stoned by religious fanatics in the city of Qom; pushed about and shot at – and driven to conduct peace talks in an opium bordello – in Cambodia; chased, with intent, by the Paris riot police; routinely expected to work through the night in Brussels and Geneva, and even to negotiate for over sixty hours virtually without sleep in Belgrade; treated on occasion by our American friends as an opponent, not an ally.

So this is an autobiography by anecdote, a description by vignette of the life of a career diplomat, civil servant and academic. The episodes and encounters which follow – however implausible some of them may seem – all did actually take place. They illustrate the true-life travels and travails, the maverick misdemeanours and misadventures, of 'Fielding of the FO', later Eurocrat Extraordinaire and Vice-Chancellor Semipotentiary, mostly far away but some of them closer to home.

The book does not cover my earlier years – at school, or in the army, or as an undergraduate. Nor my later years, part-time international consultant and part-time country 'squarson'. Nor my inner life: important things like love, marriage, money and religion are omitted – as is my affection for both Verdi and Monteverdi. Instead, the focus is on what happened in the 36 years between my joining the FO in 1956 and my leaving the University of Sussex in 1992.

Thus, Part One deals with the Diplomatic Service. Chapters 1 to 24 cover joining the FO as a crass, self-congratulatory greenhorn (2); my time in the Tehran Embassy (3-8); my assignments in King Charles Street (9 and 24); and the years spent at the 'sharp end' in Phnom Penh and Paris (1, and 10-23).

In Part Two, I move to the EU. Chapters 25-38 give the essence of inside life in the European Commission (Brussels/Tokyo/Brussels), latterly in charge of the external relations side.

Part Three (39-42) covers the return home and the reintegration into national life as a University Vice-Chancellor. In the event, diplomacy continued – not least with my undergraduates, but also in other ways; and, needless to say, old habits died hard.

Part Four (43-46) is more analytical and detached. As I did with my students and have done since in various public fora, I advance the necessity for good, professional diplomacy and debate the moral issues at the heart of it.

The Epilogue offers the benefit of personal hindsight and the Envoy signs off with a flourish of the sword (47-48).

I have suggested some background reading, for those who may be new to the game.

For a closer look 'inside Europe', the three original documents in the Annex give some finer details, written in the emotion of the moment, of my initial cultural 'shock-horror' on joining the

Brussels Commission – and my subsequent conversion.

The mood, and the degree of seriousness, varies. The episodes are, in turn, boastful and brash; meditative and mysterious; eyewitness-and action-oriented; flippant and foolish; egregious and exotic; sentimental and schmaltzy. Some are parodies of pomposity; most are self- mocking; but all of them are as true to the event as both retrospective recollection and contemporary documentation will permit. In a few instances, they 'raise the lid'; say what is normally never said.

Composing the above words about a finished manuscript, I am seated at ease, as an honorary fellow in the library of his Cambridge college. The book-lined upper floor is empty and tranquil, in the vacation. My mind inevitably goes back to undergraduate years, sitting in the same tranquil and elegant setting, more than half a century back in time; where should I go and what should I do, with a life then only just opening up before me? In my memory, those self-interrogations seem as immediate as if I had entertained them only last week.

In the event, the years which followed were to be great fun. But would I follow the same path if I were starting again in 2009? Good question. Hard question. One cannot cross the same river twice. Times have changed.

Academia, for one thing (more competitive and less well-funded than ever); Europe, for another (now with four times the original membership, but beset by ‘Euro-fatigue’ and public apathy). As for the UK (national identity, ethnic composition, social norms, religious assumptions, gap between rich and poor, economic structures, role of Cabinet and the House of Commons, form of governance, power of the media – you name it), the country has changed massively.

Whitehall has certainly departed from the 19th century Northcote-Trevelyan reforms. Sixty or so well-paid ‘political advisors’ have been introduced into the machinery of government – a scale of personal patronage at the public expense (not to mention the ninety or so sub-cabinet junior ministers) not seen in England for almost two centuries. The public service itself has been diverted from policy-making, not only to ‘delivery’, but also to a business administrative paradigm associated with the name of the late Sir Peter Kemp. Senior officials, some of them, have been driven to become courtiers of the Prime Minister, rather than servants of the state. Successive Cabinet Secretaries have been powerless to prevent this. Thatcher and Blair did not always welcome civil servants who spoke truth to power, but preferred to make policy in more restricted circles, sometimes with individuals not chosen on merit, nor required to have served any serious apprenticeship.

The FO, too, has suffered, not least from parallel diplomacy and seat-of-the-pants policy making by media-focussed counsellors and cronies under the well intentioned but unfettered new presidentialism at No. 10 – and the bloated Cabinet Office which supports and surrounds it. The knowledgeable professionals in King Charles Street have been hard put to it, at times, to cope with tragically misguided but mandatory directives from on high. All of that is probably here to stay, alas, at least for the time being.

But, to answer the question. 'Yes' to being a Vice-Chancellor again, at an institution like Sussex. Education is the key; young people are our future. 'Yes' to the European Commission – despite a large degree of UK public indifference towards the EU. There are no longer any world powers in Europe; its medium and small member states simply must hang together if they are not to hang separately, in the far from reassuring world of tomorrow. And the FO? Affirmative too. Despite everything, the British Diplomatic Service still is, and is likely to remain, among the most respected in the world.

All in all, therefore, I would not have led any other kind of life. So, in the spirit of the Prologue on the next page, I undertake to "look well to this day"; and invite you, the gentle reader, to do likewise.

Emmanuel College

Prologue

"Look Well to This Day"

Look well to this day,
For it is life,
The very best of life.
In its brief course lie all
The realities and truths of existence:
The joy of growth,
The glory of action,
The splendour of beauty.

For yesterday is but a memory,
And tomorrow is only a vision.
But today, if well lived, makes
Every yesterday a memory of happiness
And every tomorrow a vision of hope.

Look well, therefore, to this day.

(Ancient Sanskrit poem, attributed to Kalidas)

PART ONE: THE DIPLOMATIC SERVICE

1

DIPLOMATIC UNIFORM

The gold spike had a sharp point. The bubble burst. The Soviet Ambassadress cursed me in Russian. In English, I cursed my choice of tropical diplomatic headgear. Would a Third World War ensue?

Diplomatic uniforms are a legacy from the past, and a bit of a joke today. Most of us wore them with reluctance, aware of the anachronism and just a tiny bit apprehensive of public derision. The uniforms were, nevertheless – and probably still are, from Oslo to Tokyo – associated with monarchies and courts, and formed a natural part of their traditional pomp and circumstance.

In temperate climates, the kit, if expensive, is not too bizarre. Navy blue cloth, gold laced stand-up collar and cuffs (with extra oak leaf confections, for the most senior ranks, such as ambassadors and ministers); large gilt buttons bearing the royal coat of arms; slim, gilt-hilted court sword, safely sheathed in black patent leather; fore-and-aft cocked hat (with ostrich plumes, for the oak leaf brigade). We wore all this in Tehran, when the Shahanshah of Iran received the diplomatic corps on his official birthday or at the New Year Festival. After the bowing and scraping was over, and we were all back in the British Embassy compound, and after the Ambassador had stalked off into his Residence, the rest of us usually assembled on the lawn for a party of our own. Fooling around, pretending to be pirates, we junior diplomats would turn our fore-and-aft hats sideways, draw swords and pose for the photographers.

In tropical countries, one was required to wear a white duck jacket (tight fitting, without baggy patch pockets, but lots of gold buttons) and a choice between white duck or lightweight dark blue trousers (the latter with a fetching strip of oak leaf patterned brocade down the outside seams). The court sword was standard, too. But there was a difficult choice of headgear. The classic option was a large white pith helmet, similar in design to that worn by a bandsman in the Royal Marines, but with a tall, gold spike on the top. No chin strap, so one had to be careful not to allow the solar topee to wobble when one spoke. The fall back, for those with odd shaped heads or with weak neck muscles, was a white topped service cap, with a black lace horizontal band and patent leather peak (oak leaves round the edge, naturally, for the seniors). Also, a neat 'EIIR' gold and blue cap badge.

Appointed Head of Mission in Phnom Penh, and required on occasions to wait upon HRH, the Prince Head of State in full fig, I opted for an all white uniform. (Later, for formal *soireés dansantes*, I improvised an unauthorised but convincingly fit-for-purpose combination of white monkey jacket with gold epaulettes, plus dark blue gold striped trousers, plus dashing royal blue cummerbund). So far, so good. But my big mistake was to opt initially for the old-fashioned pith helmet, from a desire to be faithful to the traditions of the Raj. It provoked a diplomatic incident in its own right.

In 1964, the diplomatic corps had been greeting a foreign potentate embarking on a State Visit to Cambodia. At the conclusion of the ceremony, we Heads of Mission fell out of our line and began to shamble off towards our limousines. I was holding my solar topee sideways under my left arm. I turned suddenly and inadvertently bumped into the Soviet Ambassador's wife, denting her slightly. She was a very large Wagnerian woman, with plaited peroxide hair worn round her head in a halo, who habitually sailed through life like a galleon, preceded by an immense corsage. I don't think she felt anything. But she did yelp and utter a Cyrillic oath. The German Ambassador, next to me, subsequently swore that the right bosom deflated with an audible escape of air – perhaps even of a disabling or toxic gas. Was she really, he speculated, a KGB hit man in drag?

But that speculation came later. At the time, I bowed, kissed her pudgey hand, apologised profusely and retreated rapidly backwards, the solar topee held out of harm's way, while the Ambassadress, for her part – composure restored – giggled graciously – even, I suspected, pleasurably. Clearly, she had got the point.

Me too. I instructed my St James' Street hatter to send me out in the diplomatic bag the alternative headgear.

But how had I come to be wearing uniform at all? What was this all about?? In the next chapter, I shall go back eight years, to the very beginning.

2

'FIELDING OF THE FO': OUT OF THE DOOR AND ONTO THE STREET, IN CARLTON HOUSE TERRACE

Pride comes before a fall. Arrogance is its own worst enemy. David Wilson (later governor of Hong Kong and now Lord Wilson of Tillyorn) discovered that, in 1958. His few well-chosen criticisms of what he had found on joining the Foreign Office were met with the put-down: 'We like our young dogs to wag their tails.' Much worse had happened to me, two years earlier.

In the spring of 1956, while completing my undergraduate studies at Cambridge, I succeeded in the open competition for entry into the fast stream of the Foreign (later re-named Diplomatic) Service. Indeed, among the many hundreds of mostly Oxbridge Bright Young Things who then made application, I had come second equal on the list. Initially, I was a little disconcerted. I could read four foreign languages, but actually spoke none. My only real ambition, at that point in life, was to take a little walk in the sun, away from the Church of England. If possible – this was before the revolution of the 1960s so memorably summed up by Philip Larkin – also to make the personal acquaintance of Miss Suzy Wong, or one of her younger sisters. British Petroleum would have offered at least the sun (although they were reliably reported to be prejudiced in favour of Blues, like the old Sudan Political Service); perhaps even the Metal Box Company (which had assured me that they entertained no such prejudice). But, in the end, the FO it was. Uncoiling myself, also a respectable result in the Tripos.

So I walked on air down King's Parade, casually acknowledging the plaudits of my envious academic contemporaries, quite the undergraduate hero. (At Cambridge, these days, of course, you are only the latter if recruited to Canary Wharf, on a six figure starting salary – although the crash of 2008 and its sequel may serve to bring back some sanity and sense of public service to the career plans of the young). My uncle duly introduced me to a Sackville Street suit-maker. With new sophistication, I sipped Spanish champagne with my daily ketchup and chips. Nonchalantly – but most unwisely – I chose to report at the FO a few days later than suggested. Surely not a problem? The Foreign Secretary, Mr Selwyn Lloyd, was as likely to be free one day as another, to congratulate me warmly, and walk me across Downing Street to shake hands with the Prime Minister, Sir Anthony Eden. (Kissing hands at the Palace could wait – I was too busy, just then, to flog up to Balmoral).

Unaccountably, however, no such agreeable encounters were announced – admittedly, I consoled myself, because of the Suez crisis. So I had to make do with the suggestion that I pay a call, as the other eight new entrants already had, upon the Training Section in Carlton House Terrace. After a quick nod round the door of the Hon. John Henniker-Major, MC, the 'Toff' head of personnel, I was sent to a plywood cubicle down a back corridor to see some sort of departmental clerk, possibly a junior member of the (non-graduate, slow stream) 'Branch B' of the service.

We new entrants to 'Branch A' had all heard on the grapevine that we should each be asked to select what the FO called a 'hard language', to study in a leisurely and agreeable fashion in comfortable surroundings for a couple of years, before assuming our ultimate high responsibilities. With Miss Wong and Co. in mind, I had already earmarked Chinese, or possibly Japanese. Irritatingly, the clerk, a Scotsman, offered me a choice between Russian, Persian and Amharic – Burmese having already been allocated, and it not being the turn of Siamese, that year. But Chinese or Japanese, I asked? The Clerk explained that Chinese was not needed in 1956 since the FO already had a Chinese speaker coming in, on transfer from the Malay Civil Service; while the Japanese slot had been given to a man a little lower on the list, who had been 'temping' for the past twelve months in King Charles' Street. Casting my elitist eye around the cheap calendars pinned to the cardboard partitioning, I must have conveyed to the Scotsman some intimation of well-bred English surprise and delicate displeasure. After a pregnant pause, to let the rebuke sink in, I told the 'Branch B' chap what he could do with his Amharic; and indicated that I would get back to him, during the following week's FO induction course for new entrants, about the remaining choice between Russian and Persian.

In the event, I tossed a coin with the other late arrival on the induction course, suggesting 'heads' for the Czar and 'tails' for the Shah; but he argued, quite rightly, that it should be 'heads' for the Peacock Throne and 'tails' for the Kremlin and evil Uncle Joe. 'Heads' came up and I braced myself for departure to the School of Oriental and African Studies in London, to join the first year Farsi course. But I consoled myself with the prospect of being able to read Omar Khayyam in the original; and gain a deeper insight into the influence of Iranian Zoroastrianism on medieval Manichaean heresies in the Balkans and Western Europe – part of a recently discarded PhD project of mine.

Meanwhile, back in the cardboard cubicle in Carlton House Terrace, it was time for some further paperwork. I duly signed the Official Secrets Act; notified the FO of my next of kin; and agreed to small monthly deductions from my salary towards the in-house medical scheme. These formalities completed, I rose to leave the cubicle.

Hand on the brown plastic doorknob of the plywood door, however, I was arrested by the *obiter dicta* of the Scots clerk:

'Ye ken, Mr Fielding. No matter how rigorous and searching and exigent we make the selection process to 'Branch A' of the Service, we still find that the percentage of idiots in the intake remains constant. Good day to ye!'

Whoops!

I was then directed down the steps and onto the street. (Gosh, how irritating the Lowland Picts can be. And I feel amply qualified to suggest that; on my mother's side, I'm one-eighth a Campbell of Cawdor from Nairn).

For 'Fielding of the FO', it was not to be the last hard lesson in personal modesty and self-abasement in the Diplomatic Service. But then, I have always prided myself hugely that, like Solon, I grow old learning – something in which, to be frank, I think I can with total justification take immense personal self-satisfaction.

3

HORSE SENSE: 'UP', WITH THE QASHQAI

'Mitarseh!' they said, disparagingly.

Four horses, in a vast, rocky and inimical desert, somewhere in South Persia. The Qashqai khan, sitting easy in the saddle, the reins loose in his right hand, his vertical left arm touching the flank of his pony, asked his two loyal tribesmen (grizzled, grey-eyed, deferential and alert) how they had found the Englishman. This last, looking like a sack of potatoes, perched absolutely petrified in the saddle (manifestly, all too relieved that his steed was at last stationary), offered an uneasy grin, squared his shoulders and attempted a jaunty, cavalier, nonchalance of the kind traditionally displayed – with a broad yellow stripe down the side of his tight blue breeches – by John Wayne of the US Cavalry, to the tune of 'When Johnny comes marching home again'.

It was November 1957. Having completed an academic year studying Persian (with elements of classical Arabic) at the School of Oriental and African Studies in the University of London, I had reported for duty as a language student at the British Embassy in Tehran, in September that year. After three weeks briefing and indoctrination, I had been told to get lost and put a gloss on my language skills. More precisely, I had been dispatched to Shiraz in the deep south of Iran, billeted in the empty quarters of the former British Consulate in that city; and placed in the care of a distinguished, retired, Iranian consular official, as my supervisor of studies. He, in his turn, and at the suggestion of my Tehran masters, had sent me up-country, to join the Qashqai tribe and their khan for a week or so. The latter was a Persian gentleman of the old school – and anglophile to a degree, on account of his service, during the First World War, in the South Persia Rifles, an anti-German, anti-Turkish force, raised in theoretically neutral Iran by the British Raj, and led by British officers from the Indian Army so proficient in horsemanship that even the Qashqai were impressed.

Thus, the khan casually questioned his followers about 'Fielding of the FO'.

Horses, of course, are hell. Emotional, stupid, much stronger than we are, perfectly capable of standing on one's foot and breaking one's toes without even noticing – let alone saying sorry. Certainly, not fitted with either foot or hand brakes or even a steering wheel. If you have to ride them, better do it cowboy-style, with long stirrups – not knee-under-your-chin, in the manner of jockeys and the English landed gentry. The Normans, nine hundred years ago, knew even better: William the Conqueror and his men, quite rightly, rode small ponies with the warriors' legs vertical, grazing the ground on their very small ponies. (Brakes, after all? Or at least so as to dismount more easily, in a moment of panic??).

I confess, when equestrianism comes up, to a triple deceit. The first, as to my claim that, if I had to be re-incarnated in an earlier age, I should have wanted to be a political officer of the government of India on the north-west frontier. I do speak the languages; and shoot really rather well (see chapter 35); but was definitely not born to live in the saddle. The second, as to my having galloped at the head of the Qashqai tribe across the deserts of Fars in 1957 (of which the sad truth, and cowardly mendacity, will emerge from what follows). The third, as to my pretend happiness with horses. Not merely do I mistrust them; but, also, I never ride them from choice; and (unlike wife, son and daughter) happen to have a very poor 'seat'.

My first experience of our four-footed friends was riding a donkey on the sands at Bournemouth at the age of five. I quite soon fell off. My next experience, at the age of seven, was astride a carthorse in Devon – the motion made me seasick. After that, I gave such animals a wide berth. Until, that is, the Qashqai, with whom I scored adequately for marksmanship, but was judged absolutely bottom of the class for horsemanship.

Later in life, I was to show, Mr Wayne-manner, 'True Grit'. Or, at least, 'True Love'. In 1978, after a six-month, whirlwind romance, I married a Fellow of St Hilda's, who played polo for Oxford. Me, the tweedy Visiting Fellow of St Antony's; she, at Kirtlington, a Mills-and-Boon figure, in tight white breeches and gleaming black boots. The first part of our honeymoon was spent on my spread in Devon. We had boxed down her two ponies (my stables were, as you will understand, empty of equestrian existence and thitherto available only to overflow hippy guests, with their sleeping bags). We rode out over Dartmoor. With, at the end of the day, a couple of pints of real ale at a rural pub, as both incentive and reward. My child-bride, generous in her tankards, commented, with satisfaction, on my life-embracing, physically exultant, broad grin at the 'collected canter'. (It was, of course, a rictus of fear – but I kept that to myself, as a Qashqai should).

Back to the Persian desert in 1957. Unlike in the movie, 'Lawrence of Arabia', the Persian version was not soft golden sand, welcoming a tumble; but sharp and hard, promising to break every bone in one's body if one fell from the saddle. And the Qashqai nag, like an Icelandic pony, proved to have at least five gaits, most of them disconcerting and some of them a-rhythmic. My accompanying tribesmen, grinning wolfishly through their blackened teeth, urged me on through a painful bump-trot, and a rocking horse canter, to an all-out gallop; then back to a walk, for the pony to catch his breath; then yet again trot/canter/gallop. Determined to be British, I did not actually scream. But I probably sobbed quietly, through stiff upper lip. In intervals, at the walk or trot, I laid down a defensive oral barrage between them and me by saying how much more difficult it was, back in Good Old England, to take the bend in a Maserati at Goodwood or to 'Do the Ton' on a Harley Davidson on the bypass.

The two tribesmen assigned to me evinced not the slightest interest in my self-propaganda. At the end, to the khan's question, they responded simply, 'Mitarseh!' meaning: 'He's scared!'

Please don't tell 'The County', though: Shropshire (which is a tad Qashqai in outlook) might drop its collective monocle into its multi-leguminous potage.

4

THE TERROR OF THE TONGS

The orchestra began to play a Viennese waltz. Nodding confidently, I strode forward to do my duty to Queen and country.

The occasion was a charity ball at the Tehran embassy in, I think, 1959. Possibly, to raise money for Iranian earthquake victims. Glitterati from the Imperial Palace, *évolué* Persian aristocrats, senior government officials and some cabinet ministers (those of the latter who could dance, western-style, that is to say – I think two or three) were present; as also the diplomatic corps, along with senior representatives of foreign business and banking.

I had begun life unable to dance – too clumsy, and above all, much too shy. As a young national service subaltern, a shambolic shuffle around the floor with the colonel's wife was the best that I could manage at the regimental ball. (Something for which I subsequently earned the pained reproach of the adjutant). Having decided, at Cambridge, to become a diplomat rather than join a religious order, I naturally bestirred myself, did a make-over and went to evening classes for two whole terms at a suburban academy. I learned the modern waltz, the quickstep, the foxtrot, the tango and much else – and ultimately acquired a silver medal in ballroom dancing. But your actual continental, common-or-garden Viennese waltz had unfortunately not been on the agenda – notwithstanding paternal and grand-paternal links with Austria.

Fast forward then, to Tehran in 1959. As the junior Third Secretary, on such festive occasions my duty was to dance with all the wallflowers – I, correctly attired in tails, with a neatly tied white tie and a pair of thin soled and slippery patent dancing pumps.

That evening, I stepped out; selected a daughter of the nobility as my partner; and – ahead of all others and as a shining embodiment of youth, beauty and adroitness – started off round the dance floor, turning and turning, with a confident half-smile and a gracious inclination of my pomaded head to the ambassador's wife, as I swept passed.

Second time around the floor, things began to get slightly out of control. I suspect that I entered mazurka mode. And then I slipped, crashing into the ambassador's very large fireplace, with a great clatter of fire irons.

Mercifully, it being late spring, the fire was not lit. Also, my partner fell on top of me and was unhurt, notwithstanding the utterance of a very loud squeak. I was bruised, but unbowed, rising swiftly to my feet as if nothing had happened, to return my partner to her parents and a convenient chair for her recuperation. The head of chancery (who reminded me of that adjutant) swiftly inspected the damage to the fire irons and, at a discreet later moment, reported the damage to Their Excellencies, the (cold, slightly eerie, very Wykehamist) ambassador, Sir Geoffrey Harrison and his (much more giggly) spouse, Lady Harrison.

In the event, however, it was alright, because the latter had a soft spot for me. As I took my leave of her that evening, at the end of the ball, she whispered 'Well done, Leslie – quite the Terror of the Tongs'!

5

A VOICE CRYING IN THE WILDERNESS

No one likes 'Fundis'.

In Iran, in the 1950s, there were more than a few. At one point, in the holy city of Qom, stones were thrown and I had to do a runner. In the holy city of Meshed, deep and dark in the busy covered bazaar, I bumped into a couple of mullahs, one of whom spat at me, while the other hissed *nājes* (meaning 'unclean'). These days, in modern Iran, the clergy are more likely to be spat at by their own people than to spit at foreigners, such is popular resentment of theocratic kleptocrats. But, in Qom and Meshed then, fifty years ago, it was I, the Englishman, who was at the receiving end.

Looking back in anger, I can nevertheless understand why – I was the very icon of the ethnic and cultural outsider. With red hair, blue eyes and a white face with freckles, I stood out in the crowd. Indeed, an elderly but waggish Persian language tutor, in the southern city of Shiraz, likened me to the *Dīv-e-Safid*, or 'white devil' of Persian legend, whose spotted and sinister portrait was painted over the main gateway of the local prison. (The building, formerly the palace of Karim Khan Zand, is today a fine municipal art museum, so the reader can safely check it out). I remember protesting to this tutor that, whatever the other commonalities, I did not have horns like the *Div*. But he reposted: 'Are you quite sure?', ruffling my thick curly hair.

On the other hand, everyone likes the Sufis. In Tehran, I knew a Sufi circle and occasionally sat with them as they meditated – periods of silence broken by ecstatic monosyllabic pieties or the recitation of sonorous verses from the Persian mystics.

I thought of those Sufis early one evening in the Alburz mountains to the north of Tehran. A high-pitched voice echoed eerily through the hills, the singer invisible behind some fold in the terrain. The voice sang sorrowfully, about the human passions. For this was a passionate love song. But, who was the beloved and what was the courtship?

It was the short, spring season in Iran. The normally parched and barren desert was briefly spread with wild flowers. The hill pastures were green. Flocks of goats wandered, greedily grazing under the eye of their guardians. I was with a party of young people from the embassy, on a country picnic. The sun was still warm. Soon it would be time for us all to pile into our land rovers and head south for Tehran. I had taken myself off for a short, solitary walk, watching the shadows begin to lengthen on the hillsides, admiring the bold contours of the green and khaki landscape. On the horizon to the north was the smudged blue of a high range of mountains, still topped with snow. It was then that the singing began. Perhaps a shepherd boy. His words seemed to convey something like this:

> 'Where are you, my beloved? Everywhere I seek you.
> But you hide yourself from me.
> My love of you knows no bounds. I am your devoted one, your slave.
> If only you would turn your gaze upon me'.

Taken together, the voice and setting were compelling. I stopped in mid-stride. No crunch of the desert beneath my boots, the stillness of my immediate surroundings broken only by the bleat of distant flocks. Reality was *the voice* – unimaginably beautiful. As it seemed, all else was illusion. Listening carefully, I realised that it was not the secular, lovesick dirge that I had assumed. Certainly passionate; almost erotic. But the language was pure poetry, in classical Persian, rhythmic, repetitive, hypnotic. I could not get the detail – my knowledge of the language was not then up to it. And the voice ceased singing as abruptly as it had begun.

Yet the song sang on in my mind and memory. It came to me that this had been, in reality, Sufi stuff. I did not know the literature well enough to judge. Nevertheless, probably something from Rudaki or Maulavi Rumi? And I had caught one particular word: *Elāhi.* The shepherd boy's song of longing and devotion was in fact addressed to God.

As we gathered up our bits and pieces, preparatory to moving off, a girl asked 'What was that spooky voice about?' I could not find the right words to reply. Human kind, as T.S. Eliot reminded us, cannot bear much reality. So I answered, 'Just some local lad, with a crush'.

6

ALBURZ AMBUSH

Sometimes, oratory is the obvious oblation. And rhetoric can have its reasons.

Early one evening, on another picnic, the embassy party, in their three long-wheel-based land rovers, ran into a little local difficulty. A wayside village would not let us through. Some sort of festival was in progress, feisty in atmosphere. Tambourines were tapping and stringed instruments straining. Bare-torsoed wrestlers were flexing their pectorals. Beefy village strongmen in leather breeches were whirling heavy wooden clubs. The main thoroughfare was crowded. Our path was blocked.

It seemed to me, sitting beside the driver in the leading vehicle, that this was slightly more than rustic rumbustiousness. There was an edge to it. While the women in their long colourful *chadors* or veils stood back, the men and boys pressed forward to peer through our dusty windows and point at the young European girls of our number. Coming to my window, a senior figure, possibly the village *katkhoda* (headman), told me that we had no permission to pass through. His companion, a massive Neanderthal figure with a neck almost as wide as his shoulders – apparently the village strongman – then contradicted his headman; *indeed* we nevertheless *could* move on; but only over his own body.

The Iranian driver beside me was expressionless. Our leader, the head of chancery, George Hiller (who had won a DSO with SOE during the war, alongside the French partisans in the Languedoc, and was not normally easily fazed) seemed a tiny trifle nonplussed. Glancing back for guidance that was not forthcoming, I therefore told George that I had better try saying something to the crowd, in Persian.

Accordingly, I slid out, to stand on the running-board, strike a Ciceronian posture, and give tongue to the village fiesta, as if before the Senate of Rome; I naturally also adopted the affected accent and lengthened vowels of an official spokesman on Tehran radio, when delivering a formal announcement to the nation. Progressively, a silence fell – initially curious, later approbatory, ultimately enthusiastic.

I have always enjoyed practising oratorical flourishes and conceits, saying something sonorous but empty of meaning about absolutely nothing at all. Enemies say that I rarely do anything else (but they are mistaken). I still recall, with pleasure, the insubstantive 'political speech' in 'Beyond the Fringe' in the 1960s. Even in the '50s in Iran, I was wont, if provoked to do a party piece, to launch into long discourses, composed of pompous and purposeless phrases replete with abstractions about Common Causes, Sempiternal Verities, Noble Political Purposes, Ultimate Objectives and other resounding and grandiloquent solemnities. I could even do so – up to a point – in Persian as well as English. Now was the moment at which the proof would be in the pudding. And in Iran, language matters; words have emotional substance, independently of their narrow and literal meaning.

> 'My friends and fellow citizens.
>
> I convey to you the cordial and heartfelt greetings of Her Britannic Majesty's Ambassador Extraordinary and Envoy Plenipotentiary to the Court of His Imperial Majesty, the Shahanshah of Iran, upon whose Person, as upon all his loyal and devoted Subjects, and all of you gathered together on this most auspicious occasion, let every blessing descend from Almighty God on high and every humble token of Admiration and Respect for His Imperial Majesty's and your friends and admirers from around the planet and indeed from every corner of the known world, the Galaxy, and – to mention merely a few – the entire created Universe.
>
> It is a demonstrable delight and a profound privilege for us, your visitors, to be present with you

on this egregious, and outstandingly elevated occasion... How dazzled we are, at the glories and splendours of your village! How we share your justifiable pride in these superb athletes, outstanding wrestlers and amazing manipulators of clubs!! You and they recall to us – your unqualified sempiternal admirers, today and always – the grandeur and glory of this most ancient of civilisations, this most successful of societies, this most eminent of exemplars of high human culture, this most effulgent of each and every rural economy throughout the world that is known to man... Looking to the future which is to come, in the light of the past which lies behind, but in the sure and certain possession of the pristine present that so happily employs us at this very moment in time – enfolds all of us, each and every one, upon this Day of all Days – shall it not be here and now agreed, confirmed and proudly proclaimed, that we shall, from this moment onward, address together the common challenges of the age in which we live? So that, step-by-step and shoulder-to-shoulder, we may embrace together one Shining Common Destiny and receive, as one, and in its fullest glory and plenitude, our shared Common and so well Merited Reward!

It is, therefore, accordingly, and on that account, a matter of extreme, sorrowful and sharply bitter regret that we, your visitors, shall be unable to remain long with you, this evening… But you may count on us to carry your fame, and fairest of all reputations, to the capital city of your country, to the High Diplomatic Mission from which we hail, to your National Authorities, nay even to the very ears of your Imperial Head of State……'.

The crowd broke into first ragged, then vigorous and substantial applause – tears in the eyes of many. Mothers held up their children to catch a glimpse of me. I gave pause to the headman and the strong man to reply.

They graciously consented to our further passage, save only the proviso that we should allow at least one of the front wheels of the leading land rover to run over one of the strongman's forearms, that all might recognise what a true champion he was. I assented, with every fraternal manifestation, including the offer (accepted with alacrity) of my woolly pullover to wrap around the said mighty forearm, so as to avoid any unfortunate indentation from the chunky, all-terrain tyre. That manoeuvre effected, with no damage to either the land rover or the forearm, we prepared to edge down the street, as the crowds began to divide ahead of us. I asked the head of chancery to pass me the equivalent of a £20 note, which I presented to the headman, with a flourish, as testimony to our undying esteem, and as a modest contribution to the costs of their fabulous festival.

Once safely out of the village, and well on the way back to Tehran, I asked the driver what he had made of it. He replied in English, so that the head of chancery would understand, that there had not in reality been the slightest difficulty: it was always like this, every year, in the outback. While these occasions were best avoided by embassy vehicles, the crowd were entirely friendly and wished us not the slightest evil.

'So twenty quid was far too much' interjected the head of chancery.

The secretaries, then apprehensive but now emboldened, began to titter. A rather badly brought up girl from (naturally) the commercial section, who knew me better than I ought previously to have permitted, went so far as to say: 'BLA-BLA-BLA-BLA-BLA'.

On cue, the German Consul's secretary chimed in with: *'Ja, das ist es, eben. Er redet immer Quatch!'*

Even the rather better brought up and very pretty PA to the French Ambassador, whom I would have permitted to know me better if she for her part had permitted, simply shook her curly head and said *'Lesslee .... tu racontes n'importe quoi'*.

I saw my chance of winning the DSO vanish down the pan, and slumped, deflated, in my seat.

‘But the political speech, George, you have to admit it wasn’t too bad a spoof’, I muttered.

‘No idea, as I don’t speak Persian’, came the reply, asking ‘Driver, what did you think of Mr Fielding’s oration?’

I gave Ali a nudge and a meaningful glare.

‘Mr Fielding spoke as if he were the Iranian Prime Minister, addressing the Majles – or even H.I.M. the Shah himself, on an important state occasion’ came the edifying and exemplary reply.

Gratified, it seemed to me that the honours were even. But it cost me ten quid, for Ali, when we were next alone together.

7

TALKING TO TURKOMAN

I am in a yurt on the Turkoman steppe in Iran, talking to nomads in the Persian language, through a Turkish language interpreter. It is the spring of 1959; and a privileged moment. First, however, a little *aperçu historique*, as the Guide Bleu likes to put it.

From the foothills of the Alburz Mountains in the north east of Persia, there stretches further northward an extensive plain, which reaches along the eastern shores of the Caspian Sea, deep into Turkmenistan. It is one of the land bridges leading toward the European world from Central Asia. Across it, in prehistoric times, the first Aryans are believed to have poured into the Middle East, the Balkans, the Mediterranean and ultimately Western Europe. King Cyrus pushed up this way north to the Oxus in the 6th century BC, to set the outer bounds of the first Persian Empire. Alexander the Great marched through from west to east. Moving in the opposite direction, the Parthian archer-horsemen pressed into Anatolia and the Levant to harass Greek settlement and Roman Empire alike. In the Common Era, the tramp of foot soldiers and the thunder of cavalry never ceased – from the Sassanians restoring the northern frontiers of the Persian Empire, to the Huns, the Seljuq Turks, the Ghuzz Turks, the Mongols, the Uzbeqs, the Turkoman and finally the Russians. Houses, fortresses and walls were built, destroyed and rebuilt and destroyed yet again; piles of human skulls thrown up, cast down and trampled underfoot; slaves, booty and cattle rounded up and driven away.

In modern times, there remains a grimness as well as a melancholy beauty to the sweep of the largely empty plain, the horizon broken only by a watchtower or monument here, a grouping of black nomad tents there, the occasional band of horsemen. It is the territory of a proud, pastoral people, Turkish speaking, and largely ignorant of and indifferent towards the outside world. The Turkoman women ride unveiled and 'in-your-face', with their Mongolian good looks, their golden bangles and headbands, and their clothes in blood-red and maroon. The men who ride with them, of an even prouder bearing, wear black sheepskin hats, which stick upwards and outwards from the backs of their heads and are topped in glowing green or purple velvet. They all carry daggers; the men usually also a loaded rifle in a saddle holster. They canter into village markets, to sell what they produce and barter for what they cannot. They are constantly on the move; despise fixed dwellers in houses; possess little philosophy beyond their tribal code. They seem to have few relaxations – hunting and equitation; plaintive, simple music and poetry; opium, when they can get it; fighting, when they feel in the mood. Altogether, a wild bunch.

In the spring of 1959, the area north of Gorgan and Gonbad-e Qabus is difficult to penetrate from the rest of Iran. Outside visitors require special security passes. The international border with Soviet Turkmenistan is not far away. There is occasional gunfire, directed by Soviet frontier guards at man, beast, bird and bush. There is a 'buzz' to being here, with a colleague from the Tehran embassy, on a mixture of business and pleasure. We are accompanied by an Iranian paramilitary, his rifle loaded, with one 'up the spout'. He both watches us, and watches over us, ostensibly as our Persian/Turkish interpreter – the Turkoman themselves speak very little Persian and we speak even less Turkish. (Up there, none, naturally, speaks English).

I am the driver. I decide to push north from Pahlavi Dezh, directly to Alexander's Wall and the Soviet frontier beyond it. We move off-road, across the trackless plain itself. The smell of grass, bruised thyme and wild flowers reaches up through the open window, as the wheels roll over the smooth alluvial soil and the short turf fresh with rain. In the sunlight, the plain looks like an immense misty green sea, in a dead-flat calm. We feel somehow exposed. There are no trees or buildings or hilltops to reach up to the heavens and prevent the skies from falling in. A man becomes a mouse, scurrying across an open field, hoping that the owl or the eagle will not pounce.

We reach Alexander's Wall. In its prime, it stretched for over a hundred miles from the Caspian shore to the mountains of Khorassan. It was probably built between the 3rd and 5th centuries AD by the Sassanian kings, to keep out the northern barbarians. Square, machicolated watch towers were placed at intervals of around 1,000 yards. An occasional strongly built postern permitted Sassanian infantry and horse to make offensive sorties. *Vaut le détour*, we think, observing left and right the stretch of what appears to be a tall earth mound, pierced only by the track north to the frontier and varied in outline by the piled up ruins that once were towers. Of the actual wall itself, we find only a rubble of clay-baked bricks remaining. Builders over the centuries have carted off these bricks for their own dwellings and dug the floors of the keeps to recover ancient pots for their modern domestic use. Nevertheless, some heavy lumps of stone and brick remain. Lifting one with great difficulty and then letting it fall, our guard smiles at us, curiously proud. 'What champions the Iranians were in the ancient times, to be strong enough to build with heavy blocks like these. Our race is no longer, today, what then it was'.

We re-embark and press further north across the grass and the flowers, towards a cluster of tents. A slit-eyed young tribesman emerges to intercept us. He seems to want us to push off. However, our paramilitary says soothing things. There is a show of boorish reluctance. But we are shown into the largest tent.

These tents, sometimes called yurts, and by the Turkoman themselves termed 'alachigh', are impressive structures: mobile, yet warm and weatherproof dwellings. The alachigh inside which we find ourselves is eighteen feet in diameter (being of circular shape) and is constructed of black felt supported by a wooden framework. Round the walls (which must be from four to five feet tall) is a trellis of wooden staves held in a tight grip by beautifully patterned hand-woven tent straps, about three inches wide, which circle the whole tent.

The flat domed roof is formed of poles arching from one side to the other and tied where they cross in the middle, so that from below they look like the arms and legs of a union jack. At the apex of the dome, where the staves are lashed together, there is a hole that acts as a chimney. Elsewhere, thick black felt shuts out the light. Underfoot, felt mats in maroon and brown and black, and the more familiar Turkoman gelim, completely cover the stamped earthen floor, except for the space in the centre devoted to a rough hearth of ash and stones. On this hearth there are charcoal embers, from which rises a wisp of blue acrid smoke. There is a background odour of dust, old clothes and dried curds.

Of the five Turkoman in the tent, two are female – a shy but richly adorned young woman who fans the embers to brightness and prepares our tea; and another, older, woman who squats quietly spinning sheep's wool onto a spindle by the fire. The three men recline on their sides in a slightly ungainly way, more like bourgeois guests at Trimalchio's Feast than highborn Greeks at a Socratic symposium. An old, rather silly man nods benignly throughout and eventually accepts and begins to smoke my gift of a box of cigarettes. The second man, the one who came to bar our way, turns out to be the husband of the tea maker. He is an oafish but a handsome youth. (The Turkoman can produce boys and young men of amazing good looks, with smooth cheeks and regular features of rather a Chinese cast: they seem to have fascinated the Persian ancients, and Hafez himself wrote, in a famous couplet, 'If that Turkish boy of Shiraz would accept my heart, I would give away the riches of Samarqand and Bokhara, just for the mole on his cheek'). Finally, there is an authoritative man in his middle thirties, who sits up on his heels to do most of the talking. He is smooth featured; but with a typically Turkoman goatee-beard hanging from the tip of his chin. This gives him the appearance of a Chinese mandarin.

Early in our desultory conversation, we are served refreshments – not only the strong, sugary tea but also slightly bitter yoghurt and the most wonderful thick cream. The latter, our gendarme explains (perhaps with more diplomacy than truth), is a special token of respect for visitors of distinction. Tea-making over, small clumps of camel thorn are dragged over and thrown on the fire. As they blaze up, the dimness passes and the shadows of the tent recede. We can see metal pans hanging tied to the trellis work round the wall; and a jerrycan inscribed 'Imperial Chemical Industries Limited' which has been converted to domestic use. Also, an ancient earthenware flagon with a slender neck that has obviously come from The Wall. (We are later told that these pots are especially prized by tribesmen, who dig them up from the ruins to keep their drinking water cool in summer).

The pleasant rounded commonplaces and the formal politeness of Persian conversation afford the participant a refined pleasure and possess a great deal of courtly charm. Such subtle intercourse is not to be ours in the alachigh. We exchange with our Turkoman hosts the Arabic religious tags and phrases which the Turkish and Persian tongues have in common – Praise be to God; God willing; We take refuge in God; It is God's will; etc. But this is almost the limit of our small talk. Otherwise, through the translator, the simple and direct thoughts of the steppe Turkoman come straight across at us.

All too soon, however, we need to take our leave. For a moment, something like a smile creases the unemotional Mongoloid features of our hosts, their suspicions no longer in play and their crude sense of humour asserting itself in the face of our oddness of opinion and incongruity of appearance. But as we stoop out of the alachigh into the bright afternoon sun, there follows us, from the shadows within, an uncomprehending gaze. The life of the Turkoman nomad of the steppe is assured by certainties – by Islam, by the earth's annual cycle of fertility, by the discipline upon which a self-sufficient nomadic community relies for its survival. The world outside offers them many momentary wonders, about which, however, their insular and incurious minds are essentially unspeculative. They know themselves to be Turkoman and care as little for other peoples and other lands as they do for politics and governments. The Turkoman whom we have met cannot really consider themselves citizens of

Iran: they can hardly speak Persian. None there that day admits to having ever seen even the Caspian Sea thirty miles to the west, and only one has moved off his native steppe – to make the pilgrimage to Mecca. It is enough that they acknowledge Iranian rule over them as a remote but established fact; for the rest, the propaganda of Russia and America and Peacock Throne goes over their heads, as something both inexplicable and irrelevant.

So, what did this goatee-bearded, slit-eyed fellow in the yurt actually say to us, beyond the pious small talk? I still have my notes, which read as follows:

> 'Why do you come here across so many mountains, from your own land and people? The camels and sheep have gone away for pasture, otherwise we should be slaughtering a beast in greeting and for your honour. Surely there must be Turkoman where you come from? And surely your country cannot be full of these English, as you claim? Yes, I have been to Mecca, and there I have indeed seen many English. For Mecca is a part of England, or at any rate under British rule. I have seen teachers there, such as your friend with the glasses (he refers to my brown-haired, well-tanned embassy colleague – I am red haired and freckled and inevitably look like nothing on earth to the Turkoman). Yes, I think I have heard of Americans: they have visited others of us on the steppe and are the same as you – except that they come to instruct and to interfere and not as our guests. They are the children of Iskandar, who long ago came to build The Great Wall. Do many of your people make the pilgrimage to Mecca and is there a good road from England? You say there is *sea* between England and Mecca? I have heard that this sea is here also. I have not cast my eyes on it; only my father has seen it. But there must surely be some sort of *road* for pilgrims who travel from England to Mecca across the sea or else how should they complete the Haj? Is it a long road? How many hours' ride? How many

governments stand in the way? If, as you say, there are so many governments along the road, you live in remote parts indeed. Tell us, how then did you cross such a great distance and what brought you here today? Hardly any goats and camels on the green fields of England, you say? No Turkoman to tend them? How then do the English *live*?'

8

THE TEHRAN TAXI MEN

I couldn't afford my own car, initially, as a young 'Third Secretary' in the Tehran embassy. So, I took taxis everywhere, several times a day – they were cheap. It was good for my Persian, and I learned a lot about ordinary people, how they lived, and what they thought of the regime of the Shah. I must have chatted with over a thousand of the 16,000 taxi men in town. I found them resourceful, lively and sometimes of unexpected utterance.

To judge from them, the urban proletariat in the capital, in the late 1950s, was not an independently explosive force. But some listened intently to Radio Moscow, others to the mullahs and yet others to whatever they could capture of the golden west – and all felt increasingly aggrieved. I saw no sign of the focussed, powerful popular dissidence that was one day to end the monarchy – even if it was thereafter to place the Iranian people under a theocratic durance more harsh.

It was, however, frequently possible to let loose quite a dirge from the average taxi driver on the subject of living conditions.

I recall only three or four drivers who considered that they lived a comfortable and full life. Two of these were fleet owners in their own right, able to take the road, or not, as they felt inclined and enjoy plenty of time off for meals and refreshment. A third was a large gorilla-like man who had saved up enough, working as a driver for 'Armishmaag' (the United States Military Advisory Group), to buy himself a Mercedes Benz taxi. Women and food he proclaimed to be his sole interests, on which he spent all his money – allegedly, a habit learned from American soldiers. He claimed (in picturesque down-town Persian) to have three mistresses, and four square meals a day; and he left tomorrow to look after itself.

These men were exceptional. A more typical conversation ran as follows. Rather a pathetic broken-down middle-aged man, poorly dressed, said: 'I get up before dawn, plonk myself behind the wheel and drive solidly until noon. I have a quick bite at a café for eight Rials and then resume my work until sunset. I cannot drive after sunset because my eyes are weak and the headlamps do not work properly. That's what my life is like – if life you can call it. I barely exist and have no time for leisure or pleasure'. Or there was the example of a young man, well dressed, who had some sort of clerical job in an office. Having married, however, and acquired two children, he was obliged to become a taxi driver as well, to make ends meet. 'Now I am married, I have to take life seriously and I can't spend money on the girls as I used to. From what I earn, during the 18 hours a week that I put in with the taxi, I have to give 60 Tomans to the owner. The cost of petrol and oil is anything from 10 Tomans upwards, but on a good day there is often 30 Tomans left over for myself. With that I can buy food and clothes for the family and provide a roof over our heads. While I am in good health, we make ends meet; but I save nothing and, if I am off work, we go hungry'.

Naturally, the authorities frequently got it in the neck. Most taxi drivers disliked the police. *'Pedarsukhteh'* (the equivalent of 'bastard') was often muttered, as a taxi swept by the policeman on point duty. A frequent complaint was against privileged vehicles belonging to the army, the customs, and government ministries (in that order). The Tehran United Bus Company (in which the municipality are important share holders) was also fairly high on the 'hate list' – apparently because it was impossible to secure from them any compensation for damage to other vehicles which their buses might cause, even where the bus driver was clearly in the wrong. The same applied to the large number of military lorries of all shapes and sizes driven around Tehran, mostly empty, by ill-trained peasant drivers. The arrogance of some army officers had to be seen to be believed. As a corpulent uniformed colonel cut in front of us, the horn of his brand-new Chevrolet blaring, a sour and burly taxi driver turned to me and muttered 'In Mossadeq's day, these chaps used to creep about like mice'.

The attitude to Britain was usually favourable; most of the fire seemed to be drawn by the Americans. But I met three taxi drivers who expressed very forthright criticisms. The first driver took me up for casting aspersions at the new statue in Ferdowsi Square, which I compared unfavourably with the old statue, and which I did not consider worth the expense to the municipality. I was accused of attempting either to stir up the people's discontent against the government, or to elicit an expression of disloyalty to the Establishment from the driver and then betray him to the security authorities. In either case, I was told that the British interfered far too much in this country and should mind their own affairs. In some ways, I thought the snub was deserved. The second man said quite politely, but persistently, that the British were Iran's worst enemy. He enquired why my government interfered in Iranian internal affairs, why it stole Iranian oil and why in general it worked for his country's weakness. I was, he assured me, a spy. For proof, it was enough that I worked in the British embassy. A third taxi driver shrugged when I complimented him on his smart 1959 model Vauxhall Victor, with its newly designed, more comfortable seats. He said that the roads of Tehran were blocked with traffic because the British made a point of sending their cars here (he spoke as if we were unloading unwanted junk). All the troubles of Persia were attributable to the British. The British, he said, think that they are the only people who need oil. (The implication was that the British had cornered it on the pretence that no one else wanted it!) Iran would be better off if it had no oil, because the people did not benefit and the profit of the oil industry merely went to swell the corruption of the ruling class. He said, in his parting shot: 'You British are incredibly cunning. You twist the Russians and the Americans round your finger, and here in Iran the Americans are spending all the money and the British reaping all the rewards.'

The Iranian Establishment as a whole came in for criticism on any and every score from most taxi drivers, an element among whom tended to be politically conscious to a degree, especially on the points where the government touched their own lives. Passing a military band playing in Tupkhaneh Square, I commented favourably on the spectacle and brought down on my head the scorn both of my taxi driver and a young government official who was travelling in the same vehicle. The taxi driver said: 'You don't enjoy music on an empty belly. Look at the sort of life we have to lead here. How much do your London taxi drivers make a day? Enough to live on, that's certain, which is more than we get… the government are corrupt and have no interest in our welfare… all they do is to set up statues, construct fountains, plant lawns and lavish millions of Rials on an army, just so that it can make a noise in Tupkhaneh Square.' The other passenger, who was well dressed and well spoken, cut savagely in: 'I am in the same position myself. A government official, I can't even begin to live on my salary. I have to find a job in commerce to work at in the afternoons and evenings. Is that how a government should treat its employees?'

One man said: 'It's all very well for you to tell me not to drive so fast. I *have* to do so. The governing class compel the people to hurry, and taxis too, in order to find bread for their mouths. That's how the government keep the people from thinking about the injustices imposed upon them'. Another said: 'We are a clever people – naturally cleverer than any other people on earth – but we lack a leader. The government have forsaken their claim to leadership because they have no interest in our plight'.

Criticism of the Shah and his entourage was less often voiced by taxi drivers. Their chief preoccupations were with the dishonesty, incompetence and ineffectiveness of the government departments and authorities who had most to do with their daily life – the police, the Mayor's office, the Ministry of Roads, etc. Nevertheless, one or two taxi drivers chose to speak up. One said: 'The tragedy of Iran is that the Shah and his advisers are ignorant of the people's fate. They do not know what we have to suffer through the corruptness and inefficiency of the administration, who can successfully conceal their shortcomings from above. The Shah would not permit police officers to muck me about like they do, but he does not know what is happening, so nothing can be done.' Another was more severe. He accused the Shah and to a lesser extent his ministers of hopeless corruption and self-aggrandisement, which had grown worse rather than better as a result of the Mossadeq shake-up. The taxi driver concluded with a sidelong leer of a broad, brutal and unshaven face 'But we'll put this right in the end. Don't you worry. The time is coming…'

In the end, of course, that time did indeed come (in 1979 to be precise), to our and their sorrow. I see that the Shah probably had to go; but am not entirely sure that the Ayatollah, and the theocratic dictatorship and kleptocracy which followed, were what the long-suffering Iranian people deserved or truly desired. And the UK, so notorious among the Persians for interference in their internal affairs? We had forsaken our evil ways, ceased to follow internal Iranian politics quite so closely, and gotten used to devoting ourselves largely to export promotion.

Glad I wasn't ambassador in Tehran, for what William Shawcross has called 'The Shah's Last ride'. Fortunately, I was by then the EU's representative in Tokyo... concerning myself with - yes - export promotion. And in London? The outgoing Old Labour government was divided and in disarray, while the incoming Mrs Thatcher inexperienced in office and - on this front, at least - uncertain and irresolute.

It was time for the Persians to make their own decisions and for all of us to live with the consequences.

9

RESIDENT CLERK - WHAT A LARK!

It was always my nightmare.

In my flat in the Foreign Office, I being off duty, a crowded cocktail party would be in progress. A sprinkling of my Ministry of Defence colleagues and military friends, among other guests, were helping me to whoop it up in the drawing room overlooking St James's Park and Buckingham Palace. Mistakenly, the switchboard had put through a call to the green telephone on the large mahogany desk. Before I could get to it, a drunken dragoon or giggly grenadier would pick the receiver up. A plummy voice from no 10 would enquire whether the Foreign Secretary was dining at Brooks's that evening. The dragoon or grenadier, fazed if not actually fuddled, would enquire who was calling. The plummy voice would announce himself as Harold Macmillan. The dragoon/grenadier would reply: 'If you are the Prime Minister, then I am the Archbishop of Canterbury'! And put the phone down. Fortunately, it never quite happened to me. But tradition had it that one of my predecessors had been so betrayed – possibly, it was Philip Ziegler (I must ask him).

To put this in context, I should explain that for three years in the early '60s, I was a 'Resident Clerk' in the Foreign Office. They don't have them any more. They were finally phased out, after various transmogrifications, in 2003. New technology and management structures had finally made them redundant. But, back in 1961, with three other colleagues, I shared sprawling accommodation on the top floor of the FO tower. In that lofty and commanding architectural eminence, each of us had a drawing room and a bedroom; we shared a magnificent dining room; our basic necessities were delivered by Harrods (at our expense); but the accommodation was rent free and they paid us £300 per annum on top of our salaries – a lot of nightclub money, in 1961!

During the working day, we had our 'desk' jobs – I myself was then engaged in multilateral diplomacy in the Western Organisations Department. Each night, however, we took it in turn to be on call. Some evenings, I dined in tranquillity and slept undisturbed. On others, the telephone would ring in the early hours; the corridors would echo to the clatter of containers and the shuffle of boots, as frock coated and deferential messengers brought urgent diplomatic telegrams incoming from the ends of the earth. Three missionaries had vanished in the Congo; please inform next of kin. An ambassador proposed last-minute modifications to the instructions he had received for his call on the president the following day. Our representative at the United Nations was on the direct line (at 8pm his time, but 1am on my watch): a new situation had arisen in the Security Council and he proposed to act thus – did the Permanent Under-Secretary of State concur? The Prime Minister wanted to know where the foreign secretary could be found that evening. A businessman was at London airport preparing to fly off to Berlin to clinch a major contract; but he had left his passport behind in Newcastle. Tribesmen from across the border had raided a village and massacred the guard post in the Fezzan. Could the RAF Commander, Aden, call down an air strike on the retreating band at dawn, before they crossed back into neutral territory; if so, could the Hunters use their rockets or only machine guns? Sometimes the Resident Clerk could give the answer, either at his own discretion or on the basis of comprehensive advice left with him overnight by a Foreign Office department that was on the ball; more often, he had to consult speedily the senior officials concerned, get the blessing of a minister, summon advisers into the building at all hours to cope with a complex and changing situation.

I have more vivid memories, even, than those. One Saturday morning, a prominent member of the National Front had been sprung from prison, and stormed up Downing Street, demanding to present a petition against coloured immigration to the Prime Minister. The man and an NF junior crony were expeditiously ushered across the road to the Foreign Office front door, and thence – escorted by two elderly and apprehensive security guards – to the rooms of the Resident Clerk. Coincidently, it was the Trooping of the Colour, and we clerks and our girlfriends, the latter fragrant and attired as if for Royal Ascot, were crowded to the windows. I received the man in the dining room, took note of his remarks and accepted the petition (scrawled on sheets of cheap lined paper, although not in purple ink). I had never met anyone as ill-favoured or malevolent; the sidekick with him, too, would have given Pol Pot a fright. Through the windows, the mass bands played, 'Men of Harlech', since it was the year that the colour of the Welsh Guards was being trooped. As I shook their hands, I shook my head: 'Bloody Scots, Irish and Welsh. But ours has always been a mixed-blood country'. If they had understood, one of them would probably have taken a swipe at me; but the pair were ushered out before the penny dropped.

On another, calmer, occasion a key figure – and predictably a dodgy one – in the Profumo scandal called to see me. He was to pass on a discreet oral message for the Permanent Under-Secretary of State, about the grave misdemeanours of Miss Keeler. This won me an anonymous mention in the subsequent White Paper.

But my most felicitous intrusion was from Ted Heath, then Lord Privy Seal in the Foreign Office and No. Two to Lord Home, the Foreign Secretary. When his private office was working flat out, mid-evening, and Edward Heath, momentarily unemployed, was driving them all mad with his fussing about, his aides not infrequently sent him up to the Resident Clerk's Mess on the top floor, to cadge a drink, and pick up the latest news about the outside world.

As no war was being declared at that moment, and the telephone was silent, I was lounging in my window seat, gazing through the mist at the lamp-lit bridge that crossed St James's Park. The view could have been drawn by Hiroshige. Some Vivaldi was playing quietly on my gramophone. As was his custom, Heath burst in unannounced, demanding gossip and refreshment. After I had fixed his gin and vermouth, he wandered around my drawing room, looking at my pictures (one of them, a more than halfway respectable early Trevelyan). Coming to the white marble mantelpiece, with its Ming vases and French carriage clock, Heath found, propped against the Pugin wallpaper, an open copy of a book of poems, in the Persian original, by Hafez. Pointing at the elegant kufic calligraphy, he barked 'I bet you can't tell me what that lot says?'

Joining him, my index finger tracing the flowing script, and my lips moving silently, I studied the ghazals carefully.

'Hafez writes: "The Vizier dips the crystal goblet into the blue tiled basin of the Fountain of Life. Turning to the Sultan's silken concubine, beside him on the damask divan in the Paradise Garden, the Commander of the Faithful whispers, upon the cooling wind that blows, that all fame, all beauty, all riches and all power are evanescent, flowing fleetingly, as this water, into the Darkness of Destiny", as far as I can make it out, Sir.'

The Lord Privy Seal grunted. 'A gloomy lot, those Persians', draining his glass and returning downstairs to resume the harassment of his housecarls.

I should explain that classical Persian poetry, even more than Chaucerian English, requires much construing and thumbing of large dictionaries. As I had not yet had a spare hour or three to construe that particular page, in my regular efforts to keep up with the language, I had had to make it all up for Ted Heath's benefit. On occasions, necessity can prove the mother of invention.

10

'THE NUMBER ONE TWISTER OF CAMBODIA'

'Put not thy trust in princes'. But this does not mean that diplomats do not have to deal with them.

From 1964-1966, I served in Phnom Penh, as Chargé d'Affaires *ad interim*, at the head of a British Embassy to Cambodia which – shortly before my arrival, to pick up the pieces – had been trashed by a Government-directed mob. The head of state, Prince Norodom Sihanouk, had furthermore declared it treasonous for any of his loyal subjects to have social (as opposed to business or official) contact with 'Anglo-Saxon' diplomats (i.e. British or American). By mid 1965 the Brits (although not the Yanks) were beginning to come back into favour. The head of state wanted to be nice. But how could he rescind his interdict, without losing face?

One evening, to help celebrate a royal wedding, I was invited to the palace, where I was greeted by the sound of revelry by night. Cambodia's beauty, her chivalry and her diplomacy were gathered in a single gracious setting. Fireworks cascaded across the indigo midnight sky, illuminating the wide waters of the mighty Mekong River and the fringes of sugar palm trees which stood along the banks. Tropical flowers released their slow perfume upon the balmy breeze. The chandeliers shone over fair women, brave men and rotund ambassadors. A thousand hearts beat happily. His Royal Highness Prince Comrade Norodom Sihanouk, dressed in an impeccable dark-blue silk tuxedo, conducted the palace orchestra as they played a dance number of his composition.

Then, a change of mood; a different sound struck like a rising knell. Hush! Hark!! Was it the remote thunder of a B52 bombing raid across the Cambodian frontier with Vietnam???

Happily, that night, not so. The Prince having handed over his baton and withdrawn to mingle with his guests, and the normal conductor taking over, the band had struck up an entirely novel – even alien – rhythm, fresh from the West: Chubby Checker's 'Let's twist again, like we did last summer'. The elders and chamberlains froze; the generals looked to their aides; the young Cambodian lords and ladies glanced around them for a lead; the cabinet ministers and parliamentarians seemed puzzled; the diplomatic corps hesitated politely, taken by surprise. It was my cue, my only moment of greatness, ever.

The bride happened to be quite the loveliest young woman at Court – and the prima ballerina of the royal corps de ballet. I had often admired her, in traditional head-dress and costume, dancing at the head of her troupe – on one entirely unforgettable occasion, in the open air, against the backdrop of the floodlit temple of Angkor Wat. A favourite daughter of the head of state, Bopha Devi was a royal princess over whose petite figure and bejewelled but diminutive fingers the giant figure of General de Gaulle was to bow low during a forthcoming state visit to Phnom Penh. But this moment was mine, not the General's.

Like most intellectuals, and some theologians, I am a disco devotee. A habitué of Hélène Cordet's 'Saddle Room' in Park Lane throughout the early 'sixties, I was well up to speed in these matters. The palace soirée had hitherto proven rather stilted. A self-conscious and slightly worried Chargé d'Affaires of a mere thirty-three summers, I had been zealously over-doing the diplomatic hard graft. In a moment of recklessness and release, I nodded briefly to His Highness this and His Excellency that with whom I had been talking in my stilted French, crossed the ballroom to the Princess and swept her wordlessly onto the floor. After a minute of bewilderment, she caught my rhythm; after two minutes, was twisting elegantly but with enthusiasm; and after five minutes, found herself alone with me in the middle of a wide circle of spectators – some agape and a-goggle, others smiling cheerfully, yet others (mostly the communist heads of mission) envious and disapproving.

When the music stopped, the Princess giggled and withdrew, while I struggled to recover my breath. On the MC's mike, the unmistakably regal voice of 'Monseigneur' cut through the speculative murmurs of the court, declaring that Monsieur Fielding was then and there awarded the title of *Le Twisteur Numéro Un du Cambodge*. The orchestra broke into a ragged fanfare, and a chamberlain was sent running for a prize which the head of state duly handed over – in the shape of a silver Cambodian cockerel in a crocodile-skin box bearing the crest of the Khmer monarchy. I bowed and withdrew with appropriate self-deprecation into the surrounding throng, where enemies offered me reluctant congratulations, friends slapped me on the back, creeps ingratiated themselves, and two newspaper editors asked me for my view of the foreign policy implications.

The apotheosis of the (admittedly slightly pseudo) so-called 'playboy Chargé d'Affaires' was thereby complete. Eighteen months after my first arrival in a less than welcoming Phnom Penh, the dog-house was now behind us. It was Sihanouk, not Checker, that I had to thank. Royal edicts sending foreign embassies to Coventry are rarely formally rescinded; they tend simply to be air-brushed out, when convenient. So the end of the story had a twist to it.

11

UNCLE SAM AND THE NORWEGIAN MARINERS

In November 1965, on my watch in Phnom Penh, a big-time British peace envoy arrived in town, master plan in pocket. No less than The Right Honourable Patrick Gordon Walker, ex-Oxford academic, ex-MP and ex-Foreign Secretary, sent my way by Prime Minister Harold Wilson.

Mr Gordon Walker's mission? To guarantee Cambodia's neutrality, and open the door to a negotiated settlement to the war in Vietnam. Gosh! The Great Man was (deliberately and rather rudely) denied an audience with H.R.H. Prince Norodom Sihanouk, the Cambodian head of state; but did get to see the Foreign Minister (later, in a convenient opium den – see chapter 12 – I myself got to see the Prime Minister), to put across Her Britannic Majesty's Government's seductive proposals. While all the key figures in the Cambodian cabinet liked our ideas, Prince Sihanouk did not – suspecting a trap by Uncle Sam. Diplomatically, you could have heard a pin drop; would the Cambodians cut a deal – or kick the card table over?

By design, not accident, all hell broke loose shortly after Patrick Gordon Walker, Douglas Brown (his accompanying private secretary) and I had left the Foreign Ministry. A noisy demonstration took place outside the American Embassy, followed by a serious mob attack on its premises. It had been ordered (at a safe distance – he was communing with the spirits of his ancestors in a remote summer palace in the mountains) by the said Norodom Sihanouk.

As the Chargé d'Affaires in the British Embassy, I was Our Man On The Spot, responsible for Patrick Gordon Walker's sanity and safety. Both were quickly called into question, because Gordon Walker's first reflex was to hurry off to the US Embassy, and place himself between the mob and the mission, bearing his breast, and exposing his dome-like and donnish head to the brick bats. Knowing the Phnom Penh mob all too well, I told him politely that his plan was utter madness (although I think I used the words 'unprofessional and liable to be counter-productive'). If injury were to befall him, we should have to say goodbye to the peace conference that Mr Harold Wilson wanted.

Nevertheless, PGW had to be given something to do, by way of distraction. I secured The Great Man's assent to an alternative plan of action, in two phases.

We had already been in touch with our besieged American friends by telephone and knew the scene which surrounded them – thousands of screaming rioters blocking all the streets leading to the US chancery; a rain of missiles against the building; the flag torn down from a balcony; the windows broken; relays of people battering at the main door. Our first step should therefore be, however deaf the ears of the authorities, at least to make an attempt to get belated police protection for the Yanks. PGW and I divided forces. To keep him occupied and out of trouble, I sent him off on an intentionally time-consuming and pointless mission, to call on the Soviet Ambassador. The latter was then the Dean of the Diplomatic Corps and therefore the spokesman of all the foreign embassies in all matters affecting their general relations with the Cambodian authorities. Predictably, the Russian – a foxy man, with a KGB back ground – shrugged the matter off, saying that he had no knowledge that a riot was in progress. At the same time, I myself shot off on a recce, and then made my way to the Ministry of Foreign Affairs (closed in the afternoons, as is frequently the custom in tropical countries), to call on the duty officer. He received me, suitably shifty and shamefaced; admitted that he was aware of what was afoot; and assured me that he had already notified the police. I told him in no uncertain terms that, if so, there was precious little result to show; on my way to the ministry, I had been able to observe, mingling as unobtrusively as I could with the outskirts of the crowds, that the police were conspicuous by their total absence. The duty officer said he would telephone again.

Back at my house, PGW and I and the private secretary compared notes together and concluded (as I had secretly expected) that we had got nowhere. I had already telephoned through to the US chancery an account of what I had been able to see of how the attack was developing (they could not judge this too well from inside as they had to keep clear of the upstairs windows, and the ground-floor windows were obscured but protected by metal shutters). This completed Phase One.

Phase Two of my plan, after the tactically prudent and carefully judged elapse of wasted time, was to track the mob more closely. We went first – another privily time-wasting exercise – to our own chancery, some distance from the American, to make sure all was well. In the anticipation that trouble might arise, I had already told everyone to go home and stay out of sight, while arranging with the Military Attaché, the Vice-Consul and other male staff for regular surveillance of the chancery premises. These were completely locked up, everything stowed away behind locks and bars, and the shutters drawn. The transport yard was empty, the official vehicles dispersed. A quick inspection showed that all was well; the streets were clear and there was hardly a sign of life to be seen anywhere. The servants quarters were empty and locked up too; men, women and children, they had all departed with such of their possessions as they could carry, having chalked on their doors in Cambodian a plea that their houses should be spared.

A Fabius Cunctator with no more excuses not to proceed to the scene of action, I slowly drove the three of us in an unmarked car to the nearest quiet spot. Patrick Gordon Walker, Douglas Brown and I then threaded our way along a side street which I had explored earlier, leading up to the cross roads where the Americans were located. The mob grew numerous and noisy and we began to attract glances that were initially merely curious but, soon, frankly disapproving. A solitary policeman told us that we should not be there and then turned away to talk to someone else. We sidled forward, quite close by now to the US building; but then got stuck in the press, which swayed this way and that, as the stones flew. Above the din, some people yelled at us. We avoided eye contact. It was all starting to turn a little too 'hairy'. We started to get jostled. Being the youngest and perhaps also having been half-recognised by a local thug, I received a shove in the ribs, which I took care not to return. Accordingly I exchanged shrugs with Douglas Brown, and decided that we should pull out, discretion being the better part of valour.

Pursued by catcalls, we slid back down the street and turned into a dingy, dimly lit and vaguely disreputable bar which had just decided to open its doors. So we ordered three beers – in French, so as to excite no anti-Anglo-Saxon sentiments – before starting to speak among ourselves in pseudo-Norwegian. (I had given the other two, before we came in, the cover story that we were crew from a visiting freighter in the port).

I said, as one does, '*God dag. Hoora for den Norske Fiske*' (an expression which I had picked up, naturally enough, while reading Persian as a post graduate student at the School of Oriental and African Studies in London in the 1950s).

On cue, bless him, Patrick Gordon Walker came in, slowly and with seafaring melancholy, on the broad line of: *'God dag! Ja! Ik bin enkapteinen van der 'Oslo'!'*.

Douglas followed in similar vein, with something like: *'Hvordan har De det? Et stort glass mørkt øl. Skål!'*.

We then got going one of those brooding Scandinavian conversations, punctuated by long pauses, Nordic *'Ja-Ha'*s and penetrating gazes into the middle distance, that Ingmar Bergman had made familiar to all. I did a running translation into French for the barman. (*'Snakker De fransk?'*) But as the gentle reader will already have realised, we none of us really spoke Norwegian. Struggling with fits of the giggles, we started eventually to lose credibility with the barman. It was time to go to the loo (*'Hvor er toalettet?'*), pay up and go outside to take another look.

This return to the charge was to carry us clear to our objective. The roar of angry voices was abating; the crowd was beginning to thin out; the police were becoming more numerous; the missiles, more sporadic. We edged up to the corner of the crossroads just across from the US chancery's front door. There we found another bar, with a telephone. I at once got on the blower to the Americans to tell them the latest on what was happening and where we were. Less than a quarter of an hour later, the roads cleared immediately to our front, the mob having broken up and gone away. The acting head of the Political Section, Doug Perry, accompanied by a US Marine Corps NCO, came down to the ground floor, by pre-arrangement, to let us in through the battered front doors. The latter had resisted very well but took some opening. We walked as casually as we could across the street as the last half bricks sailed overhead.

Upstairs, the first man we met was Mr Alf Bergeson. Alf was young to be a Chargé d'Affaires. But he was an ex-Naval Academy (always a recommendation), Boston Brahmin-style diplomat, in the old tradition – courteous, conciliatory, shrewd, endowed with both a saving sense for the ridiculous and a sense of humour. (Almost an Englishman, in fact). Originally First Secretary and head of the Political Section in the US Embassy in Phnom Penh, he eventually became the Embassy's appointed chief, following the gradual removal of his seniors. The last American Chargé d'Affaires before the Embassy was finally withdrawn the following month, it was therefore Bergeson who saw out the final mob attack. We found him calmly supervising the damage control, with a lop-sided grin. In an office in which the windows had been stove in, the furniture smashed and the floor littered with stones and rotten fruit, we heard his account of what had happened. Then he gestured, with an apologetic shrug, at the shattered air conditioning apparatus in the corner that was groaning and shuddering its last moments, emitting irregular blasts of noisy, hot air. Through the gaps in the window frame, the recessional roar of the retreating mob could be heard. 'Sorry about these modern machines of ours,' he said, 'don't seem to make them like we used to'. Then Patrick Gordon Walker, Douglas Brown and I went the rounds, shaking hands with the rest of the staff and laughing – a shade too heartily it was true

– at all the jokes. The Yanks were in good heart and had conducted them selves with admirable Anglo-Saxon phlegm. (Quite like 'Norwegians').

I gave a dinner that night for Patrick Gordon Walker, attended by members of staff and my principal foreign diplomatic cronies. Alf Bergeson managed to make it after the soup (having had a hectic period clearing up, reporting to Washington and leaving the necessary instructions). It was a light-hearted affair, with everyone in a mood for relaxation. So there were no speeches. But I did propose one toast – 'Uncle Sam!'

Gordon Walker departed. I then went back to the Cambodian Foreign Minister and gave him, for the first time, and last, as it happened in our professional relationship (and the poor man was to be swept away, later, along with his Prime Minister, in Pol Pot's pogrom) an unvarnished piece of my mind. I reported all that, bitterly, by telegram. The Foreign Secretary replied, laconically, 'You spoke well'.

12

ON HER BRITANNIC MAJESTY'S DIPLOMATIC SERVICE, CHEZ MADAME CHHUM

Diplomacy, East of Suez, can on occasion be a dodgy business.

Dinner that evening at the French ambassador's is fun; interesting and articulate people; chilled Rosé de Tavel. But I have another subsequent assignation. My Cambodian chauffeur, and my huge Austin 'Princess', have been given the evening off. In white tuxedo and black tie, I slide into my little open-top white motor and move quietly away from the Ambassador's elegant house, into the tropical night. I head south, for the ill-lit outskirts of Phnom Penh. Most of the real estate round here is owned by *Maman Vénérée* – more correctly known as the Queen Mother of Cambodia. I park, self-effacingly, one hundred yards short my objective. Ahead, there is a large wooden building, surrounded by trees, and lit by candles and spirit lamps. Further up the un-tarmaced street, leaning against a lamp post, is a Cambodian gendarme – not that the capital city is dangerous to walk at night, but nevertheless an outward and physical sign of Her Majesty, the Queen Mother's inward and spiritual concern that her property should be fully respected. And, indeed, three or four official-looking limousines are already parked, closer to the entrance (their drivers absent, or leaning back in their seats, sleeping, open-mouthed).

I walk up onto the veranda, and receive whispered greetings. First, I am ushered into the presence of Madam Chhum, whose fingertips I kiss, and who signifies to the staff that I am *persona grata*. I shed my European clothes, wrap one of the house sarongs around my hips, order two *Trente-*

Trois, ice-cold French lagers, and enquire after His Highness. As agreed, he is expecting me.

An exceptionally pretty Vietnamese girl (Madame Chhum's was said to be more than a mere opium den, although I never checked that out) leads me down a wooden corridor carpeted with rice straw, to one of the top class chambers. Within, lying prone upon the floor, a wrinkled Cambodian crone of advanced age (possibly even over 50), with the illumination of a rush light, is preparing the opium.

First, she makes it bubble and boil, over a spirit lamp. Then, she transfers the oleaginous lump to the ceramic bowl of a bamboo-stemmed pipe. This, in turn, is passed to the Minister, himself lying prone, in a sarong, on a low bench to one side. Within the chamber, as throughout the house, there permeates the sickly-sweet smell of top-grade opium on the boil. His Highness, an habitué, has already in the course of the evening, consumed several pipes; no doubt he is proposing to take one more, before going home.

I myself have never found opium (once, some years before, gingerly essayed at a Qashqai feast, in tribal Iran) offers me anything approaching the charms of a gin and tonic. But there is no accounting for taste. Anyway, sharing the *Trente-Trois*, we begin to talk frankly and at ease.

Yes, 'Monseigneur' (i.e. Prince Sihanouk, the Cambodian Head of State) has acted arbitrarily and without consultation. The Chinese have leaned on him. But the entire Cabinet, while ultimately powerless in confrontation with a *deva reja* or god king, nevertheless wishes to accept the latest proposal of the British Government for a peace conference. They are grateful to Prime Minister Wilson, to Mr Patrick Gordon Walker and naturally also to me. So, would I like a pipe? (I decline, politely).

Slowly, gently, without any manifestation of egregious emotion or horrible hurry, I withdraw, pressing my palms together and bowing, as Cambodian good manners require. Resuming my tuxedo and its accessories, I settle a grossly exorbitant bill for two beers; I once more kiss Madam Chhum's fingertips; I slip away in search of my Triumph. Back at the residence, I scribble some notes on the pad by my bedside table, and fall asleep, free (after my final hot shower of the day) of the clinging odour of opium. Tomorrow, at 8am, will be soon enough to send off my cipher telegram to the Foreign Secretary.

13

FRIENDLY FIRE

Some cats have nine lives. I myself, these days, rather less than nine.

The incident took place one sunny day in 1966 on the Cambodian frontier with South Vietnam. No diplomatic attaché was hurt, except in his dignity. But there was a certain amount of dry-cleaning and renewal of wardrobes to be done afterwards.

The Khmer village was a mess. Bomb craters. Slight residual smell of cordite and burning generally. Trees uprooted or chopped by machine gun fire. Straw huts on stilts, blown over. Farm implements scattered. Untended chickens pecking around in the mud. Dead buffaloes with distended bellies, legs pointed stiffly at the sky. A dead human or two, rattan screens flung over the messier bits, to keep the flies off. Otherwise, on the broader landscape, a tranquil and traditional Cambodian setting. Bushy topped sugar palms. A chequered pattern of dark green rice fields, divided by earthen tracks and wayside ditches. In the middle distance, a line of low, steep-sided hills covered with scrub. Flashes of water here and there, running along the irrigation channels. Somewhere not far away, an ill-marked international frontier. A blue sky with a few fluffy white clouds.

The day before, the village had been attacked by the Americans, more likely by navigational error than in Hot Pursuit of Red Hordes. The village was apparently without military association. The International Control Commission (ICC) from Phnom Penh was now on the scene to investigate – Indian, Polish and Canadian diplomats, accompanied by assorted attachés from the British, French and one or two other embassies. A column of jeeps and land rovers was neatly drawn up on the laterite road just outside the village proper. Altogether, twenty or thirty foreign observers and Cambodian officials, all in smart civilian clothes, wandered through the village with maps and cameras and notebooks, assembling material for a report on yet another 'Frontier Incident'.

Not far away, just within Vietnam, our gallant allies were still at it, in defence of democracy. There was a crump of bombs and a rising column of smoke, not too far distant. Also the sound of aircraft. One of these, a Skyraider with US markings, flew across the border to inspect us, stirred by curiosity. We must have looked like a Sunday School outing or a Swan Hellenic tourist expedition – Panama hats, white shirts, old school ties, neatly pressed lightweight suits. The Skyraider pilot had clearly seen nothing like it before in Vietnam, or even back in Alabama or Tennessee. He'd already dropped his two bombs, but still had some ammo left and five minutes more flying time over the area. After another circle to make sure that we really were a Viet Cong force on the march to Saigon, he straightened up, entered a shallow dive, took a bead and opened up. ZOOM, ROAR, TAT-TATTA-TAT.

Well before that, the Skyraider had attracted everyone's wholehearted attention, even that of Mr Bindra – the very fat and frequently quite confused Head of the ICC. The Vienna Convention on Diplomatic Privileges and Immunities appeared, there and then, more a scrap of paper than a cast-iron guarantee. The Sunday School scattered – Brits first, being better trained and more professional – diving for cover in the village ditches. Mr Bindra was on top of the Brits, who could hardly breathe. But that suited them just fine and dandy. To either side were Russians smelling of BO and Poles of cheap scent – also good protection.

The Skyraider, mission accomplished, flew off back to Saigon and (possibly) one of those tinny medals the Americans shower on their military heroes. After a few minutes, the diplomatic observers all emerged diplomatically from their various places of diplomatic hiding, brushed some of the mud off their diplomatic ducks, waved away the last of the Polish aftershave and looked around them. Mr Bindra had won the gold medal – he was already almost within reach of his jeep. The rest of the party followed at different speeds, the Anglo-Saxons affecting a nonchalant stroll. No one had been hit.

At the back of the crocodile, the laid-back, laconic voice of the Australian military attaché rose above the shuffle of Gucci moccasins:

'Yeah. US pilots. I reckon either they're green, or they're yella? That one was green!'

14

THE CROCODILE PRINCESS

The girl was gulped down, regurgitated, buried upriver. But she still speaks and is spoken to. I was one of those who spoke.

Just over twenty miles up the Mekong River from the town of Kratié, at a jungle village called Sambaur, there is a tomb of importance in the beliefs of the Cambodians. In it repose the ashes of the Princess Nucheat Khatr Vorpheak, who met a tragic death in 1834 while still of tender age. Bathing in the waters of the Tonle Sap near the then royal capital of Oudong, she disappeared. Some months later, her body, somehow preserved from decay, was discovered inside a crocodile killed many miles away up the Mekong at Sambaur. The beast had evidently swallowed the child whole, and carried the body undigested for miles down the Tonle Sap to Phnom Penh, where the river flows into the Mekong, and then upstream beyond Kratié, a journey of around one hundred and ninety miles.

The Princess was duly cremated, as was and still is the custom; a 'stupa', or conical funerary tower, being erected in her memory and over her ashes at Sambaur. She was highborn and beautiful, of royal descent; she had died while still immature and hence, as the Cambodians see these matters, unmarked by sin; the recovery of her remains seemed little short of miraculous. These qualities, taken together, indicated the special favour in which she stood with the 'Tevodas', the mysterious divinities which presided over and protected the Kingdom of Cambodia. It was not long before the spirit of the dead princess made contact with the living through the person of a 'Hora', or medium, at the Royal Court.

Through a succession of clairvoyant astrologers, the Princess came to assert a benign influence on a succession of kings and rulers. The most potent of all the human spirits of the realm, her special care was said to be the national survival and prosperity and – in that light – the conduct of Cambodian foreign affairs. Princess Vorpheak was credited with having tendered sage advice throughout the trials and indeed near-extinction which threatened the country in the 19th century; while in more recent times, she had predicted the success of the 'Royal Crusade' – the campaign against the French Protectorate, conducted by the King of Cambodia, which was to result in the grant of national independence in 1953.

I was enchanted by the legend of the princess when I first heard it on taking charge in Phnom Penh in 1964, and fondly thought of her whenever I made a major move in my relations with the Cambodian government. What would she think and how would she advise? Would she look with favour on my efforts, such as they were, to patch up old quarrels and help Cambodia in her struggle for peace and survival? I never knew the answer to these questions. Her presence was not widely spoken of. Few foreigners knew of her existence. No diplomats went to Sambaur. Nevertheless, I decided, within a few weeks of the conclusion of my diplomatic mission to Cambodia, to visit her tomb.

It was the season of heavy rains and dark grey clouds. I set out with a couple of scholarly Australian friends across flooded rice fields, along muddy river banks and through foetid dark jungle, on an arduous seventy-two hour round trip.

Close to sundown, we came to a halt where the laterite track disappeared under floodwater. Here, we took a boat; a long pirogue with an outboard motor, plying as a sort of Green Line bus between riparian villages. Stopping here and there on our way, we slid up the Mekong, finally coming to a halt at Sambaur. Disembarked, we wandered along soggy paths between the wood-framed, rush-walled houses. Few people were about in the late afternoon: one or two dark-skinned peasants loped by, wheeling bicycles; some Chinese shopkeepers stared blankly from their dark interiors; a group of children scampered along; dogs barked. I exchanged some

Cambodian with those who would listen, but received only baffled smiles. Eventually, we came into an open space where a rather dilapidated and apparently deserted monastery stood in the clear grey light. A large wooden building, the temple itself, stood in the middle of the square, surrounded by lesser buildings of leaf and straw where the monks no doubt lived when they were at home – we could see newly-washed yellow robes laid out to dry. To one side stood the stupa of Princess Nucheat Khatr Vorpheak.

I chose not to approach the stupa at once, but walked into the temple and stood looking up the length of the dim nave to the figures of the Buddha that stood elevated on their thrones. To them I mentally addressed my message, explaining why I had come. I have always felt at peace with the Buddha, in his simple Cambodian effigy; serene, but deeply human. I felt so at that moment, in that empty and decaying temple, in that remote retreat from the world of my origin.

I then plucked up courage to walk towards the stupa. A tall conical structure, it stood, in a clearing apart, on a stone terrace of its own. Although restored in 1956, the tomb was already showing the erosion that time brings so speedily in its wake in tropical countries. The mosquitoes sang in my ears as I approached and the heat seemed the more stifling for there being no sun. Behind the stupa stood the dark green of the jungle and the khaki of the hutments. Above the stupa's needle point, house-high in the air, the thick oily grey clouds sat overhead, heavy with more rain. A slight drizzle began to fall.

My mind felt blank, despite a quickening of the pulse. Perhaps I was screening it from self-conscious and superstitious melodrama or, worse still, from disappointment and bathos. But as I looked up from the foot of the stupa, I felt suddenly quite sad; it was not a distinguished edifice, being patched up here and there with cement, and covered by patches of light green moss; and I was struck by an emptiness, as of the tomb of Christ on the day of His ascension. Then something happened. My foot slipped on the wet steps of the terrace. I took this for the accident it was and walked a step or two nearer. After I had looked about me for a few minutes more, my foot slipped again. I could see that the stones beneath my foot were wet with rain. And I knew that the rubber soles of the comfortable jungle boots on my feet were worn smooth with long service. Yet I had been standing still when I slipped. Slipping and sliding a third time, I apprehensively backed down off the terrace, walked some distance away from the stupa and turned squarely to face it, like an Anglican looking at the altar at Matins in a Norman parish church in Shropshire.

My mind then cleared. I felt rebuffed and resentful. Without either bogus reverence or caucasian condescension, but certainly with an edge of reproach, I laid my thoughts calmly and consecutively before the Princess Vorpheak, as if I had been speaking aloud.

I said that I was a foreigner who did not know the Khmer customs, who had lived for less than three years in Kampuchea, and who would shortly leave for a destination at the further end of the earth [Paris], never to return to Sambaur. But I had come as a friend of the country and its people, and as one who respected the legend of the Princess. This legend was the property of Khmers and not of the British, and it was not for me to believe it or to disbelieve it. It was true that in the mental world in which I lived and had been brought up, I found it hard to see how a child long since dead could be active in the affairs of the living. Yet my civilization laid no claim to all knowledge and to all wisdom, and my personal over-scepticism could well be mistaken or, perhaps more probably, misplaced. In electing to visit the stupa, therefore, I had chosen to accept the legend as it stood; and I had had the presumption to offer the Princess, although I was an alien, some portion of the gratitude and respect which was unquestionably her due from all Cambodians.

The Princess, if she existed, and could receive my thoughts, would know with what a heavy heart I had first come to Phnom Penh and how initially critical and ill at ease I had felt there. The Embassy's chancery had been sacked by a government-directed mob; the Ambassador had been withdrawn and embassy dependants evacuated. Sent up from a comfortable and interesting job in Singapore to take charge of the remnant, I had found that my attachés and I were in Coventry. Cambodians – apart from servants and language tutors and Cambodian ministers and senior officials in the security of their offices – had been forbidden contact with us. My French had been initially rusty, my Cambodian limited, and acquired only after a prodigious white-hot effort. So, my mission to Phnom Penh had not been of my choosing, and was no bed of roses. The responsibility which I then shared with the Foreign Secretary and his advisors in London was no mean thing for a young diplomat at the outset of his thirties: the attempt, through the Anglo-Russian co-chairmanship of the Geneva Conference on Indo-China, to win international recognition and respect for the neutrality and territorial integrity of Cambodia, and to count her out of the Vietnam War.

Her Highness would know that I had laboured to understand and to help. I had been grateful for whatever benevolence the Princess might have felt towards these efforts and I hoped that she would share my satisfaction that at least something had been done. I knew that there were tight limits to the effective action which my successors, as I myself, could take to advance the interests which it was the Princess's charge, under the 'Tevodas', to protect: the survival and happiness of the Khmer nation. But I asked her to be prepared to judge us fairly and generously, and to give us the credit of good intentions. Also I invited her, if she felt so disposed, to help the men who should come after me.

For a brief moment I had the impression of contact, of a message not merely sent but received. Then the emptiness came back and the everyday world once more took me in hand.

I walked up to the stupa again – this time without slipping – and tried to decipher the inscription in squiggly Cambodian lettering on the base. My friends approached from the monastery and we exchanged one or two commonplace remarks. I bent over my camera and took some photographs. Then we strolled back to the riverside in search of our boat. After a few minutes, the pilot took us away for half an hour upstream to deliver a passenger and a bundle or two on the last of his rounds. We smoked and gazed at the setting sun. Then the pirogue cast off for the last time and, turning into midstream, ran swiftly south with the current. It was dusk when we passed by Sambaur, silent in the shadow of the trees, one or two huts aglimmer with lanterns. I stood on the roof of the cabin searching the skyline. Briefly, I glimpsed what I was looking for – the top of the stupa standing out in ghostly grey contrast to the black jungle beyond.

Once again, the veil briefly lifted. This time, a wave of gentle emotion seemed to reach me from across the water. I felt that the Princess was sending me on my way with a message. For what I was, as such I had been accepted: a friend of Cambodia, within that wider discipline which made me before all else the servant of another country, the subject of another Crown.

15

TAMOURÉ IN TAHITI

'Not one of those chilly mortals then, Sir, are we?' It being the run-up to Christmas, H.M. Customs and Excise at Heathrow were being unwontedly jocular. Earlier, I had provoked the same reaction at a snowbound Orly (*'Décidément, Monsieur n'est pas frileux'*). All because, as a disciplined Government Official, and a Commissioned Officer of the Queen, I always declared everything, when passing through Customs, whether in this country or any other. In the end, I became so embarrassed that I felt I simply had to dispose of it honourably. Of course, I refer to my skimpy Polynesian grass skirt, a gift from a young lady of good family in Tahiti.

Travelling steerage with Qantas from Sydney to Los Angeles, I once found myself briefly stranded in French Polynesia. As a tourist on my first visit, this troubled me not a whit. The more so, for the fact that the local Qantas manager in Tahiti, taking pity on the pommie waif-and-stray, invited me to stay at his house until the strike was over – explaining that his wife would not mind, as she in her turn was stranded in Sydney. The object of the exercise was that, while the cat was away, the mice should play. We had 'barbies' on the beach, in front of his sprawling residence. Cartons of tinnies (which he termed 'heart-starters') came out of the deep freeze. The neighbours were invited in. Also Mme Lou-Lou, his chubby, pushing-fifty, cook/housekeeper. And her daughter, Mlle Leila, a slim lady in her early twenties, together with an even prettier companion. The first evening was decorous and restrained. The 'barbie' on the second night, however, to celebrate the lifting of the Qantas strike the following morning, was more exuberant. It was announced to the manager's circle as a pyjama party, although the Polynesian ladies wore native dress, because it was so much cooler, while the Australian gentlemen wore Y-Fronts, because they felt too hot.

After an al fresco meal and a frolic in the pounding surf, it was time for some music. The beat of the 'Tamouré' boomed out to the swaying palm trees and across the moonlit ocean. All Aussie eyes were upon me, to see whether I knew what to do. The Polynesian ladies giggled nervously, not knowing what to expect.

Fortunately, I knew the form. The dance had been all the rage in the Saddle Room at the bottom of Park Lane in London, the year before. The slender and beautiful Hélène Cordet, who ran the show, and her current Beau, an overweight middle-aged gentleman wearing a guardee blazer of many buttons, had demonstrated the steps. The underlying and emphatic drumbeat was Oomp-di-OOMP, Oomp-di-OOMP, Oomp-didi-OOMP. To this accompaniment, the man's movement was to stomp his feet more or less on the spot, bending the knees downwards and outwards, then up and down, while his elbows were held akimbo, in a simian posture. (Not entirely a pretty sight, in the case of the Beau). The melody, on the other hand, went Da-DA-da-di-da-da, with variations, to which the ladies waved their arms gracefully above their heads and shivered (or shimmied) their hips. A fetching sight, in the case of Mlle Cordet and an even more remarkable sight with Mlle Leila, who had, like her lady friend, inadvertently forgotten to put on anything more than an exiguous grass skirt, and nothing in particular above the navel except a garland of orchids. (Their mothers really should not allow them to go out like that – alas, it is even worse today, and not only in French Polynesia).

So, to protect her from Aussie testosterone, I took Miss Leila's hand and led off the dance – I (too prudish to follow the Y-front fashion) wearing a baggy borrowed pair of Hawaiian shorts in a vivid floral pattern, and my Polynesian partner in her native dress, trembling and twirling, the two of us barefoot on the beach. Gentle reader, it was not a waste of space, I promise. The evening did assume a dream-like quality. For me, it was back to the Garden of Eden, before The Fall, when all was innocence and delight. (For Leila, perhaps, it was wondering when she could get the chance to dance with her friend. But I don't think so; in the dance, at least, we were at one. Anyway, we are all created in God's image; patience is a virtue; hope, on such occasions, springs eternal in the masculine breast).

I left the following morning on the Qantas plane just in from Sydney. With the returning manager's wife, my path never crossed. Just as well, because I was holding a grass skirt in a paper carrier bag as I went through check-in. Hence the mirth at Orly and Heathrow in the hails and snows of a Northern Hemisphere in December.

For years thereafter, I honoured my promise to Leila and wore the skirt with pride, whenever climatic conditions permitted.

That skirt, then. What final fate befell it? Alas, it got a trifle torn, one night near St Tropez. And then, there was the awkwardness of all those uncalled for remarks in Customs Clearance. So eventually, we bade each other a fond and final farewell. The skirt was offered up to Odin and Thor in a Bonfire of the Vanities on Dartmoor.

But the first owner still lives on, her youth perpetual, in memory undimmed. Quite right too. And all thanks to Qantas. So, *Vive la Grêve!*

16

TOE-*MAY*-DOE KETCHUP, IN TENNESSEE

The Germans have this expression: 'One is what one eats'. True, in a way, of China, India and Japan. Quite true, of Italy, Mexico and New Zealand. But supremely true of the United States, in my experience. I will expand on that.

These days, as we all know, everyone's kids have been over to the US before their 'A-levels', or in a 'Gap Year' thereafter. But in the 'forties, America was a faraway country of which we knew only what we had gathered from Hollywood, or from observing G.I.s in uniform on our streets and railway platforms during the war.

Generally, the image was beguiling, the people sympathetic. So, in later years it felt natural to work closely with US colleagues – perhaps more natural than with any other nationality, at least until Britain entered the Common Market. And, as a diplomat and a Eurocrat, I have in fact travelled across the length and breadth of the US, as well as in and out of Washington and New York on official business more times than I can remember. I like the people and admire the country.

But it was not until the 'sixties, in my early 'thirties, that I first contrived to cross the Atlantic – or more particularly, the Pacific, since I was travelling east-about, from Asia, making first landfall in San Francisco. For the tourist in me, it was a great adventure; but, for the diplomat, not in all respects what I had anticipated.

I was certainly warmly received. Strolling down the San Francisco waterfront, ludicrously over-dressed in my smart, Singapore two-piece suit, white shirt, striped tie, and beribboned Cambridge boater, I was greeted by a young woman (not a lady of the night, but a nice College kid, on the arm of her Beau) with the words: 'Oh, you look so BEAUTIFUL!' The next day, on a visit to the campus at Berkeley, I took the precaution to dress down – joining in, on the fringes of a student demonstration, with the refrain: 'Hey, Hey, LBJ, how many kids did you kill today?' On the tourist bus to see the redwood forests, anonymity was not possible. Each passenger was asked to declare where he or she came from. When it was my turn, I said 'London, England'. To a gratifying, and as far as I could see warmly spontaneous, cheer.

I had less than two weeks to spend in the US, on this first visit. So I flew over the mountains of Nevada and Colorado down to Texas and then took the Greyhound bus – with casually selected stopovers – up from Houston. New Orleans was sleazier than I had expected it, and much more run-down, but nevertheless a delight – embracing the inevitable tourist clip joint on Basin Street, with a brassy, middle-aged, white stripper and a rather sad black trumpeter playing 1920s Blues. An even greater delight, when I eventually reached it, before flying on to London, was the city of New York – I goggled at skyscrapers, iridescent in the rays of the setting sun, spectacular and of great beauty.

Although not, in those days, much of a 'Foodie', there were nevertheless some decent meals, by the standards of a ravenous 33 year old on the travel trail. Seafood, naturally, on the quayside of Fisherman's Wharf in 'Frisco; an enormous Texan steak, on its home territory; a treat at the Pierre in New York which even a Parisian would have found passable; even a jolly good traditional English breakfast at the Hay Adams in Washington (although inevitably with 'easy-over' eggs).

But the most memorable gastronomic encounter was in a roadside café in Alabama (or was it Tennessee?), where my Greyhound bus made a pit stop for twenty minutes. It was 'Hicksville'. The white, overweight and unhealthy looking waitress behind the counter, was sullen and disobliging. She took an instant dislike to me – quite rightly – though I still maintain it was through no fault of my own. I managed to secure a mug of weak American coffee. Rejecting her 'nondairy creamer', I solicited proper milk (a congealed and cheesy carton was produced, reluctantly). I asked for brown sugar, rather than white saccharine (she waved at a bowl down the counter, around which some flies were buzzing). In my most ingratiating English English (which only made everything very much worse), I inquired whether I might possibly have a little 'Toe-*Maa*-Toe' soup? With a snort, she tipped some tomato ketchup into a bowl, added hot water from the kettle, slammed it down in front of me, said 'here's you toe-may-doe soup, Mister', and then flounced off into a back purlieu.

I took a run for it, leaving a ten dollar bill behind me (far too much, but – despite myself – I felt sorry for her. *Man ist was man frisst, nicht?*)

17

BEIJING TEXTILE MILL NUMBER TWO

I have always had this 'thing' about China.

My father used to take pleasure in a small collection of attractive if not particularly valuable Chinese vases. He took me to look at more serious objects in the Victoria and Albert Museum. I had always wanted to go to the 'Middle Kingdom' (and not only to meet Suzie Wong – see chapter 2). After popping in and out of Singapore and Hong Kong on several occasions on business and pleasure, I finally made it to People's China in March 1966. I had things to discuss there, about the prospects for the continued neutrality of Cambodia (I was still then in charge of the Embassy in Phnom Penh). And I wanted to extend my credibility with the Cambodian 'Establishment', for whom China was the 'Number One' player in their region: some ostensible if shallow familiarity with China was what they looked for in foreign diplomatists with whom they did serious business. More than that, I wanted, for my own curiosity and satisfaction, to see something of the great China herself. And more particularly of Beijing, the seat of the feared and famous Chairman Mao Tse-tung, supreme icon of western 'Lefties'.

Everything went as I wished. An easy rail journey up to Canton by train. Everyone very respectful on the Chinese end of the platform at Lo-Wu. There was the usual if naïve little piece of theatre, in which a Chinese official would run after foreigners from the waiting room to the carriage, waving a half-empty packet of western cigarettes and enquiring solicitously whether they had inadvertently left it behind. The packet was not, of course, mine, nor indeed that of any other western traveller that day. The object of the exercise was simply to demonstrate the common honesty of People's China. There was a lot to see through the carriage window – for example almost no mechanisation of Chinese agriculture at that time. Buffaloes or even coolies pulled the plough, and tractors were few and far between.

After taking a good look round Canton, equipped with a Cantonese phrase book, it was up to Beijing and into the care of the 'Office of the British Chargé d'Affaires' – in reality, our Embassy. (We were not in those days welcome to accredit a full-scale Ambassador Extraordinary and Plenipotentiary to People's China, notwithstanding the fact that the UK had been among the first to grant diplomatic recognition to the Communist government when it first assumed power). In my spare moments, I bicycled everywhere. I was lodged downtown in a little house with a walled courtyard, normally lived in by a Chinese-speaking British diplomat, currently then on leave. His two servants spoke little English and I even less Mandarin, but we got on famously together; the choice of bacon and egg for breakfast is readily conveyed in almost any language. Also, apart from arranging Embassy briefings and calls on the Chinese Ministry of Foreign Affairs, our people had very kindly laid on a sensible and instructive programme of visits: to the Forbidden City, the Great Hall of the People and the Museum of the Long March, as well as to various factories and other economic features outside town. Also, the Great Wall of China and the Valley of the Tombs of the Ming Emperors (with picnic thrown in).

Somehow, however, there was something missing, that I could not quite put my finger on. There was a formality, a preciousness, at times even a touch of pomposity in what Chinese apparatchiks had to say. There was always a little speech by some boot-faced and brutish official (invariably, a veteran of the Long March) wherever I went. Typical of such insincere utterances was the introductory address of the general manager of Beijing Textile Mill Number Two. Traditional links, ancient understandings, contemporary common concerns, people shall speak unto people, popular rejoicing in the arrival of the amazing and impressive visitor from outer space, etc. This was then followed by a dreary troop round a succession of machine shops and sheds, and a meaningful inspection of the factory canteen (every kind of delicious and healthy food on offer to the workers in the People's Paradise, cauldrons of rich beef stew, piles of nourishing noodles, etc. – but my Chinese-speaking companion from the Embassy pointed out to me quietly that no one was eating the expensive stuff, no doubt because they could not afford it, or because it was for display only). Eventually, the tour concluded. We walked down a long corridor along the walls of which the clerical staff of the mill had been lined up, to applaud the distinguished visitor and bow low as he passed. By some instinct, reaching the end of the corridor, I suddenly turned and looked back. To my delight, one of the women workers had her tongue poked out at me. Embarrassed, she was overcome by giggles.

I walked out into the sunlight, overjoyed. So, they were human after all. It made a nice little anecdote for me to drop, when I got back to Cambodia. Basing myself on five full days in Beijing, I felt that I completely understood everything about China and the Chinese; took them at friendly face value; and came to suspect that even Mao (now of course known beyond peradventure to have been an absolute monster) had been a trifle misrepresented, not to say misunderstood, bless him. Well-informed and highly intelligent colleagues in the Chargé d'Affaires office, though sympathetic to the symptoms I was exhibiting (not uncommon for first- time British visitors, they said – particularly Labour back bench MPs) gently but persistently attempted to modify these gifted and insightful impressions. Inwardly, however, I knew I was right.

The next month, without warning, Chairman Mao Tse-tung launched the 'Cultural Revolution'. The 'Red Guards' were unleashed on the streets and on the countryside. Senior party officials were arrested, publicly humiliated and (if they were lucky) sent for re-education purposes to work on pig farms in the remote provinces. As for the office of the British Chargé d'Affaires, it was attacked by a mob, the British staff beaten up and the building trashed. (There was a fashion for that sort of thing, in Asia at the time – the British Embassy in

Cambodia, for one, had been raided, and the US Embassy attacked twice, in the mid 1960s – see chapter 11). Back in Phnom Penh, I found that the civilised and communicative Chinese Ambassador, and his elegant wife, had had to ditch their wardrobes and start appearing on all public and state occasions in loose-fitting, poor quality denim overalls; and that they had begun to find it difficult to control the provocative activities – antithetical to the Cambodian government, notwithstanding the Head of State's professed public belief that China was his 'Friend Number One' – of their own Embassy juniors.

None of which, of course, meant (I told myself) that, at rock bottom, my first impressions of Beijing were not admirably perspicacious and totally on target. True, it is unwise to derive generalisations from inadequate data – i.e. don't pontificate if you don't know what you are talking about. Yet, timing is everything – one is always right, in the end; it is just that, sometimes, the end is a long time coming.

18

'DOUBLE-O' DANGER MAN

I have never looked anything like James Bond, or indeed had anything to do with the fellow.

I admit that I do have a good tailor – but only to disguise the flab and conceal my sloping shoulders. 'Double-O', to me, is something to do with toy train sets. (Possibly manufactured by Hornby, commonly on sale at Gamages in Holborn, sixty years ago). Personally, I would not know a dead letter box from a live one. Although a serious rifleman and competent with a sporting shotgun, I have always known side arms to be inaccurate beyond five yards and more dangerous to the holder than to the target. Particularly if accidentally discharged from inside a trouser pocket – best left, therefore, to kinks and obsessives. Latterly, I am not even licensed to shoot game birds, now that I have sold my side-by-sides to fund my wine cellar (it was either that or sell the Utrillo). 'M' surely has to be the first initial of Lady Thatcher. The only women who have ever come flocking to me in life have done so merely to put my rattle back in the pram. My training in martial arts was confined to lying groaning on the mat, nursing bruised ankles, in Judo classes at the School of Oriental and African Studies in London. My skill at cards goes no further than 'happy families' and 'snap'. I know myself to be a complete physical coward, except in moments of panic or when bravery is otherwise completely unavoidable. Some evenings, I can't even open my front door with its proper Chubb key, let alone a bent paperclip. I prefer my bedtime cocoa stirred, not shaken. Low-slung, high-powered motor cars – especially any with a leather belt across the bonnet – say strictly nothing to me. I much prefer the 'sit-up-and-beg' saloon cars of yesteryear. (If anyone knows where I can pick up a 1946 Ford Popular, would they please let me know? I mean one of those with wind-down windows, and windscreen wipers that slow down and stop when you step on the gas and accelerate from 30 to 35mph. No independent front wheel suspension, or Sat Nav equipment, please). I much dislike heights (even from a chair lift on the lower slopes at Verbier). I cannot fly helicopters, and have never knowingly been parachuted anywhere (except from the FO to the Brussels Commission in 1973). On water skis, on the Mekong, I could never follow a straight line and sip champagne at the same time. Codebooks are a complete enigma – except the one we were given in the Boy Scouts, requiring us to smile and whistle simultaneously, and be as pure as the whispering wind.

In August 1989, happily installed in Sussex as Vice-Chancellor of the University there, I received a letter from the security department of the Foreign and Commonwealth Office, alerting me to the publication, by some sort of oddball or anarchist group, of a 'Who's Who of the British Secret State'. It was, apparently, full of mistakes; but listed the names of some 1,800 officials and others who the publishers alleged were closely connected with, or actual members of, the security services – serving, retired, or (believe it not) in some cases actually deceased. One of the 1,800 was Fielding, Leslie, of 'MI6', whose last assignment was listed as 'First Secretary, FCO, 1970-'. I was told, as presumably were the many other ex-Diplomatic Service recipients of the same round-robin, not to attach too much importance to such rubbish; but to be alert and consult the local police if I had any anxieties, or in the event that the publication attracted the attentions of investigative journalists, or 'Smersh', or other equally ill-intentioned individuals or institutions.

I was not, as Vice-Chancellor, or in any previous incarnation, whether as a member of HM Diplomatic Service, or on the permanent staff of the European Commission in Brussels, a member of 'MI6' or what is more properly called the 'Secret Intelligence Service' (SIS). Of course, I would say that, wouldn't I, even if it were not true – such are the supposed wheels-within-wheels of the secret state? You can't win. Perhaps this is as it should be – although, in the 21st century, senior members of the SIS are as likely to appear as such in 'Who's Who', as they are to remain veiled from the public gaze. Nevertheless, the fact remains that I was a 'dip' and not a 'spook', all my life. The anarchists had registered yet another of their many and egregious errors.

Reflecting, at my desk in the University, I thought I could guess where all this nonsense originated – namely, my three years as Chargé d'Affaires in Cambodia. Phnom Penh in the 1960s was not only a place (at least at the Royal Court) of necromancy and superstition; it was also commonly held to be a centre of international intrigue, espionage and secret intelligence gathering. Let me begin with professional elucidation, for the benefit of the innocent or ill-informed.

As the British Government now openly declares, but formerly was reluctant to admit, there are at least three active secret intelligence-gathering organisations in this country. The first and best known is the Security Service, sometimes called MI5, accountable to the Home Secretary. The second, and necessarily the least known, is Government Communications Headquarters (GCHQ), whose main office is in Cheltenham, and which is understood to engage in international electronic surveillance. The third is the SIS, whose impressive new headquarters on the South Bank in London is now a tourist landmark. In addition, there are various other bodies concerned with intelligence, including – on the technical analysis side – a dedicated intelligence staff in the Ministry of Defence and – at a much higher and more general level – on the Joint Intelligence Committee (JIC) in the Cabinet Office.

As regards the Diplomatic Service and the Secret Intelligence Service in particular, these are two distinct organisations which offer their members quite separate careers. The two respect one another and work closely together. But 'each to his own last'. And there is a clear-cut distinction between ends and means. The ends of secret intelligence are determined by the FCO and No. 10 and the means are, within given guidelines, the business of the SIS.

I myself joined the Diplomatic Service – then, before the merger with the Commonwealth Service, called the Foreign

Service – in September 1956, on being successful in the open examination for entry to the senior branch. My subsequent career was classic, copper-bottomed diplomatic; initially in Tehran, London, Singapore, Phnom Penh and Paris; and later (with the European Commission) in Brussels and Tokyo.

It was against this background that I arrived in Phnom Penh from Singapore in May 1964, and took over the Embassy as Chargé d'Affaires the following month. I replaced both the Ambassador (who had been withdrawn), and the Head of Chancery (who had done a direct swap with me and gone to join the staff of the UK Commander-in-Chief in Singapore, as one of his foreign policy advisers). Consequently, the residual diplomatic staff in Cambodia consisted, apart from myself, of only two others: a Defence Attaché from the Intelligence Corps in the rank of lieutenant colonel, and a Vice-Consul concerned with visas, administration and accounts. Everyone else – three Second Secretaries for political affairs, trade promotion and press and information – had already been withdrawn, like the Ambassador himself.

This new profile provoked a certain interest among the Soviet, Chinese and other communist bloc embassies, to say nothing of the omnipresent, proprietorial and ever-inquisitive French. Who was now what the Russians would call the 'Resident'? Had British Intelligence turned its back on Cambodia, where it was assumed still to have secret agents and 'assets'? Or was Intelligence Colonel Robson, or that suspicious Monsieur Fielding, the new master spy? After all, our French allies reasoned, over their evening glasses of Pernod, Fielding was clearly some sort of military intelligence officer, because he had been sent direct to Phnom Penh from the British base in Singapore. (The French, in particular, have always been slightly baffled by the way the British Government machine works – in particular, by the ease with which our civilians and military talk to each other at every level, and the different government departments work together as a team). The 'Deputy Defence Attaché' in the French Embassy in Phnom Penh therefore came sniffing round me, to the point of requiring active discouragement.

Even in the Chinese Embassy, with whom we had paradoxically very correct working relations, mainly over Hong Kong, people were similarly exercised. At Chinese receptions, I was pressed, in an arch sort of a way, by someone I took to be their senior intelligence officer, about the nature of my duties. People at the Russian Embassy, likewise.

But it was the French who most strongly suspected, on what they considered their 'patch', SIS operations in Cambodia directed (and perhaps dramatic new intelligence initiatives undertaken) by person or persons not only unknown but – worst of all – also undeclared to *les services français*. In what was still, in some respects, a village as well as a capital city, the buzz went on for some months in the bistros, cafés and bars, among the cannier journalists as well as the *barbouzes* (intelligence and security officers) and the military types. Whenever conversations edged that way, I myself offered arched eyebrows and a puzzled stare to all comers, until I finally perfected a Gallic shrug and a sphinx-like facial expression. But I continued to be closely observed. My chosen *figura* as a 'play-boy Chargé d'Affaires', seemingly somewhat out of kilter with the normal comportment of a British Head of Mission, served only further to fuel suspicion. My not infrequent excursions up-country and to the border regions were assumed to be part of a sleuth-like professional search for military secrets and clandestine Viet Cong bases, or for clearing 'dead-letter' boxes, or for placing cunning transponders or fiendish tracking devices.

And so, to my surprise and initial embarrassment, the 'walk-ins' began. A well-placed resident French journalist sought me out, offering to sell privileged inside information about domestic Cambodian politics. Someone from an east European embassy indicated that he was toying with the idea of defection to the West. Unexpected intermediaries popped up, with suggestions for the negotiated release by the Viet Cong of hostages and prisoners, through clandestine channels. Somebody else altogether had yet something else to offer or suggest. What did I want? What would I pay? I could not begin to evaluate any of this, let alone handle it. But I imagined other people could, who were competent in these matters. So I learned to cope as best I might, with a word here and a nod there, and advice from somewhere else, without personally engaging in activities incompatible with my status as Envoy.

After nearly three years of such, I was transferred back to Europe, and settled down to routine diplomatic life in the Paris Embassy, for classic across-the-board liaison with the Quai d'Orsay on foreign policy issues. But, for some, this could only be a blind. That dodgy Monsieur Fielding must be up to something deep and undeclared. (One only had to look at his nightlife: all those bars, nightclubs and discothèques. An expensive man to tail. Who was he meeting? What were his targets?) Even the expatriate press corps got wind of these suspicions. The late Sam White (gossip columnist extraordinaire of the Evening Standard, long-serving 'Lunch Time O-Booze' at the Crillon Bar and self-designated Doyen of the Western Press Corps in Paris) once found himself unjustly threatened with libel proceedings by a particularly unsavoury *barbouze*. It was therefore to me, over a pig's trotter lunch in the Marais, that the savvy Sam (ever, he believed, 'in the know' on who to go to, about what; but, as always, somewhat confused) carried his loud complaint. I naturally reported this to the appropriate quarter. Rubbing his hands with glee, the SIS Head of Station told me to carry on the good work.

But 'give a dog a bad name'. My (totally, non-) career, as an alleged SIS officer, was to linger on, by reputation, for years after assignment to other equally transparently orthodox official duties, whether as Deputy Head, from 1970-73, of the FCO 'Planning Staff' think-tank, or as a 'Eurocrat' in the European Commission, from 1973-87. (I still wonder why, when Jacques Delors became President of the European Commission, he was initially so circumspect in his dealings with me as his Director-General for External Relations. Was it that I had just won the EC rifle championship? Or was he the recipient of a solemn warning from *les services* in Paris about 'Danger Man Fielding'?)

At the University of Sussex, however, despite its left-wing reputation, absolutely no one cared a fig about their Vice-Chancellor's supposed past 'form'. For most of my students, most of the time, and even some members of my academic faculty, some of the time, anyone not a neo-Marxist, post-Maoist, Deconstructionist, Feminist Socialist was an obvious secret agent of Western Capitalism, anyway. So, what else was new? Seemingly equally indifferent are the congregations to which I, as a lay reader in the established church, have subsequently preached at matins and evensong in the Welsh Marches – like my former students, they have more important things to worry about (probably mainly the Welsh, ever threatening to surge through the Ludlow Gap in search of livestock, booze and women – in that order). And now that I have given up pheasant shooting, I have, of course, also disposed of my redundant Walther PK automatic, even if I am hanging onto some of the ammo, to help light the bonfire; and the shoulder holster, to hold my hip flask. (Don't tell 'Q'!).

19

PACIFIC 'PIDGIN'

You are never sure that you can't speak pidgin English until you have really tried. It was not, in my day, a language greatly used in the FO – more an option for those fellows in what used to be the Colonial Office, I imagine; or perhaps an outlying department of the Overseas Development Agency (now DFID). But I undertake that it can be acquired, with a little effort – and a lot of imagination.

It all goes back to that fateful day in 1963, when Charles de Gaulle, then President of France, vetoed the application of the government of Prime Minister Harold Macmillan to join the then European Community (now the European Union). The Brits returned to the charge under Prime Minister Harold Wilson, only to be vetoed by the General a second time in 1967. Eventually, under Prime Minister Edward Heath, with the consent and indeed approval of de Gaulle's successor, President Georges Pompidou, and with the lubricating (and well lubricated) good offices of Sir Christopher, later Lord, Soames (Wilson's well-chosen political appointee as British Ambassador in Paris), it was all finally fixed up. The UK duly entered the EC in 1973 – and is mercifully (or perhaps mercilessly) still there today. But in 1966 we were not there yet, and had to watch our Ps and Qs with Paris.

An enthusiastic 'European' and a Francophile diplomat, I followed all this pretty closely at the time. As the Chargé d'Affaires in Phnom Penh, I first met de Gaulle on his State Visit to Cambodia in September 1966 (see chapter 21). In a brief but unhurried private audience, I was given a solemn warning about the absolute necessity for the Americans to cut and quit in the Vietnam War – and by implication about UK foreign policy in that area. To a large extent, I agreed, over

Vietnam; but found myself simultaneously both mesmerized and repelled by the political personality of the General. As was well-known, the latter professed admiration of Great Britain, but really did not seem to like the British (perhaps he hated us for being far too nice to him after the fall of France in 1940). I met a similar attitude, when I called, two months later, on the high-powered French ambassador in Jakarta. This was the socialist apparatchik and politico, Claude Cheysson – later to become French Foreign Minister; but also, at another point, to be one of my two Commissioners (ministerial bosses) in Brussels in the 1980s. The message of both men was for the UK not to be the running dog of America, if we wished to be welcomed into the European pack.

All of this was very much germane, when the FO pulled me out of Phnom Penh to send me to join the political team in the Paris embassy. It was a compliment, because we were at 'action stations' to improve Anglo-French relations – Wilson seemed determined to pick up where Macmillan had left off. My initial job in the chancery was to take care of bilateral diplomatic relations outside Europe and to help keep the decks clear where possible. Not easy, in the event, given de Gaulle's encouragement of the Biafran cessation in the Nigerian civil war, and his espousal of separatist tendencies in Quebec, to name but two provocations. But the effort had to be made.

This was why, in December 1966, en route from Phnom Penh to Paris, I found myself island-hopping in the South Pacific. The object was to gain insight into French colonial policy in the area, one of several potential irritants to Anglo-French relations. Travelling from east to west, after visiting Indonesia and Australia, I had called first on the French Governor in New Caledonia, and was about to do the same in French Polynesia, after a detour to see how the Brits were playing their hand in Fiji. But I also needed to visit Vila, the capital of the Anglo-French 'Condominium' of the New Hebrides. Today, the place is called the Republic of Vanuatu, having received independence from London and Paris in 1980. Back in 1966, however, one hundred and fifty thousand, primitive-looking, Melanesian aborigines came under the authority of both a British and a French 'Resident' (in practice, colonial governor). There were in fact three distinct but related colonial administrations – one French, one British and one Joint. The set-up was *sui generis*, not to say bizarre in the extreme.

How come? Basically because, while the British and French felt – for once – no compelling territorial imperative in the regions before the First World War, and the islands had no significant natural resources, both countries wanted to keep the Germans out.

The first Europeans ever to visit the New Hebrides were Spanish and Portuguese. Yet it was Captain James Cook who had given the islands their name, when he visited them on HMS Resolution in 1774. Small numbers of white people began to drift in; traders, but also riff-raff and even some outright villains. Problems of piracy began to arise, calling for action by the British and French navies. The Germans, too, began to take an interest in the South Pacific, to extend the Kaiser's Imperium. In 1906, on strategic grounds, Paris and London agreed informally to join forces and establish a 'Condominium', subsequently to be entrenched in a formal Protocol signed in 1914.

But Anglo-French friction was never far below the surface. By 1966, outside the New Hebrides, the two metropolitan powers were following diametrically opposite colonial policies in the Pacific – the Brits wanted out, while the Frogs wanted to hang in. Within the Condominium, a tradition existed of French rivalry of everything British (although, curiously enough, not so much of British rivalry of the French) – all the more difficult to understand for the fact that French nationals were much more numerous than British and that, commercially, France was the dominant partner.

Differences over policy in Vila in the 1960s centred on French reluctance to accept the revision of the very outdated Protocol and of other administrative and legal practices in the islands. We would have liked to simplify things, to correct anomalies which could give rise to scandal in the United Nations, and to prepare the way eventually for some measure of local self-government (full independence being at that time still over the horizon for so small, politically backward and economically unviable a territory). Paris, on the other hand, appeared firmly attached to the status quo, arguing that things could perfectly well continue to jog along as they always had done, to the practical satisfaction of all concerned; that it did not matter very much what United Nations committees might think; and that there was in any case no sign of any great desire on the part of the New Hebrideans to run their own show. Above all, no precedent should be set which might make the French position in Polynesia more difficult to sustain – not least, because the French needed somewhere to do their nuclear testing.

Unsurprisingly, the absurdly suspicion-laden and jingoistic spirit of rivalry on the part of French officials had made the New Hebrides an unrewarding post for our administrators for many years. Everything had to be replicated and if possible surpassed. When we opened a teachers' training college, the French Resident immediately rushed to clear the jungle and lay the foundation stone (with great pomp – but at that stage without the funds to finish the project) of an enormous French lycée. No sooner the British Resident had acquired a large boat for island cruises than his French colleague bought the first larger boat he could lay his hands on in Vila harbour. A project for a joint Anglo/French hospital, for which we had pressed hard, had just fallen through; the French preferred to have a new hospital of their own. Inevitably, French officials disliked and discouraged the use of the 'pidgin' English, traditionally spoken in the islands (as indeed it was throughout Melanesia – a dialect heavily Australian in vocabulary, no doubt because so many Melanesians had served as indentured labourers in Oz). Numbers of New Hebrideans also attended English schools and colleges. The French administration was consequently working and spending really hard to even things up. Prestige dictated that the local French airline should be subsidised by Paris, although the British airline had to make its own way. The Tricolour flew over every French institution and gave the visual impression that the New Hebrides was a French colony fortuitously inhabited by a handful of British administrators.

Which is where I came in. A charm offensive had been opened, by both sides. The Brits wanted unnecessary friction out of the way, for evident foreign policy reasons. Their partners, realising that the 'Condominium' was increasingly an anachronism, unlikely to last forever, were getting scared that the UK would simply pull out unilaterally, leaving France holding the baby. The British Resident continued to live in a large house on an island offshore; the Frenchman in a large Residence in town. Melanesians serving in the French Resident's Police Force still wore képis and slim, sleek uniforms, while Melanesians in the British Force wore red tarbooshes and wide, baggy khaki shorts. But the new French Resident, a charming official of Armenian extraction, was busy soft-peddling the chauvinism; and his opposite number was only too pleased to respond.

On arrival, I was whisked off to meet our man on his island who briefed me carefully. I called on their man in the town, speaking my very best French – meek and mild, smiling and waving, butter wouldn't melt… but with my antennae out and my wits slightly less scattered than usual. I got on well with H.E. Monsieur Mouradian, who kindly arranged for his *chef de cabinet* to drive me around the countryside, to view *les réalisations françaises*.

As we drove, the man gave me an amusing low-down on the local Millenarian Cargo-Cults (mainly John Frum, inspired by the awesome impact on the Melanesians of the rich, powerful, black, US GIs descended from the skies during the war – 'Johnny from America'); noted regretfully that there were over one hundred indigenous languages still actively spoken; but denied that the Melanesians preferred to speak pidgin English rather than the language of Voltaire. Otherwise, he made some effort to be personally agreeable. I liked him, reciprocated the charm, but looked for the occasion for a gentle tease.

We saw an elderly New Hebridean aborigine trudging along the country road. He turned and appealed for a lift, without any great expectation. To demonstrate French *fraternité*, we stopped and picked him up. The fellow sat hunched and humble in the front seat next to the driver, mopping and mowing in acknowledgment of the gracious salutation of my French minder.

In a spirit of irresponsible devilment, I opened a conversation with our passenger in pidgin. (I had already dug up and digested a phrase book produced by the Australians in Papua New Guinea).

'Greetings', I said. 'How are you? Do you speak pidgin?' (*'Halo. Me talk goo-day. U fella Oke? Spik-im talk-pidgin?'*)

No reply. Perhaps a word of personal explanation was called for?

'I am a senior diplomat of the Queen of England. I have come to have a close look at this country, and am seeking information about it'. (*One fella, big big fella, offisa belong Misus Kwin, Luluai Inglis. Me bin kumant look-im look-look long dis ples, find-im talk-savvy*).

And, to impress upon him my cargo-cult qualities, I added:

'I will soon fly far away across the ocean in an aeroplane, to make my report'. (*Me bai go straight now ride em balus chop chop an tap long salt warra, go long way ples, giv-im story*).

The aborigine shifted uneasily in the front seat. Perhaps I'd scared him – made him think that the bountiful British were about to abandon the New Hebrides to the mercies of the frightful French? Better reassure him.

'I am much impressed by this country and do not intend to upset things or compromise the Condominium. Be assured, I will make a positive report, I promise. Thank you'. (*Me plenty like-im dis place. No capsize-im. No bugerup Govman. Orait, orait, me swit fella, report-im dinkum. Promis-im. Tenkyu*).

The New Hebridean then turned to the driver and spluttered:

'Qu'est-ce que c'est que ce rigolo? Qu'est-ce qu'il raconte? Je comprends rien de ce qu'il dit. Quel con! Le mec, il sait pas parler français, comme tout le monde? Il se fout de notre gueule, quoi!'

The rest of my conversation took place in French. The Chef de Cabinet sat back and smiled. Quite rightly. Naturally,

I smiled back, in a world-weary sort of way. In due course, we dropped our passenger.

But I did wind down my window and say 'See you'. (*Look-im yu*). If only to put the Frogs in their place, one does well to have the last word on such occasions.

20

A 'SIXTY-EIGHTER', AND PROUD OF IT

On the evening of 26 May 1968, having nothing better to do, I was standing quietly in a corner of the Place de la Bourse in Paris, watching a large group of demonstrators attempting to set fire to the Stock Exchange.

The latter had been under some sort of occupation and was flying black (Anarchist) and red (Communist) flags. As a member of the political section of our embassy in Paris, one of my duties was to keep an eye on what was going on, so that my Ambassador, the gentle and scholarly Sir Patrick Reilly, a fellow of All Souls, could keep London fully informed. A news flash on a pirate radio station had tipped me off. The Stock Exchange was no more than half a mile from my flat in the IIe Arrondissement, opposite the Bibliothèque Nationale, so I finished my cognac, changed out of my chancery suit, donned polo-neck, jeans and sneakers, and slid out unobtrusively into the spring evening.

Slightly to my disappointment, the demonstrators did not succeed in getting very far with their incendiary aspirations before the riot police arrived, dressed in black and heavily equipped. Up went the cry 'CRS: SS!' A company of the latter, equipped with helmets, visors, shields, truncheons and side arms, was in the process of forming a military phalanx in a side street. The commanding Captain marched forward to issue his orders. I began to look around for an exit.

It had all started with a student demonstration at Nanterre University on 3rd of May. And the students certainly had a case. Throughout France, they suffered from ill-adapted and rigid curricula, authoritarian and remote administrative structures (the system had in fact changed little since its reworking by Napoleon) and virtually no contact with teaching staff. Although the student population had tripled in little more than ten years, from 200,000 in 1956 to 600,000 in 1968, the numbers of teachers had not kept pace. The staff/student ratio had become even more woefully inadequate than usual (in the English Faculty at Nanterre, for example, there were – incredibly – only four teaching staff for 2,000 students). Failure rates and absenteeism were high.

Unsurprisingly, when the authorities responded by closing Nanterre, the students simply moved to the Sorbonne, where they joined their fellows in setting up stalls in the courtyard. Ever the conscientious diplomat, there I was, talking to them all. Nice kids for the most part, and not without their grievances. And their posters and slogans were a delight (saying things like 'It is forbidden to forbid'; 'Imagination seizes power'; and 'The more I make love, the more I want to make the Revolution; the more I make the Revolution, the more I want to make love'). The charismatic twenty-three year old Cohn Bendit, a French-born German, was on the scene, with his shock of red hair – hence his nickname, *'Danny le Rouge'*. But shortly after I had myself left the courtyard, the police none too gently moved in, to eject the demonstrators; while Cohn Bendit was expelled from France the following morning as an undesirable alien (albeit only to return in disguise, with his hair dyed black).

The trade unions soon joined in, helping to bring France to a virtual standstill for three weeks. A chain of events was then initiated which was to shake the nation to its core, cause several deaths and many hundreds of injuries, and lead to the resignation, within less than twelve months, of General de Gaulle, the then President of the Fifth Republic.

On the 6th of May, there were major clashes with the police in the Latin Quarter. By May 11th, sixty barricades were up in central Paris, built of trees, traffic signals, motor cars and piles of chunky cobblestones. I still have, somewhere, a six inch cube of granite, picked up in the 'Quartier Latin' as a souvenir – I used to keep it in my study as Vice-Chancellor of Sussex, for didactic and admonitory purposes, in my dialogue with the students' union. Molotov cocktails were thrown, walkie-talkies were in use by the mob, and communist trade unionists were out in force on the streets. That day, 367 people were hurt and – much worse, in the eyes of the Paris bourgeoisie – 188 cars had been misappropriated. Nothing upsets the *Parisien Moyen* more than seeing his beloved 2CV upside down in a barricade.

Up till then, opinion polls had suggested, and my Embassy colleagues and I had agreed, that four out of five Parisians sympathised with the students. And why not? France, then, was more than merely bored; she was also bruised. General de Gaulle, after ten years of exercising more or less undivided power (which, as Jean Lacouture once put it, he had used with an 'inimitable mixture of sovereign haughtiness, bonhomie, crudity, boldness and skill'), had triumphed over all his opponents – politicians, colonels, terrorists and Eurocrats. But the structure of state was fundamentally fragile. Political power was too personalised, too patronising; and had become alienated from the people. The broadcasting media were state-controlled; wide sectors of the press, subservient. The nation was not comfortable in its straitjacket, and wanted to break loose. Certainly, by 1968, this was not the France of my early 20s – nor for that matter my father's own 20s either. Rejoicing in the *Entente Cordiale*, Pa had celebrated, before WWI, a France that was happy and herself; and cheerfully went off across the Channel as a Territorial Army volunteer in 1914. In 1968, it was now time for the French to breathe freely again, and revert to a more relaxed norm.

Nevertheless, as the student riots grew more serious, and the workers let rip, old ladies stopped throwing flowerpots at the police from their top floor Boulevard balconies, and the political mood changed. Ordinary people became dazed and shocked. The student revolt lost its romantic appeal. In consequence, the more moderate trade unionists disassociated themselves from the students. General de Gaulle said, *'La Réforme, Oui; La Chie-en-Lit, Non!'* (The headline in the Daily Express – 'The General says 'No' to a Dog's Breakfast' – was a mistranslation; the old boy was talking about the need for the nation not to soil its own bed linen.) There was a surprise dissolution of the National Assembly – elections were called for June, which were in the event to demonstrate a renewal of support for the Government. By 30th of May a huge procession of solid citizens, gilded youth (the so-called *'Fils à Papa'*), and the usual right-wingers staged a mass procession up the Champs-Elysées, led by a colourful collection of Mayors and Deputies wearing Tricolour sashes. The Government claimed there were 500,000 on that march; using Foreign Office techniques – an essential part of the repertoire of a diplomat in the Third World and closer to home these days, alas – I made it less than 200,000. The worst of the troubles were over. General de Gaulle, of whom I admit to having been in awe personally (he had a compelling gaze equal only to that once ascribed to Adolf Hitler) was to suffer a terminal loss of credibility, leading to his resignation – and to the election of Georges Pompidou as President in April 1969. Very good news indeed for the Brits – Pompidou lifted the Gaullist veto on UK accession to the then EC, operating in cahoots with Prime Minister Edward Heath.

But back to where I began – the night of 26th of May 1968. It was only a couple of years previously that I had still been serving in Cambodia. The Embassy there having been sacked by rioters in 1964 and I myself having been pushed around by the Cambodian mob in a major street demonstration in 1965, I had become – by 1968 in Paris – fully 'streetwise'. So, in the Place de la Bourse, I decided it was time to make a move, PDQ. The CRS Captain had just waved his stick over his head and given the command 'CHARGE!' While he had a beautiful baritone voice and a fastidious uniform, I was not too confident that his men would pay much attention to the Diplomatic Immunity card in the hip pocket of my jeans; and, in any case, as Alfred de Musset might have put it, '*on ne badine pas avec la CRS'* (you don't play games with the riot police). I was away in a flash, turning right into the Rue du Quatre Septembre, left into the Rue de Richelieu, then right into the Rue de Louvois, up four flights of stairs and secure behind my front door. Once there, however, I rubbed my hands with glee. One day soon, France would escape from the grey grip of Gaullism, to become once more herself.

As I regularly boast to any close French friends who still listen: *'Moi, je suis Soixante-Huitard – et j'en suis très fier!'*.

21

THE GAZE OF DE GAULLE

I was not sorry, when General de Gaulle lost the plot, and stood down as President of the French Republic. He was, in his declining years, no friend of Britain – if, indeed, he ever had been, even when welcomed and supported in London where he sought refuge, after the fall of France in 1940.

I was shocked as well as saddened to find, on my arrival in the Paris Embassy, how deep the resentment of the 'Anglo-Saxon' ran. The General famously vetoed, for the second time, Britain's application to join the European Community – a savage thrust at his ally. But it did not stop there. He also gave moral and (covert) material encouragement to the Biafrans, in their war of secession in Nigeria – he being jealous, it was thought, of the initial success of the British decolonising process in Africa, and apprehensive that Nigeria would come to dominate the surrounding ex-French mini-states. Then came *'Vive le Québec Libre'* and the General's flagrant interference in the domestic political affairs of Canada – a country I knew and respected, and whose fighting men had, incidentally, assisted in the liberation of France in 1944. I was to do my bit for Canada later, when Prime Minister Trudeau developed his 'Third Option' and requested a 'Contractual Link' with the enlarged European Community, after the UK had entered. (I was appointed the EC's negotiator; the 'Framework Agreement for Commercial and Economic Cooperation' which I drafted and saw through to signature, was, in both form and content, without precedent in the annals of the EC to that date. With the special consultation arrangements it included, the Agreement gave Canada what she wanted and so amply deserved.)

But the General was not misguided on everything. He was right about the futility of the US military commitment in Vietnam. Even if (ironically) French colonial myopia in Indo-China, and their defeat at Dien Bien Phu in the 'fifties, were at the origin of the trouble in Vietnam, Laos and Cambodia in the 'sixties and 'seventies.

And it was in the Vietnam context that I had my one and only brief private audience with General de Gaulle. The occasion was his state visit to Cambodia in September 1966.

The arrangements for the President's reception were the most lavish and spectacular ever known in Cambodia. Thus, 300,000 Cambodians turned out to greet de Gaulle on his arrival. Half the population of Phnom Penh were present for his open-air speech. A fabulous pageant was mounted by floodlight before the brooding temples of Angkor. The French President and his wife were accommodated in the Royal Palace itself, a personal honour totally without precedent. The associated security precautions were on an equally grandiose scale. Dubious French locals were banished by the dozen to the distant seaside. Almost every petrol station in Phnom Penh was drained, in case someone should blow it up while the General rolled by. Armoured cars stood at the street corners and steel-helmeted troops lurked in the leafy shade of the main boulevards.

International attention was mainly focussed on the significance of this visit for the Vietnam War. The world press had speculated that a major mediatory French initiative would be launched. In practice, little of practical effect was to emerge. President de Gaulle's speech in Phnom Penh on 1 September delivered a forthright attack on the American position in Vietnam, but contained no offer of French good offices. Indeed, he specifically said 'France will not attempt any mediation in this conflict'. Instead, the General simply exhorted the US to withdraw from Vietnam within an appropriate and fixed period of time.

So what the General said and did was uncompromising – and unconstructive. But, at the age of 33, I found myself struggling with an unexpected admiration for the man.

This was to be reinforced when I actually met him, face to face. The courtesy, but also the charisma, were almost overpowering; the gaze, positively mesmeric. Receiving the Diplomatic Corps, he had a word with each of the foreign Heads of Mission. With a handful, the General found time for a brief private conversation. They included myself (despite my youth; but no doubt because of the UK's Co-Chairmanship with the Soviet Union of the standing Geneva Conference on Indo-China). When it was my turn to be bought forward and presented, I found myself exposed to a positively magnetic force of personality. The General spoke unhurried and elegant French, addressing me formally, as 'Monsieur le Chargé d'Affaires'. He was not only very polite, but also quite insistent – gazing down into my eyes to convey his emphasis. He began by asking me to convey his greeting to Her Majesty the Queen, for whom he expressed a deep – and, I sensed, quite genuine – respect: we were fortunate, he said, to owe loyalty to such a Head of State. He then moved on to politics and diplomacy. I should convey to Prime Minister Wilson the necessity for the Americans to quit Vietnam and – by implication – the desirability of London conveying just that unpalatable message to Washington. (In other words, the Brits had to make a choice between Europe and America). I listened; I spoke briefly; almost imperceptibly, he nodded. I was more than flattered – I was bowled over.

Afterwards, the *chers collègues* rushed up to me, to ask why the General had taken so much time talking to a junior head of mission. But I had a telegram to send to London, who had the right to know first. So I simply said:

'Oh, the usual thing, you know. No surprises!'

22

DRACULA, PRINCE OF DARKNESS

In my experience of the human condition, there is high-life, low-life and no-life.

Personally, I prefer the latter. A gentle amateur philosopher and theologian in search of understanding and spiritual enlightenment, give me a quiet evening at home, any time, with St Augustine of Hippo or Jalal ud-Din Rumi, a gas fire and a mug of warm lemon barley water. As for low-life, that is where I get dragged, unwillingly and against my better judgement, by acquaintances who nevertheless need to be kept an eye on in their hour of need. (See 23). And, high-life? That, of course, is what goes with the job, in the Diplomatic Service.

In the late 1960s the highest high-life of all was in the Embassy in Paris of Sir Christopher (later Lord) Soames and his wife Mary, younger daughter of Sir Winston Churchill. Later, Soames was to be my boss in Brussels, when he became Vice-President of the European Commission. But in Paris he was an initially unfamiliar quantity, who took a little getting used to. It was an unusual but shrewd ambassadorial appointment by Prime Minister Harold Wilson. In Paris, Christopher Soames was a big fish, politically as well as corporeally. A Tory toff, and former Cabinet Minister, he had been made Ambassador with essentially one purpose: to overcome the French President's veto on UK accession to the European Community. Once I had grown accustomed to the Soames phenomenon, and established what was expected and what I could contribute, I became personally devoted to both of them. But, from the point of view of my 'no-life', there was one drawback. Whereas I knew myself to be a shy and studious bachelor, the Soames's took me for a *beau sabreur*, extrovert playboy and general Deb's Delight. Yet, there were consolations: for example, a tutored introduction to serious claret and a social entrée like Clark Cable's in 'Gone with the Wind'. Never, since the days of Pauline Borghese and the Duke of Wellington, had the Faubourg St Honoré found itself so full of men of power and authority, *décolleté* and diamond-draped women and the unmistakable whiff of position and influence.

One winter, the Soameses decided to give a fancy dress ball, like no other in living memory, for *le tout Paris*. All of us in the political section, working directly to the Ambassador, were invited to make up suitable little parties of glitterati. I managed to rope in some of the usual suspects – apparatchiks and aristos, rebels and reptiles. But what was I going to wear? We were all busier than usual in the chancery, revising the traditional, annual 'Personality Report'; and I was blowed if I was going to go cap in hand to some theatrical costumier for a cowboy costume or Caligula's codpiece. Naturally, I did have a grass skirt, a present from a lady of good family, brought back from an earlier passage through French Polynesia (chapter 15); but I had already concluded that the Embassy ballroom might be too draughty. With three hours to go, I was therefore still costumeless and (worse) clueless. Suddenly, however, *le coup de foudre*. Culture and The Higher Thought came to my rescue.

Wasn't this month the Horror Film Festival in Paris? Wasn't *Dracule, Prince des Ténèbres* (with a plausibly dubbed Christopher Lee) the current Top of the Pops among *Les Filmes d'Epouvante*? Did I not possess clip-on plastic vampire teeth (a present from the Werewolf Lady at La Poubelle – which is another story – see the next chapter)? And also, somewhere, a white tie and tails. Quickly, I togged myself up. To add Transylvanian glamour, I slung the red and blue striped belt of my silk dressing-gown over one shoulder, tied to the pommel of the court sword belonging to my diplomatic uniform. But more was needed. So I pinned onto my breast the kitsch, gilt-and-glass joke Star once given me by a grateful Prussian baron. (A fellow student at a French business school, he had broken his spectacles when falling down a cliff early one morning, well before breakfast, while admiring the moon, and had had to be rescued and consoled with yet another *digestif.*) On looking in the mirror, however, it all still somehow lacked conviction, even with the fangs in position. So I covered my face with white talcum powder, brushed my hair straight back to give me a wild stare and slid a small bottle into my tailcoat pocket. The improvised make-over was complete. With some difficulty, I found a taxi driver ready to let me into his cab and convey me to my destination.

The Embassy that evening was lit with candelabra. An orchestra played. There was dancing; a delicious buffet, too. Liveried footmen in swallow tails moved softly among the guests, bearing crystal flutes of Pol Roger on silver salvers. There was a gorilla, a Mme de Pompadour, a Mother Superior, a Marie-Antoinette, an Astérix the Gaulois and his twin, several Cardinals, a Roman Centurion with hairy legs and knobbly knees, a Lawrence of Arabia, one Napoleon, two Mickey Mouses, three Vietnamese Emperors, four Mexican peasants with ponchos and sombreros, several Cleopatras. Also, I believe, a Jane Birkin (in the original) if not a Brigitte Bardot. But only one Dracula.

Time for the line-up. There was a fanfare of trumpets. Christopher and Mary Soames (conventionally attired, as befitted their diplomatic rank and their role as judges) took their place on a small dais in front of the orchestra. Guests who were competing for the fancy dress prize were invited to circle the ballroom. First time round, as it seemed to me, the eyes were on others. The competitors circled for the second time. Hanging back a little, I drank unobserved from my small bottle. Finally approaching the dais, I snarled, and allowed the tomato juice to pour down from my fangs over the white piqué waistcoat. Christopher recoiled, his expression a struggle between disgust and fascination. Mary screamed and clutched her husband's arm. The prize was mine.

Not everyone was happy.

'God-damn sonofabitch' muttered the disappointed gorilla (I think, a gentleman from the Wall Street Journal).

'C'est dégueulasse, ça' said the Banque de France.

'Quel cochon' opined the Ministre des Ponts et Chaussées.

'Vraiment la fin', concluded a Merchant of Death.

'Légèrement excessif, je trouve', whispered the high-up chap from the Elysée, cautious as ever.

But then, all my life I have had to live with the well-grounded and entirely understandable envy of those around me. So I bared my fangs one more time and returned to my little party.

'Minou, t'es devenu parfaitement fou', said the Countess affectionately.

'Dingue comme tout', agreed the Directeur from the Quai d'Orsay, likewise.

'Chouette', conceded Le Monde Diplomatique.

As for the ash-blonde ballerina from Berlin, she embraced me warmly, with shining eyes. *'Das war eine richtig gute SCHWEINEREI!'*

Or words of encouragement and invitation to that general effect. (And, in those days at least, one was always ready to go to extreme lengths to advance closer Anglo-German relations.)

23

PARIS BY NIGHT

I was always a night bird. As such, Paris was my home-from-home.

From time to time, the Soames chancery offered not only glitter and glamour (see previous chapter), but even – very occasionally – just a little time off. To the point, once, of my being able to absent myself from Paris one weekend, to become the guest of the Scots Greys with the British Army of the Rhine: Scottish dancing in full fig (gladly – I'm good at it); up in their helicopter (accepted); chance to drive a tank (super); choice of a nag, for a chukka or a canter before tiffin (firmly declined). My hosts in Fallingbostel, West Germany, Major Charles and his wife Henrietta (not their real names), were in due course invited back to Paris, for a long weekend. But I was still then unmarried. *Hinc illae lacrimae.*

I had first met Charles in Hampshire for Christmas the year before. Setting out from Paris at five in the morning in my two seater rag-top, I was rammed amidships near Saint-Denis by a *camionette* performing a U-turn. Hell of a bang; driver's door stove in; steering wheel a bit bent; protesting rib cage. But, happily, no damage to the boot (where the godchildren's presents were stowed) and nothing to stop my onward progression, a fraction crab-wise (the chassis was later found to be a trifle out of true). With a length of Embassy red tape to keep the driver's door closed, I caught the car ferry, and arrived in time for pre-lunch drinks. As soldiers were present, it was a matter of 'Fielding of the FO' maintaining a stiff upper lip and keeping completely mum; after all, it only hurt when I laughed. Taking a stroll together out of doors after lunch, Major Charles, ever alert, promptly spotted my two-seater.

'Good Lord: what happened there?'

To anyone who might enquire, I had been rehearsing the answer on the ferry.

'Rats, Charles. Just rats'.

My 'street cred' rose; I was invited, on the spot, to a Highland Ball on the north German plain; and so, to my story.

When Charles and Henrietta arrived one Friday in Paris, for their return visit, I had found myself summoned at short notice – as chance would have it – to fill a spare place at one of the Ambassador's smart dinner parties. Black tie; best XVIe Arrondissement French; not too much to drink, as one of H.E.'s helping hands. So I booked my house guests that evening into my favourite neighbouring bistro, 'Aux Lyonnais', in the Rue Saint-Marc; the bill to come to me; menu pre-chosen too: *salade au lard, perdreau aux choux, gateau rustique, beaujolais de vigneron* – i.e. nothing too elaborate (they were Scots, after all, and would understand). Me absent, they duly tucked in (no subsequent complaints), while I did my stuff for the Soameses. (But, with a tedious set-to with Hervé Alphand, the Secretary General of the Quai d'Orsay, about whether diplomats were more like civil servants, or officers of the armed forces, in their conditions of service. Alphand was probably right from the outset; yet no self-respecting Parisian high society dinner can proceed without: *'Là, je ne suis pas du tout d'accord!'*).

I got back to my place, in the IIe Arrondissement, shortly after midnight. Henrietta had gone to bed. Charles was keenly awaiting my return. Could the two of us pop out, since the night was still young, to sample French culture? I explained that the Palais du Louvre, the Musée de l'Homme and the Institut Oriental were all closed and would not open until ten o'clock the following morning. But Charles persisted. Perhaps a little stroll, then, to catch the night air? As he pointed out, he was properly dressed (black tie and trews). So I consented, reluctantly.

Happily, there were suitable low-life options to hand. In the habit of walking back home from the Faubourg St Honoré after a formal embassy dinner, not quite yet ready for cocoa with my teddy bear and an Enid Blyton story, I had developed a network of personal détente. The lesbian night club in the Rue Chabanais; the depraved and ineptly named 'Oxford and Cambridge Bar' in the Rue Saint Augustin; the (mostly gay) 'Die Kneipe' beer cellar, opposite; and, finally, the (very hetero) 'La Poubelle', in the Rue Rameau, off the Square Louvois. I was proudest of my honorary membership of the first, 'Chez Fred', which had demanded persistence and a rigorously low profile. In all four establishments, it was possible for a tired professional diplomat to hunker down at the zinc and swallow a nightcap or three, without being too much pestered for his views on Proust or Phnom Penh or World Peace or even the political prospects for President Pompidou.

So off we went. The Bier Keller liked the gallant Major Charles (whom I introduced, anticipating future advancement, as *Herr Oberst*) and *Eiswein* was served in big glasses; but Charles didn't much like the Bier Keller – too reminiscent, perhaps, of 'you-know-where', on the Hamburg waterfront. So, we crossed the road to the 'Oxford and Cambridge Bar'. There, I had been the corrector of a past solecism. On the wall behind the zinc, Jules used to be proud to display, painted on wooden shields, the two coats of arms – alas, however, of the *Municipalities*, not the *Universities*. As a then honorary senior scholar of my Cambridge College, I had felt morally obliged to furnish – albeit without the formal consent of the respective Vice-Chancellors – heraldically appropriate replacements. Consequently, thereafter, I could do no wrong.

But, that Friday evening, Jules himself was absent, and almost all the ladies were otherwise occupied upstairs. So we strolled on to *'La Poubelle'* (the 'Dustbin'), where I observed through a crack in the curtains that the Werewolf Lady – quite dotty, with a pleasing lisp – was vivaciously holding court. It was the Horror Film Festival in Paris that month. The *patronne* had announced to the *clientèle* that she was a *'Loup-garou'* (werewolf). Red talons were brandished menacingly. But, as Dracula, I was nevertheless welcome. So we strode in.

'Bonsoir, Mlle! Dracule, Prince des Ténèbres, à vos ordres! On s'est déjà rencontré, vous vous en souvenez?'

'Bonthoir, M. le Baron, très heureuthe de vous revoir'.

'Puis-je vous présenter mon ami, le Chef d'Escadron Charles? Il est Dragon de Sa Gracieuse Majesté.'

'Enchantée,mon Chef d'Ethcadron'.

Then, to me, in a stage whisper.

'Il est vraiment Dragon? Mais où est thon thabre? Avant qu'il ne th'en aille, j'ai bien envie de le voir!'

Eventually, fearing untold complications, Henrietta-wise, I whisked the Major out again, and took refuge in the safer waters of 'Chez Fred'. But here, too, my luck was out. After a little time chatting quietly at the bar, over a suitable something, Charles insisted on inviting a young lady to dance. Cheek-to-cheek. He returned to the bar flushed.

'Now, guess what, Ned (for so I am known in Scottish circles)? She told me she's a lesbian because her mummy was!'

No sooner than he'd said it, than *le Chef d'Escadron* was being propelled out into Rue Chabanais by two very large ladies in dinner jackets with very square shoulders. I followed, muttering apologies. (It took me three months to graft my way back through the door).

We hailed a cab to the Champs-Elyseés area. The 'Crazy Horse' was loaded to the gunnels that evening; but I found somewhere more discreet, not too far away, where we fell in with a party of jolly journos and took our seats for the show. A lady who did not seem to feel the cold cracked a whip at us and sang a song which I couldn't quite understand. I took the opportunity to ask the 'Sunday Telegraph' correspondent (now the Earl of Stockton) what he thought about French policy towards Biafra. After a bit, the whip lady went away, to be replaced by another lady (or it might have been a gentleman who thought he was really a lady, or vice versa – by then my thoughts were elsewhere, on my next report to the FO on the Vietnam peace talks) who stood in a spotlight in the middle of the little floor and, finding that s/he was inappropriately dressed, began (quite understandably – but surely this should have been thought of earlier, before the show began?) to change clothes. A party of American peanut farmers or Mormons were in occupation of the next table and began to make a slight fuss.

'Oh NO, Wilbur, she's a GUY! Why did we COME here?'

I thought them jolly rude and leaned over.

'Well actually, I come here OFTEN. May I introduce myself? I'm Mabel and this (indicating Charles) is my girlfriend Maureen'.

'Oh my GAAD. They're EVERYWHERE. Get me out of this joint. I'm leaving, right NOW!'

Later, Charles and I wandered out into the night with the journos, who had already long since filed, and were talking of possibly going on to the 'Crazy', now less crowded. Charles decided, on mature Presbyterian reflection, that while he had enjoyed being a passive spectator, he now wished to participate more. I gave this my Anglican consideration, without great enthusiasm. We grabbed a taxi to the Ile St Louis, to my favourite disco, 'La Cabane'. As I had already deviously calculated, this splendid institution had just closed its doors (as it was on the way to 4am). So it was time for a brisk, healthy stroll over the Pont Louis Philipe, through quiet streets, to Les Halles, for *les huitres, la soupe à l'oignon, le pied de porc*, washed down with some decent Sancerre and a bottle of Pomerol. Not to mention a pot of black coffee. We reviewed the situation in the Middle East. I then explained Sufi mysticism and spirituality; Charles spoke of the co-axial machine gun, as I recall.

In due course, dabbing our lips, we emerged into the morning, heading for the Bibliothèque Nationale and my apartment, by way of the Place des Victoires. Shops were beginning to open. The smell of fresh coffee and croissants filled the air.

'What about a present for Henrietta? Perhaps, some croissants?' I asked.

Assenting, Charles was given a large paper bag of peace offerings. Eventually, we climbed carefully up the four flights of stairs and stood giggling before my front door.

'Shush. Shush, Henrietta's still asleep. Gently does it'.

Key in door. Door opening. Door open. There, in the hall, stood Henrietta, in her nightshirt, bare foot, looking ravishing as always. But with eyebrow cocked.

'Charles, where HAVE you been?'

'It's all right dear. Just popped out with Ned. Got you some delicious croissants. Here, in this bag'.

But, alas, the bag was empty. He'd scoffed the lot, en route. So I wrote down the instructions for the Palais du Louvre, the Musée de l'Homme and the Institut Oriental.

'Back at teatime', I promised. 'Cucumber sandwiches and Lapsang Souchong.'

Then I left them to it; took a quick shower and shave; and headed off for the chancery. It always made a good impression to get in early. Except that, it being a Saturday, the place was officially closed. I had quite forgotten. The security guard nevertheless let me in. The skeleton staff were on duty and busy. And, in my office, there was a long green leather chaise longue. But, once there, the telephone rang. It was young Mme la Marquise, up in the XVIe from her Chateau, unenthusiastically awaiting the still-deferred return of her elderly Marquis from a bonking… er, *banking* tour of Latin America. Marie-Chantal hadn't seen me for ages. Would I pop round for coffee or lunch, or… something?

A couple of years later, the FO moved me back to London, to the (rather serious) policy planning staff, or 'think tank', with the Rt Hon. Sir Percy Cradock as boss, Sir Roger Tomkys and Lord Powell as my juniors. Thereafter, on to Brussels to do (even more serious) economic work with Lord Soames, Sir Roy Denman and Lord Hannay. Posh people, great warriors, but tough work. Never glad confident morning again.

As for Major Charles, he did indeed became a colonel – ultimately, a full one – and also won (to boot and horse) a serious medal for bravery. Eventually, he joined his illustrious ancestors. We – his many friends and former fellow officers, his two wives and a bevy of attractive women of uncertain status but clear devotion – buried him up in the Scottish Borders, the other year. A piper of the Royal Scots Dragoon Guards played the customary spine-shivering lament. We wept buckets. Then food and drink were served, while spirits rose again.

'Dearest Ned', asked one of the attractive women, 'A penny for your thoughts'.

'Longa est vita', I replied, *'si plena'*.

24

FOREIGN OFFICE FAMILY PLANNING

It was not my choice of jobs – I had made it clear to the FO personnel department that, when posted back from the Paris Embassy, I expected a job in one of the departments dealing with economic affairs – I had had enough of purely 'political' work and wanted to diversify. But I was told to belt up and get stuck in. 'It's a compliment to you, old chap!' And so, in September 1970, I joined the planning staff as its number two. Unexpectedly, I found myself enjoying what the French would call *la tarte à la crême* for three whole, gluttonous, years.

Once upon a time in Whitehall, the FO had decided to set up what was called its 'Planning Staff'. Very small – four officials at most. Very close to the centre of power – it worked directly to the Permanent Under-Secretary of State/Head of the Diplomatic Service. Very selective, in what it did – while ready to take on almost anything on which Cabinet Ministers wanted an independent analysis or second opinion, the planning staff also produced 'blue sky' thinking of its own, on upcoming international issues on which 'The Office' had, in the heat of the day-to-day, not yet fully focussed. Despite the name, it was rarely asked to put up detailed 'plans'; but it was expected to produce new foreign policy recommendations. The planning staff was naturally in touch with 'think tanks' at home and abroad; with institutions such as the Royal Institute of International Affairs (Chatham House), the International Institute for Strategic Studies, the Ditchley Park Foundation, and academe generally. But it remained FO 'family'. The 'planners' were diplomats first and last, and each was 'one of the boys' with the rank and file of professionals working in King Charles' Street.

That September, I found myself joining three men who were each unquestionably brighter and more beautiful than I was – maybe because personnel department thought that they needed a low-brow anchor man or anyway someone with different aptitudes and insights. The boss was Percy Cradock (later Ambassador in Beijing and credited with the successful arrangements for the handing back of Hong Kong to China; thereafter, he became, for eight years, foreign affairs advisor to the Prime Minister, Margaret Thatcher; and, finally, a Privy Councillor). Originally a law don at Cambridge and thus a late entrant to the Diplomatic Service, he was intellectually one of the cleverest men I have ever worked with. In the 'Third Room' were Roger Tomkys (a brilliant 'Greats' man and University Craven Scholar from Balliol; and subsequently a distinguished FO-trained Arabist, who was later to become Master of Pembroke College, Cambridge), and the perky and engaging Charles Powell (later Mrs Thatcher's right-hand Private Secretary for eight years; now, a peer of the realm and a successful City type).

We were a band of brothers, without heavy hierarchy. We saw all the same key documents and telegrams to, from and about all parts of the world that mattered. We commented freely and easily on each other's draft policy papers. One of us was usually selected to take the lead and do most of the initial work; but we worked very closely as a team and together 'owned' whatever the planning staff finally decided to put up. And we worked flexibly – sometimes in at dawn and out in the early hours, when we needed to get a move on; but, at other times, away from the building at seminars, or talking to strange people, or travelling abroad on business. It was all exceptionally invigorating.

Yes, abroad did come into it. We held meetings with our Japanese, American, German and other opposite numbers in their capitals – and indeed once had a meeting in Warsaw to strike sparks off our Communist Polish equivalents, at their invitation, as the cold war approached the beginning of its eventual end. But we also had to cover the home front, both in London and outside the capital – I offer two examples; a bleak meeting with journalists, academics and politicians, about how to bring peace and reconciliation to the Emerald Isle, on the freezing campus of Lancaster University during a Christmas vacation; but, also, a more convivial spring conference at Edinburgh (where the Malt flowed freely) about the prospects for the European Community after UK entry.

We did indeed produce a number of think pieces. One, crafted by Roger Tomkys, took a hard look at (what was left of) 'national sovereignty' as traditionally conceived. Others bore on the future of Europe (some even circulated to the Cabinet, despite – or because of – the fact that few of Ted Heath's ministers had much real 'feel' for it). Before even setting out from Paris, to take up my planning duties in London, I joined in an exercise to answer the PM's question. 'Why can't we be more like the French?' Heath, and others like him, had not only a healthy concern with France, quite rightly, but also an exaggerated respect for the way the French did things, sometimes wrongly.

Further afield, much attention was given to Asia and the Far East (mostly addressed to what was called 'The Asian Quadrilateral' – the relationship between China, Russia, the US and Japan – but also including a particular study of the last, a rising new political and economic phenomenon). I did some very *sub rosa* work with the late Sir Fred Warner (just back from being the number two in our UN Delegation in New York), on how to wind up resident British responsibility for UDI in Rhodesia (decision deferred, so paper dismissed).

I chipped in something about the longer-term economic prospects for, and future political and strategic significance of India (a country either largely ignored in Whitehall, or else treated as if we still ran it by Viceroy; but never analysed in a detached fashion). I also took the lead in writing what we then called 'Low Level Political Violence' – meaning terrorism and how to deal with it. This was possibly my only lasting monument as a policy planner, because it had the merit of being first in the field and therefore became a small part of the intellectual foundation for subsequent and more systematic governmental reflections.

Widest of all, for which Charles Powell did most of the work, was an annual reappraisal of what we called 'Priorities' in foreign policy. The aim was to jog the elbow of traditionalists, to encourage people to examine how the world was changing (and our future place and possibilities within it) and generally to get the government to put its money where its mouth was (or where that mouth might be tomorrow – assuming that we still had any money, naturally).

Our work earned us enemies – not (I hope) for our arrogance, but for what others sometime saw as our presumption. There was once a row about whether we should spend more money on cultural activities in the Yemen (of which the planners thought the global priority too low and the opportunity cost too high – but there were, we admitted, good tactical political reasons for what was afoot). We also attracted incomprehension. Our papers always went for approval/disapproval/ directions for a re-write/whatever, to the so-called 'Planning Committee', composed of all the Senior Under-Secretaries of State. In the Committee, but slightly below the salt, also sat the Director of Research and the Head of the in-house Economic Advisors. At that time, following the merger between the (élite) Foreign Office and the (dull and dozy) Commonwealth Relations Office, there were rather more 'Commonwealthies' of senior rank than there should have been – unlike the FO, the CRO had been a top-heavy and over-promoted organisation. This contingent puffed away at their pipes, fingered their watch chains and waited for the opportunity to turn the collective discussion to personal reminisces of Chiefly Characters in Nigeria or Major Maharajahs in Malaya.

Even the FO stars were sometimes bemused. Sir Oliver Wright, the anti-egghead, shoot-from-the-hip, Chief Clerk (the Deputy Under-Secretary of State responsible for personnel and administration), debonair in his contour-hugging Saville Row suit, and with a rosebud ever in his lapel, at the end of a meandering debate on my India paper, attempted to steer the summing up from the PUS by intoning that we were not entering the European Community (then in immediate prospect) in order to put up the shutters on India (which the paper – the man had clearly not read it properly – had absolutely not recommended). The Commonwealthies nodded vigorously. I caught the eye of the PUS, Sir Denis Greenhill (a covert personal patron of mine), and blinked one eye, ever so slightly. At another meeting of the committee, we addressed what might be done, in an enlarged European Community, to strengthen Western defence. (The Commonwealthies looked detached and concentrated on refilling their pipes – altogether, it was an unproductive meeting). I recall also a third meeting, to discuss something which a senior American had recently said (probably Henry Kissinger) about Japan and China. To our misery, the Chairman ended up asking us to update our 'Asian Quadrilateral' paper, for the nth occasion in three years. Like 'The Mouse Trap', that paper ran and ran.

But by then it was time to move on. Christopher Soames had fingered me to join his External Relations Directorate-General in the European Commission, as the director for, interalia, EC/US relations. So I packed my parachute, and jumped, in April 1973. I landed safely, but sadly never returned to the Diplomatic Service, which is another story (see the next chapter).

PART TWO: THE EUROPEAN COMMISSION

25

ACROSS THE CHANNEL AND INTO THE TREES: FAREWELL TO THE FO

An odd place, Brussels, I found.

A-jabber with alien tongues and impenetrable local jargon, inhabited by ravenous anthropophagites great and small, the graveyard of many a parliamentary, political and diplomatic reputation obeying customs unknown to Englishmen and laws known only to the Gods, its procedural jungle pathways tortuous, dimly lit and beset with traps for the unwary and snake-pits for the unwelcome, the dreaded Brussels Euro-Jungle is a place where the tenderfoot can disappear without trace in broad daylight, and where even seasoned old-timers with leopard skin bandannas round their hats go pale beneath their tans if caught out in the bush after sunset.

Brussels also has some of the best restaurants and pubs, and brightest public servants, in the world.

As already noted, I joined the FO in 1956, serving in the Middle East, South East Asia and Western Europe, in large medium and small diplomatic missions of acknowledged efficiency. In London, I was responsible for the NATO and WEU desk in a *mouvementé* period; and, later on, served in the policy planning staff. It was an orderly, appetising and oxygenated existence, involving no obviously incurable diseases, little map reading or hand-to-hand fighting, and really very few unpleasant insects.

But Arcadia is never forever; Olympus is not an abiding abode for mortal men.

In 1973, on Britain's entry into the European Community, I was seconded from the FO to the European Commission in Brussels, as one of the directors (in Whitehall terms, 'Under-

Secretaries') responsible for external relations. Most of the time I was condemned, as Sisyphus might well have been, to labour ceaselessly to propitiate the United States, to appease the Old Commonwealth, and to cope with agricultural trade problems in the GATT. In addition – and as an act of malice towards the then only professional diplomat in that neck of the Commission's woods – I was assigned supervision of the Commission's protocol service, and of a new unit set up to rationalise policy on external diplomatic representation.

The initial 'culture shock' on arrival in Brussels was pretty massive, even for a professional. Language alone was a problem; to draft documents much of the time, and to speak most of the time, in French, demanded a level of effort greater than that which I had previously had to make during three years in Cambodia and four years in the Paris Embassy. The French language demands facial exertions different from those required when one mutters away in English. Consequently, my throat, cheeks and lips began to rebel after eight or nine hours non-stop; and I regularly suffered from 'French face-ache' in the first week or two back in Brussels after a spot of furlough. A greater difficulty was the shortage of Brussels staff, compared with Whitehall's ample availabilities. In consequence, the workload was consistently – sometimes absurdly – heavy, by normal FO standards. Another kind of handicap was imposed by the bureaucratic tradition of the Commission. Old timers used to joke that it was an amalgam of the worst practices of each of the civil services of France, Germany, Italy and the Benelux – the six founding members of the European Community.

Certainly, staff discipline was more relaxed, obedience to instructions less unquestioning, than in 'The Office'. There seemed little or no career planning or in-house training. I looked in vain for the kind of teamwork and the co-ordinating structures familiar to me both within the Foreign Office and between government departments in Whitehall. One had to watch out for banana skins from the ill-intentioned. Hierarchy did not seem to matter too much – the Luxembourger head of my protocol service (Grade A4) was junior in rank to his Italian Number Two (Grade 3 *à titre personnel*). There were other novelties and horrors, like giving press conferences and being grilled by the External Relations Committee of the European Parliament. Worse, I was constantly required to rush off and *do* something, instead of composing elegant and judicious 'Blue Minutes' for ministers.

As for the EC overseas offices for which I had assumed responsibility, they were few, of recent creation and operating on an improvised, even hand-to-mouth, basis. Confidentiality was less that what I had been accustomed to. One privileged external delegation was rumoured to possess an ancient cipher machine which no one knew how to use and which was therefore left locked up in the safe. There was no diplomatic bag service, or secure telephone link, to anywhere or anyone. On one occasion, I had to report to the chef de cabinet of my Commissioner in Brussels, from a slightly dodgy situation in Latin America, by means of a telex sent from the local Post Office, couched in Persian, in which we were both fortunately fluent – see the next chapter. Indeed, the Commission took pride in being a 'House of Glass'. Asked by a Foreign Office friend how I was finding things, a few weeks after my first arrival in Brussels, I recall replying that, while in London you locked away official papers on leaving the office at night, in Brussels you left your files on your desk, but locked up the telephone, so that office cleaners did not spend their evenings making long international calls to distant relatives. Internal organisation, too, could be – dare I say – inspirational. Thus, I recall the Washington delegation once reporting the same US government policy development twice to Brussels, in two separate telexes, drafted by two different officials who had not consulted each other or their boss. In another overseas office, its head – a senior German from Bonn's generally weak, reconstructed post-war civil service – occasionally assigned the same piece of work simultaneously to two separate officials, to see which one did a better job of it – a procedure proudly described by its practitioner as using a 'two-headed eagle'.

The foregoing will rightly appear arrogant and condescending. To start with, I do confess to having missed the planning staff in particular, and the Diplomatic Service in general; and to have longed for the day when I could 'come in from the cold'. Indeed, during those early years with the Commission, I must have given the impression of a fastidious and slightly narcissistic subaltern from the Sixtieth, who had suddenly found himself an outcast, on transfer to a line regiment stationed in a remote outpost of some insalubrious equatorial colony.

But these personal feelings were mistaken, and anyway faded with time. I came to realise that I found myself in a set-up which had more in common with a successful City institution, or the upper layers of a dynamic multinational company, than with a long established imperial bureaucracy. There were not a few precocious prima donnas; a good working relationship with colleagues had to be earned, rather than expected as of right; knowledge was power – you did not share it too widely (as even Lord Hurd once admitted finding, on moving from Westminster to Commerce). Average ability in the Brussels bureaucracy seemed to me to fall slightly below that habitual in top Whitehall departments. But the senior continental officials – at least in DGI, the External Relations Directorate-General in which I served – were people of marked ability and intelligence, who believed in what they were doing. These, and European colleagues from the agricultural and industrial policy departments, possessed international negotiating skills, developed over long years doing the same sort of job, that were unsurpassed – perhaps even unmatched – anywhere in the world. I came to admire them and I saw that I had much to learn: initially, they were probably less convinced that they had much to learn from me. Yet, although it took time for my face to fit, in the end it was possible to rub noses and undergo tribal initiation.

My first day in the Foreign Office offered me the comforting assurance that 'we still find that the percentage of idiots in the intake remains constant' (see chapter 2). I was to remember that, twenty years later, swinging in a hammock slung between fever trees in Etterbeek. Clearly, one had to join them if one could not beat them. There was no alternative but to go native. To keep the opposition guessing, I began to switch constantly between fancy French, barrack room

Flemish, Goon Show German, intuitive Italian, D.I.Y. Danish, survival Spanish, long forgotten Greek (mostly 'Water is Best' and 'Everything is in a state of flux'), and broad Harry Lauder Scots ('There's aye muckle a slappy steen, at ilka body's door'). I duly locked up my telephone; left my papers strewn across the desk; cast banana skins behind me; set aside hierarchy; instructed two juniors to do something which I then did better myself; dined as often as possible at 'Le Cygne', 'Comme Chez Soi' or the 'Villa Lorraine'; and generally daubed my cheeks, and other accessible parts of my anatomy, with the comitological war paints of the relevant EC tribal Indabas.

But there was a price. It became difficult, when briefly out of the trees and back across the Channel, to speak good enough English, for example, to get past the porter's desk at The Travellers Club in native dress; and, utterly unthinkable, on eventual return to Blighty after 15 years of 'Brassholes', to consider any employment exciting enough, outside the University of Sussex. But I console myself. I am glad to say, on the first count at least, that I have happily since recovered full command of my native tongue. *One must-a be dankful for ze small merçis, nicht?*

26

FROM MONTE, WITH FARSI

I don't know about you, but I have never quite been able to get on with your genuine, real-life fascist. Not even Coronel Machismo – of whom more later.

I was hidden in Hertfordshire while World War Two was in progress (the odd stick of German bombs notwithstanding – I experienced a very near miss on 22 February 1944) and so never met, face-to-face, any real Nazis. And the cheerful Italian PoWs who were allowed out to promenade the pavements on Sundays were no Benito Mussolinis. But stories of stirring deeds filtered back from the front line. Thus, I once heard about a feature of armoured warfare in the western desert. Tank commanders were under orders to be guarded over the radio, because of listening Germans. Officers who had formerly served in the Indian Army therefore developed the habit of communicating with each other in Urdu, Bengali, Hindi or whatever they had in common. While ultimately decryptable, these tongues were tactically robust, because they were very unlikely to be understood then and there. Later, it didn't matter. I was to remember that – and subsequently apply the lesson.

One of the many pleasures of the Persian language is that so few people speak it: Iranians and educated Afghans; a scattering of Central Asiatics; a diaspora of new Americans in California. And that is more or less that. Iranian resident diplomatic representation, too, beyond the world's major capitals and outside the Asian and Mediterranean region, tends to be sparse. No one particularly expects an Englishman to speak Farsi, even in Iran, let alone outside it.

I remember watching a James Bond movie, one evening in downtown Bangkok. The Iranian tourist couple next to me were running an excited commentary on the action in Persian, which became increasing irksome. In exasperation, I finally turned towards them, introduced myself with much politeness (*ta'arof*) and enquired whether it might be possible for them, without too much trouble (*bi zahmat*), to lower their voices? Staring at me in the flickering light, they slowly made out that I was a foreigner; nay, worse, a white Caucasian; nay, worst of all, probably even 007 himself, sent to get them. To my surprise and indeed embarrassment, they immediately rose up in panic, pushed away from me along the row of goggling Siamese, and stumbled out of the cinema into the scented South East Asian night, with snatched backward glances of horror.

This memory returned to me in 1974, as I sat on the opposite side of a mahogany desk of Mussolini proportions in an oppressively airless office, in a rather rococo Foreign Ministry building, in a small South American country (the People's Republic of Parazil) which around that time had been misfortunate enough to find itself under military government. On the other side of the desk was the Permanent Secretary – no suave and scented diplomat, but a stocky military man, with spatulate fingers: Coronel Machismo. I had hoped to get on with him. He was doing his duty, as he saw it. I was personally on his side, as it were, in the cold war; and had no time for Marxist guerrillas, or hard 'Lefties' of any ilk. If I disapproved of military government per se and hoped for the return of parliamentary democracy to Parazil, that was not why I was presuming on El Coronel's time and patience. Now in my third day of negotiation, he and I were still turning in circles and getting nowhere. The Colonel wanted the European Commission to pull out, or (better) withdraw protection from, the local agent running its tiny library and sub-office in his country. But he would not say why. I had been sent out from Brussels by the European Commission's Vice-President, Sir Christopher Soames, to get to the bottom of the matter, and find a mutually satisfactory solution. For the n'th time, I heard myself telling Machismo that I had not yet been told the 'why', and could not therefore recommend the 'what'.

Finally, and for the first time in our dialogue of the deaf, he was to lose his cool – and even switch to English:

'Señor Feldin, I leesen to all the telephone calls to Brassoles you make from your EC office'. (Pause for effect; flies buzzed against the dusty window panes). 'I seemply have to lift thees telephone' (pointing to the only object on Il Duce's table, beyond a large sheet of faded green blotting paper) 'and your representative will be in preeson, where I shall be able to settle matters directly… and *personally*'.

Despite myself, I began seriously to dislike the Colonel. I took a deep breath, before responding.

'You are welcome to sit beside me in the EC office, Coronel, whenever I speak to His Excellency in Brussels. The European Commission prides itself on being a 'House of Glass'. We have nothing to hide'. (Liar). 'But if you lift that telephone now, it will hit the international headlines immediately, and the consequences for the Republic of Parazil will be incalculable – but far-reaching'. (Again, liar! But I had to say *something*). 'I have been personally sent here by none other than the Vice-President of Europe, in order to be of assistance to you, Coronel; but I cannot do so unless *you* first help *me*. Between us, as officers and gentlemen (I touched my regimental tie), in the security of this office, I say once more, please state at least your *general* reasons, if you cannot adduce any confidential evidence which you may possibly have at your disposal'.

Machismo finally capitulated. With a shrug, he swept open a drawer, withdrew a photostat and passed it gravely across the table. I received the document, without looking at it; but held my interlocutor's gaze – not easy: he had black irises, like a gipsy.

'I shall need to study this carefully, on return to our office; then, once more to speak to His Excellency in Brussels'.

'By telephone, Señor Feldin?'

'Naturally, Coronel. Good afternoon.'

'Hasta la vista, Señor.'

As it happened, I was never to see the chap again – although he occasionally still visits my dreams, as a 'nasty' from Central Castings.

It was not quite as bad as we had feared. The German EC official who had acted as my interpreter with Machismo (I myself had inadequate Portuguese or Spanish or whatever the Parazilian lingua franca was) kindly translated the document for me, on the way out. Sympathy and support for the Partido Católico Democratico Populár. That sort of thing. Inappropriate, for a local agent of the EC; but not a matter for military interrogation, possibly of a forceful nature. We popped back to our sub-office, to see the said local agent, by then with a loaded revolver on her desk. After she had put it away, at my request, and had had a look at the photostat, at her request, she opted to leave Parazil, prontissimo.

My colleagues and I decided to put the sub-office into mothballs, until the political climate improved. I had to clear all this with Brussels. There was, as Machismo had reminded me so delicately, no secure communications link. It would be improper for me, a British diplomat on secondment to the European Community, to turn to the British Embassy for help; and probably unwise to invite the local French EU rotating 'Presidency' to pass messages through their own channels. In any case, too slow – action was needed within hours, not days; communication had to be not only secure, but immediate.

Accordingly, in neat capital letters, I wrote down in my hotel a brief report with numbered paragraphs and simple recommendations, and instructed Luigi (a streetwise Italian junior official in my team of investigators) to go to the central Post Office and send it to David Hannay (then Soames's *chef de cabinet*, now Lord Hannay of Chiswick and the author of the preface to this present book). The answer came back by telephone to my hotel bedroom, two or three hours later, Soames and the Director-General having been consulted. 'Your first paragraph, Bloody Hell. Para 2: Crumbs. Paras 3 and 4: agreed by all. Para 5: not more than $5,000. Para 6: as soon as possible: See you later, alligator'. An eavesdropping

Coronel Machismo was welcome to make of all that whatever he wished.

So it was *exeunt omnes*. The team and I did this and fixed that (including the local agent's instant expatriation) and generally jumped about. My Italian junior and I were the last to leave Parazil. I was disinclined to hang around, having arrived without a diplomatic visa and possessing, unlike my accompanying polyglot German colleague, no ambassadorial status in Latin America. But I had felt duty-bound to call on the 'Presidency' Ambassador to de-brief. (*'Cher ami, vous avez parfaitement raison. Il a fallu en finir'*). Luigi and I then hopped into a toy private plane and told the pilot to make for Buenos Aires, via Montevideo, with the aim of picking up the regular Varig flight to Santiago.

This last, we just managed to do, running across the tarmac to a jetliner almost with its chocks away. But the ladder was still down, the pilot cheerfully holding back, after a brief chat over the intercom with my own buccaneer of a pilot, and in anticipation of two more first class passengers. In South America, the individual still counts; and money counts even more. This, despite airport officials waving their arms like windmills and shouting 'But this is Argentina, not Parazil' (as if I didn't already know).

Before that, however, while still skimming the delta of the River Plate at wave height, there was a question in my ear from the streetwise Italian junior:

'Signore Lezz-lee, il vostro telegrammo segretto. Com'era fatto?'

It was very noisy behind the cockpit. But I managed to bellow into Luigi's ear that Hannay had once been on the FO Persian course, like me.

'Ah si, naturalmente. Molto bene. Grazie.'

27

KUKHRIS DRAWN, IN KATHMANDU

As is well known, the Brits love jokes. The only trouble is, that they are rarely appreciated – in the words of Rudyard Kipling's poem – by 'lesser breeds without the law'.

Shortly after joining the Diplomatic Service as a 'Third Secretary', I was appointed Private Secretary to a slightly intimidating Wykehamist ambassador (see chapter 4). One of his pieces of advice to a new boy was: 'Never make English jokes to foreigners – they always misunderstand them'. Indeed a major drawback, but also one of the many stimuli of working in close harness with real foreigners (for example, in the Brussels Eurocracy or with the NATO, UN, WTO or OECD Secretariats) was often to prove to be the grievous absence of a common sense of humour.

So it was, initially at least, with Ruprecht (now dead and not his real name). A relatively young German official, absolutely brilliant and newly promoted, he had been appointed Head of the North American and Diplomatic Division in the re-shuffled External Relations Directorate-General of the Brussels Commission, when the Brits arrived there in early 1973, on UK accession to the European Community. I was among the parachutists from Whitehall. Having stowed my chute and taken post, I found myself under a first class Dutch Deputy Secretary and an even more impressive Dutch Permanent Secretary (Director-General); but saw little of either of them, quite rightly, except when the going was really rough – they mostly left me to get on with my job. Below me, were three Divisional Chiefs: a seasoned and tough Frenchman, a competent if charmless Luxembourger, and the said Ruprecht.

('It's because you are a green British newcomer, and an ignorant diplomat to boot, that they've given you the best heads of department going', said a cynical and malevolent Belgian in-house colleague).

Ruprecht turned out to have a frighteningly strong academic background; an impeccable early track record in the Commission; stilted, but fluent and intelligible, mid-Atlantic English; bilingual French (he had a beautiful French wife, Sophie, and multilingual children). From Hamburg, with a father who had been a regular naval officer, Ruprecht was not only an internationalist but also an anglophile, imbued by his father with a great respect for the Royal Navy. (He was a little taken aback, when I quoted Sir Winston Churchill on the traditions of the latter – rum, sodomy and the lash – but soon recovered, usually knowing when he was being teased). The two of us held in common having been bombed during the Second World War, I in London, he in Hamburg; and the consequent personal commitment to making post-war Europe come together and stay that way. He worked night and day with total loyalty to me, his Director – not the universal rule in the Berlaymont Headquarters building. But was he really human? Was it not my duty, as an Englishman, to enlarge his narrow continental horizons?? Conscious of the White Man's Burden that birth, privilege, rank and history had laid upon my admittedly entirely deserving and capable shoulders, I started to 'bring him on' – beginning with instruction in *British*, not American, English. (*La mission civilatrice du perfide Albion, quoi?* quipped a French subordinate.) But Ruprecht was a quick learner.

In 1974 the two of us were in Tokyo, to conclude the inter-governmental convention which was to permit the opening, later that year, of the intended new EU Delegation in Tokyo. On our way back, with the long-suffering Sophie's consent, we took ten days' furlough, so that I could give the man a quick *aperçu* of the British Imperial Experience – Kashmir, Kathmandu and Kabul, to be more precise. We took priest bread from the Sikhs in Amritsar; camped on a Kashmiri house boat; glimpsed the peak of Everest from a mountain pass; plunged in and out of oriental bazaars and bussed up the Khyber and back. Western Europe (where Ruprecht commanded four languages) it was not. Nor the YMCA in Tintagel, where he had consolidated his English as a young man. Nor a junior leaders scholarship to the US. Nor student work-experience in Canada. Nevertheless, the man took a deep breath and drank deep.

The real 'switch-on', (or should I say 'switch-over'?) came in Kathmandu.

In those days, there was only one halfway decent hotel; an improved, yet still appalling, airstrip; a few hippies looking for a 'fix'. Otherwise, still much its old self. We watched the dead being cremated on their pyres on the riverbank; heard the monkeys chattering in the woods; examined erotic temple sculptures, with few surprises; explored the bazaars, the side alleys and back streets. But in the latter, my comeuppance. I was wearing a pork pie hat from Lock of St James's Street (to keep off the fierce tropical sun), a khaki riding mac (bought in Kashmir, against fierce tropical downpours), my late father's Artists' Rifles tie (he had bought a new one just before he died, and I thought it was safe to get some wear out of it East of Suez, if not in Whitehall) and highly polished black brogues from Duke Street, St James (because I had calculated that polishing up their toe caps would keep me out of mischief in the evenings). Ruprecht, as usual, was arrayed in white shirt, sober alumni tie, and a dark blue suit – like a Gnome of Zurich or an off-duty Guards officer in Birdcage Walk. We were wandering along a muddy road, near the football stadium, from which came confused cries and the distant wail of oriental music. In the opposite direction, there approached a commanding figure in jodhpurs, long-skirted buff jacket with stand-up collar, and a velvet Nehru cap. It came to a halt, puzzled but intrigued, before us; hesitated, looking first to one, then to the other; finally, it saluted Ruprecht and enquired whether he was, by any chance, a 'British Officer'? If so, would he care to join the Colonel Sahib, at the regimental party? Ruprecht, Chelsea accent by now to the fore, and Boston Brahmin temporarily banished, replied that he would be delighted; but asked, with a nonchalant gesture in my direction, whether the Colonel Sahib might permit him to bring with him his Second-in-Command? (The figure took a second look at my pork pie hat, flashed white teeth in a broad grin, and courteously assented.) He led us into the stadium, talking volubly to Ruprecht about – I think – the Japanese army in the Burma campaign, having learned that we were just in from Tokyo.

A Nepalese Ghurkha battalion was celebrating the Festival of Dashain, in honour of the goddess Durga. The officers, all in regulation Nepalese civvies, sat in the grand stand, where we too took our seats and were plied with sugary tea (no milk) and pistachio nuts. On the opposite side of the stadium, the regimental band was playing ragged but stirring Nepalese music, which proceeded hypnotically and without pause. On the stadium floor, the battalion colours were planted firmly in the sand. The soldiers themselves sat tidily on their benches round about and observed the action attentively, murmuring among themselves and giving voice, at intervals, to lusty shouts of wild acclaim.

Animals were being led out one by one to the centre, where groups of Ghurkhas awaited them. A flash of a kukhri, and a goat's head parted from its body, describing a complete turn in the air before being deftly caught. The headless body was then dragged by its tail all round the colours, leaving a red circle of blood in the sand. Always, a decapitation in one swift blow. Goat after Goat. Cheer after Cheer. Bang-Bang, the drum; Waily-Wail, the clarinets and brass; Clash-Clash, the cymbals. Then water buffalo were led forward. Kukhris were sheathed; new, long, two-handed scimitars produced. Scimitars swept, ox heads dropped to earth rather than span in the air. But, always, the neck completely severed with one blow. Twitching carcasses were dragged by several soldiers round the colours, in fresh circles of gore. All in homage to the demon goddess, Durga.

Having had fried eggs and bacon for breakfast back at the hotel (but Ruprecht, on Sophie's orders, only fresh fruit and yoghurt), and feeling the sun though my rubber riding mac, and smelling the blood on the sand, I began to think, after some time had elapsed, that the moment might have come when, Pukka Sahib or not, with or without the Artists' Rifles tie, I might need to retire to a more private place. I so whimpered, in German, to Ruprecht, who smoothly took leave of the Colonel Sahib in correct Camberley form, and led me away, hand at my elbow, but with a final lordly wave of thanks to the regiment from the stadium exit.

'What d-did you make of it, R-Rup?' I stammered, trying not to gag.

Now it was payback time. He saw his chance.

'Bloody good show, Leslie', he replied. 'What with this lot and the rum, you chaps had all the cards in the war. My father was absolutely right'.

Ruprecht was one of my best friends in the European Commission, and an honorary Englishman of whom even Gunga Din could have been proud. Whether I in my turn became a 'good European', I rather doubt; but Ruprecht at least showed me the way.

We all thought that he would make Director-General, one day: but he died in mid career, from skin cancer. Some said: too much time sailing in the sun off the Spanish coast (he and his wife had a family villa down that way). But I thought: privation and malnutrition in wartime Hamburg – the Brits knocked the hell out of the place, you know; and, in the London Blitz, I had had the easier part.

28

WORKAHOLICS, LIVING IN RABBIT HUTCHES

I once organised a turbulent press conference in Tokyo for one Sir Roy Denman, a boss man from Brussels. Just before we entered the crowded room, he turned to me and said. 'In the event, Leslie, that I see a man enter the room and come towards me, with a gleam in his eye and brandishing a samurai sword, I shall turn to you with the words: 'As you were saying, Sir Roy!'

I have in fact never quite liked having things pointed at me. Not fingers. Certainly not samurai swords. Especially not Sten guns (one was levelled at me, years ago, by a trainee who had met with a stoppage on the firing range, and had turned clumsily in my direction for advice). But not even – since Tokyo in 1979 – zoom lenses and television cameras. Let me explain.

Life in Tokyo at the head of the 'EC Delegation', from 1978 to 1982, was much of the time to do with securing the opening up of the Japanese market to European exports of goods and services.

In terms of formal customs duties on imports, Japan was not so widely out of line with its other industrialised partners, certain tariff peaks excepted. A badly briefed Japanese cabinet minister even declared, at a high-level GATT meeting, that Japan had one of the most open markets in the world – provoking, even in dull and diplomatic Geneva, an audible gasp in the conference chamber, and not a few politely suppressed guffaws. For the fact was, high tariff or low, open market or not, Japan's actual imports of common-or-garden, manufactured goods were virtually nil (other than low-volume, high-cost, luxury items like Rolls Royces and French perfumes). Imports of services did little better.

Japanese official spokesmen blamed the Europeans and Americans for lack of effort in understanding the Japanese market, in learning the Japanese language and in meeting idiosyncratic Japanese consumer requirements; also, for going instead to easier export markets elsewhere in the world which required less understanding and exertion. There was a grain of truth in this. But no more than a grain. The then prevailing Japanese mercantilist mentality was 'exports, our duty; imports, unpatriotic' and tended to view international trade as a 'zero sum' game. In the spirit of 'export or die', anything that the Japanese could make for themselves should for that reason not be imported. To the sound economic principle of the international division of labour and the merits of global competition on a level playing field, the Japanese government paid lip service only. The Japanese had in effect made trade in manufactures mostly a one-way street, by means of a raft of regulations and hidden administrative practices which limited or excluded foreign goods not judged to be vital imports. The distribution system, once foreign goods had passed through Japanese customs, was archaic – and, to a high degree, inaccessible. The Japanese consumer paid the price for this; but the system of tied outlets and inefficient 'mamma and papa' stores was too deeply entrenched – and too difficult to disrupt, in terms of domestic politics.

Yet the giants of Japanese industry expected free access to European and North American markets. They engaged in 'laser beam' export drives, narrowly focussed and intense. Binoculars, cameras and motorbikes came first; followed by motorcars and electronic consumer goods. They could be quite predatory, seeking to squeeze the life out of their European and American competitors.

Their trading partners' response was only to be expected: informal, 'voluntary' export restraint agreements (VRAs) were negotiated, governing certain key Japanese exports, so as to prevent economic disruption, and to allow indigenous Western industries temporary 'breathing spaces' in which to adjust and adapt. As a free marketeer myself, I did not like this kind of undercover dealing. European industries never fully used their breathing spaces. And the Japanese paid no real penalty. If they exported fewer of their excellent, largely fault-free products, then they could charge more for them.

A better approach was to persuade the Japanese to start assembling and where possible actually manufacturing in the European markets to which they found it so lucrative and attractive to export. In the UK, they eventually established plants for motorcars in Sunderland, and television sets and video tape recorders in Wales. But initially, they needed some persuading. And, of course, their trading partners continued to be faced with the flagrant import imperviousness of the Japanese domestic market already referred to. It was epidemic and systemic, admitting of no exceptions. The US – Japan's closest ally, politically and militarily – was treated no better than anyone else. Exports of American skis were blocked, on the grounds that Japanese snow had different characteristics from American snow; US baseball bats, for equally impenetrable local or ethnic reasons.

In Brussels, the Commission, which sent me my instructions and to which I made my reports, began to lose its temper. There was talk of withdrawing GATT privileges from Japan, under a key clause in the founding treaty, relating to fair trade and 'Nullification and Impairment of Benefits'.

The Director-General in Brussels was Sir Roy Denman, a former Board of Trade official and Second Permanent Secretary in the Cabinet Office. Well over six foot, with a voice that one felt could ring out over a battlefield, he had a commanding presence. Meeting him, one was conscious of his self-assurance and of forceful emotion kept under control - but revealed at moments of exuberance (and, at times, in recklessness). A man thus to be reckoned with - and (for all that he spoke excellent German) one hard for his lazy, self indulgent political master, Vice-President Wilhelm Haferkamp, a German trade unionist, to cope with. Willy Haferkamp was the kind of political leader who, when faced with a hard policy choice, preferred to adopt the easiest course or to take no decision at all. The relationship was bound to end in tears.

Denman had great respect, not only for the Germans, but also for the Japanese, whom he came up against in Burma during the Second World War. They had fought bravely and believed in absolutes, as he did himself. Without the disadvantage of actually having had to fight either of these peoples, I, too, respected the Japanese and the Germans. This fact did not escape Sir Roy, with whom I had established a good rapport, despite his love-hate relationship with the FO. Quite unpredictably, we became allies and friends. I liked the way he called a spade a bloody shovel; he (mistakenly) took me for a Foreign Office renegade who had defiantly jumped ship, to join the European Commission. Whenever he was in Tokyo, I plied him with round-the-clock, drip-fed weak whiskey water; he in turn pretended to listen to what my staff and I had to give him by way of advice (even if he had already made his mind up, as was usually the case).

Roy Denman had, however, a particular weakness with the press. In Brussels, he liked to show his policy papers to selected journalists, and share gossip about life in the Berlaymont headquarters building. Eventually, the pigeons came home to roost. The story got out of Haferkamp's abuse of the vice-presidential expense account (huge, constantly overdrawn, yet repeatedly replenished by a reluctant President, and indiscriminately and ineffectively spread about). Also, such tittle-tattle as Haferkamp having spent three days in Geneva for a Ministerial Meeting; but turning up only once, for an hour or so; and otherwise dividing his time equally between two separate hotels, housing different companions. ‘The Economist’ magazine - ever with its ear to the ground in those days, on European matters - came out with Haferkamp's picture on the front cover, and some such slogan as 'Hey, Big Spender!'

At that, not only the unfortunate Vice-President but also the Commission President himself felt the imperative to do something. As also the German Ambassador to the EC: (*'Ordung soll sein'*). Denman was promptly transferred to Washington, to be the EC Representative (a task which admittedly appealed to him, and which he ably discharged), while I was summoned from Tokyo to take over (with reluctance) Denman's job in Brussels. Once there, I backed him against all comers, and our comradely rapport continued, until eventually I left Brussels for Sussex.

Well before all that, however, the Japan team in Brussels had written a paper about EC policy towards Japan for circulation throughout the European Commission, into which Denman inserted a number of pithy and pointed phrases which were gratuitously provocative. (My staff and I in Tokyo had not been consulted on the final text). One of them was to the effect that the Japanese market had about as much propensity to import foreign goods as there was to be found any semblance of party spirit on a wet Sunday afternoon in Glasgow. Knowing Glasgow a little, I could see what he meant. But he then went on to say that the Japanese were a 'nation of workaholics, living in rabbit hutches' (a comment he had made to me, as he viewed Japanese housing from the back seat of my chauffeured Mercedes, as we drove into town from the airport on his first official visit to Japan). The report was quite deliberately leaked to the press. It was immediately all over the European newspapers and – after a short delay – the Japanese. The comment was seen (wrongly) on the Tokyo streets as racist; but recognised (rightly) by the Japanese authorities as commercially threatening.

Trade tension rose. Popular resentment in Japan also. My delegation began to receive threatening phone calls and letters. The Tokyo police, to their credit, stepped up their arrangements for our protection. To take the unintended sting out of the situation, I appeared on a Japanese TV talk show with a top Japanese industrialist, he wearing made-up, furry rabbit ears and I offering him a bottle labelled 'Workahol'. The Japanese sense of humour started to reassert itself. Syndicated columns began to comment that it was perfectly true that Japanese housing was cramped and substandard.

The European trade issue nevertheless became the talk of the town. Heads were shaken and fingers wagged. At the gymnasium where my wife and I went regularly for a workout, a new Japanese masseuse appeared, to manipulate my joints and walk up and down my back in bare feet, as is the practice. Stocky, middle-aged and ill-favoured, she did her job well, until the point came when she asked me, in Japanese, what my job was. I told her *'Eeshii daihyō desu'*. She sucked in her breath in shock and disapproval. Was it I who had written about rabbit hutches? Luckily, the session was near to its end, because I began to get a much rougher ride.

And so it was, almost immediately afterwards, that Sir Roy Denman and his team of his advisors flew out to Tokyo, for negotiations with the Japan authorities, giving the latter a severe jolt. The question of the nullification of Japanese rights under Article XXIII of the GATT was the main item on the agenda.

After the talks, I organised a press conference for Sir Roy at the Delegation. The press room was crowded out, my (highly strung, French) press attaché apprehensive and unable to cope. Many of the journalists and cameraman had never been seen before. My ever-loyal Japanese staff, too, seemed anxious and on edge.

The tension in the room was immense. Zoom television cameras and telescopic lenses pointed first at Denman and then at me.

'Are you sure we are safe?' whispered Denman in my ear. 'Are these cameras really *cameras*? Who is that chap with staring eyes at the back, holding a knife?'

Then came the first press question. A strained gentleman, mouth flecked with foam, glared first at Denman and then at me, unsure whom to address. He barked, in staccato basic English,

'When-Will-Trade-War-Begin?'

Devices once more zoomed and pointed. First at Denman, then at me.

Denman smiled, turned to me graciously, and said: 'Would you care to take that, Sir Roy?'

29

ROY DENMAN REMEMBERED

The greatest of all directors-general in the European Commission, before or since, was Sir Roy Denman KCB. (See previous chapter).

He had been an influential member of the team that took Britain into Europe and was a passionate champion of European integration. I first met him in 1973, when he was in the Department of Trade (having been a key player in the negotiating team which fixed the conditions of UK entry into the European Community), while I was about to leave for the Brussels Commission, on secondment to the Directorate-General for External Relations. Before setting out across the channel and into the trees, and against everyone's advice (he was said to be a prickly character, with little time for flannelled fools from the FO), I sought Denman out and asked for his advice. He gave it, vividly and in full measure: what he thought of everyone I would be working with, from Sir Christopher Soames downward; what to do and what to avoid; what to expect from Brussels in general. It proved spot on. After that, I got on with my job for a time. In 1975, Roy Denman became a Second Permanent Secretary in the Cabinet Office with overall responsibility for European affairs. In 1977, when I heard that Denman was transferring to Brussels to take over as Director-General, I decided to return his compliment, and wrote him a letter through FCO channels to tell him exactly what to expect, tactically, once he had hit the ground and folded up his parachute. He read it attentively and asked for more. I went over to London to see him, to answer his supplementaries, but also to ask him some questions of my own. Much later, he told me that he had found mine an accurate guide to the terrain, and the best advance briefing he had had from any one source.

I tried to live up to the best of his example (but avoid his few and rather frightening shortcomings) when I succeeded him in 1982. At his funeral in June 2006, St Luke's Church, Chelsea was packed not only with Brits, but also with a mighty phalanx of Roy Denman's friends and former associates from the continent of Europe and from America. There were many press obituaries. I, for my part, contributed the following to the Times:

> 'Your obituary of this highly effective, but controversial, public servant is accurate but deserves to be completed. I called on him in the cabinet office (prior to his posting to Brussels – to the ill-disguised relief of not a few in Whitehall – as Director-General for External Relations) to find out what the rest of us who were already in the Commission could expect from him. He told me to pass the word that he would arrive with a sword of fire and a bottle of whisky.
>
> We were not to be disappointed, in either respect. His impact was electric. Some shone, others shrank, but morale rose. He reinvigorated and redirected the Common Commercial Policy of the EC. Almost single-handed at the European helm, he committed us to a fresh attempt at the liberalisation of world trade, precisely at a time when protectionism was on the upswing, following oil crisis and recession.
>
> Not everyone liked him. His idle and ineffective Commissioner – the late Vice-President Wilhelm Haferkamp – constantly plotted to get rid of him. Yet, despite a well-deserved contrarian reputation, Denman could be kindly to his subordinates and was by no means a sworn enemy of the Foreign Office. He admired what he once described to me as the 'Coldstream Swagger' of Sir Michael Palliser, the then UK ambassador to the common market. Denman sent me, a professional diplomat, to Tokyo, to help avert the trade war then in the offing; and later put me

> up to succeed him as Director-General in Brussels, when – after one too many rows with Haferkamp – he got sent sideways to be EC Ambassador in Washington.
>
> Denman's real ambition, for most of his career before Brussels, was to become Cabinet Secretary. He had the ability – he could master any brief in no time flat, and draft impeccably at speed. But he would never suffer fools gladly, or tolerate unconstructive ambiguities. (What would he have said – and done – about Iraq?) The Commission, and ultimately Europe, were to be the beneficiary – Sir Roy Denman proved a Prince among Eurocrats, at 'the sharp end', where it matters – and where by no means every Whitehall Warrior emerges victorious.'

There was certainly no doubt about Roy Denman's sincere and long-held European convictions – unusual, if not rare, in the Home Civil Service in his day and age. The following is what he wrote, on his retirement from Washington in 1989:

> 'After the last farewell dinner on the last night, after Moya had gone up to bed, I sat and thought. This was my last day as a Government servant. At midnight I would be free. I thought of the time fifty years ago when Europe had first caught my heart. The towers and spires of the European Union could now be seen across the plain. I was proud to have been one of the baggage train on the long march.'

I share Denman's pride, and am glad to have marched with him. May he rest in peace.

30

ISE-JINGU OUT OF SEASON

I am not a great one for dialogue with the spirits of the dead. Only one of the latter, and then with slight misgiving, have I ever directly consulted. (See chapter 14).

In my undergraduate years (in a psycho-scientific rather than superstitious sort of way – with instruments of detection and measurement), I was an investigator of haunted houses, as a member of the Cambridge Society for Psychical Research. Later, I was the occupant of three such houses myself. But they held no fears for me and were – almost all of them, anyway – psychically dead. From my mid-forties onwards, as a lay minister of the established church, I have lingered little in country churchyards, and certainly composed no elegies there. The Cenotaph, for me, is no more than a lump of limestone in Whitehall. The Pyramids of Egypt and the pharaohnic monuments of the upper Nile, though fun to visit, nevertheless convey no supernatural thrill or sense of continuity with an unseen world. The Valley of the Imperial Tombs of the Ming Dynasty, outside Beijing, lights no particular light bulb. The ruins of Graeco-Roman antiquity, idem – although, as an admirer of Rome at its apogee, I tend to feel a little sad in Hadrian's Villa or strolling among the ruins of the Roman Forum or standing amid the remains of Leptis Magna.

Ise, in the Kii Peninsula in Japan, was different. Throughout my four years as the EC representative in Tokyo, I had never previously been there. Partly because I had other things to do and professionally more relevant places to visit; but also because of a certain mistrust of Shinto, Japan's oldest religion, the 'Way of the Gods'. Despite being overlaid by Confucianism, Buddhism and the many Modernisms of the scientific and technological era, Shinto was nevertheless part of the Emperor worship and militarism which had inspired, in my lifetime, the invasion of China, the assault on Pearl Harbour, the suicide missions of the young kamikaze pilots, the cruelties of the Imperial Japanese army in South East Asia, the savage and sadistic disregard of the Geneva Convention. Furthermore, Japan's unwillingness to follow Germany's example, admit her past misconduct, and face the truth rather than repress it, is something which I have never been able fully to understand, let alone forgive. On occasional visits to the Yakusune Shrine, near my official residence in Tokyo, my purpose was solely to push my little daughter in her pushchair in spacious surroundings, not to venerate the spirits of Japanese war criminals. True, the Emperor of Japan is today considered by no one – except a small under-class of extreme right wing illusionists – to be descended from the Sun Goddess Amaterasu. Nevertheless, the latter's shrine, and those of some ancestors of the imperial family, are located at Ise, the Mecca of the Shinto faith, the recipient of much national respect and many pilgrimages.

One day, I learned that I was to leave Tokyo for Brussels – where working life, on promotion, would be decidedly difficult; normal married life, a miracle.

It was then that I had second thoughts about Ise-Jingu. I had long been a student of comparative religion. I liked to think that I felt personally at home whenever, wherever and through whomsoever the spirit of God whispered to creation. If only in terms of respectful farewell to the country in which I was still living but was soon to quit, and in which I had felt happy and at home, I concluded that I should be better able to depart in peace by making some sort of pilgrimage to Ise. In the event, I found the shrine and its surroundings of remarkable aesthetic appeal; but also quite moving.

It was midweek in late spring. I was accompanied as guide by one of my Japanese staff. But she was silent as she paced beside me along the riverbank, through the trees, across the humped-back bridge, and into Geku, the outer shrine. (The mysterious inner shrine is not normally open, even to Eurocrats). We wandered among the various wooden temple buildings, all of them endowed with strong, pure profiles, in the mode of the Fourth and Fifth centuries AD – the pristine essence of ancient Japanese architectural inspiration, innocent of the Chinese models which were to influence Japan in subsequent eras of artistic evolution. Uniquely, these remarkable temples had always been – and still are, to this day – rebuilt and replaced every twenty years – always identical and unchanged – in order to preserve their ritual purity, and in celebration of the bounty as well as the beauty of nature.

That day, the setting was special. Light wind, soft rain, the shifting play of light and shadow, the noble lines of the cedar timbers, the gentle curves of the roofs, all came together for me, without my asking. The place was plangent. It being out of season and at the wrong hour, almost no one was about. But somewhere, an unseen visitor clapped hands at a shrine, no doubt before bowing and praying, as so many Japanese generations had done at Ise, over fifteen past centuries.

There was nothing spooky about Ise. Yet here was the essence of the Japanese aesthetic genius – simplicity, elegance and restraint. Here too, nobility, loyalty and honour. But I also picked up something else, which I had not expected. Was it my deep Celtic response to a common, prehistoric, transpolar Shamanism? Was it some wider commonality, to do with simply being human? To me as a Christian, it was the presence of the Holy Spirit, observing, sustaining, interceding – as in all ages, at all places and with all men, outside as well as within the catholic and apostolic community. Perhaps Cardinal König, Archbishop of Vienna and the Belgian Jesuit, Jacques Dupuis, had they been present, would have felt this too. And the words in the back of my mind, at Ise, were those of the psalmist: -

> 'If I take the wings of the morning,
> And dwell in the uttermost parts of the sea,
> Even then shall thy hand lead me,
> And thy right hand shall hold me'.

I stood quietly. This was the still point of the turning world. But my colleague shifted uneasily. Maybe, as a Westernised, foreign-educated young Japanese, she felt embarrassed and out of sympathy with the whole thing. Or perhaps she was afraid that I would simply dismiss Ise, as a mere exercise in off-piste tourism. Or perhaps even thought that neither of us should be there at all. I did not find it in me to ask her. So we took our departure.

I shall never go back; but I shall never forget.

31

YAKUZA!

While still thinking about things Japanese, let me rush forward in time to the summer of 1991.

The fit and physical, dark-blue-suited young man with cropped hair, is standing very close up indeed to the elderly ticket collector, and whispering intently into the latter's ear. The ticket man himself stands rigid, with a blank expression, but in a state of manifest anxiety. The young man's right hand gently moves up and down the older man's spine, as if counting the vertebrae. But the tips of the young man's little finger, and of the finger next to it, are missing – the mark of a gangster, an enforcer, or what the Japanese call a 'Yakuza'.

We are in Japan. I am in a first class compartment of the famous Bullet Train. In Tokyo, I have just awarded, in full fig as Vice-Chancellor of the University of Sussex, an honorary D.Univ. upon a generous Japanese benefactor, the ceremony taking place in the presence of the British Ambassador, in the hushed and umbrageous surroundings of the private garden, at H.E.'s Residence. I am now travelling to Kyoto, to make a speech, and to bestow an honorary doctorate of science upon an academic of international standing at the top University there.

My Registrar, a hard-bitten Yorkshire man on his first visit to Japan, is with me in the carriage. He is impressed by the train – punctual to the second, rock steady as it whispers along at speed, the compartments spacious. We are sitting on the right side of the aisle, one third of the way along, next to a large window through which we hope to glimpse the summit of Mount Fuji. Apart from ourselves, there seem to be almost no other passengers. But two characters further down on the other side of the aisle seem to have some problem. They have just beckoned to the dark-blue-suited young man (outwardly some sort of factotum but in reality, it later emerges, their very own on-board martial arts bodyguard). The bodyguard in turn is earnestly engaged with the ticket collector.

After a pregnant pause, and some Japanese hissing in of breath, the collector and the young man move to talk to an elderly Japanese gentleman further down on the left, who is then conducted (or, in fact, virtually frog-marched) out of his reserved seat, down the aisle and into the next carriage, to find another seat and disappear from this narrative. Returning, the ticket collector swings the abruptly vacated seat round through 180°. The two dissatisfied passengers then take new seats, facing each other. There they sprawl arrogantly, as if they own the whole Bullet Train, and proceed to banter together, with the occasional raucous laugh. One is quite tall and dressed like a bookie. The other stocky and of sombre attire. They wear rings on their fingers. They are not the sort of men one meets at the Emperor of Japan's annual Garden Party. I conclude that they are probably gangsters of the highest possible rank.

This probability becomes a certainty. At each of the Bullet Train's infrequent station stops, and at precisely the appointed place (markings on the platform indicate where each carriage will stop and almost to a foot where any particular seat is located), a line of tough-looking bullyboys bow low just outside the window. They receive barely a glance from the bookie and the sombre suit. The bowing low apparently continues, until the train has drawn clear of the platform, on the next leg of its journey.

During my earlier four years as head of the EC Delegation in Tokyo, I confess that I myself had more than occasionally caught a glimpse of leading gangsters in their Lexus limousines in the Ginza, driven by blank-faced thugs wearing white gloves; but I had hitherto not consciously shared a railway carriage with any such. Sadly, my 'street cred' with the Registrar has been shaken. He heard me say at some length, the day before in Tokyo, what a safe city it was; how criminal violence against the person – as opposed to suicide or self-inflicted injury – was virtually unknown; how you could walk almost anywhere by day or by night in total safety; how friendly and efficient the Japanese police were, etc. Clearly, I have some explaining to do.

Sotto voce, I say that, as anywhere in the world, there is organised crime; but it operates in Japan within very strict limits and understandings, closely monitored and enforced by the authorities. As to the young man's hand, he would have severed the fingertips himself, not as an isolated act of machismo, but as a sign of absolute loyalty to his criminal master. Probably, the lad is as thick as two short planks, with little education and no other prospects in life; this is how he comes to terms with himself and finds some sort of place in society. Apart from the two short planks, perhaps we had found here an example for our own professoriate, back at Sussex University. A finger-tip-free pro-vice-chancellor or deputy registrar, for example, would be a colleague upon whom reliance could be placed in all circumstances – even if the individual might, as a consequence, miss out a little bit on Campus *Fingerschpitzen-Gefühl*. The registrar nods thoughtfully, but seems unconvinced.

Most body contact in Japan is publicly avoided. People may shove each other, packed like sardines in the Tokyo subway during rush-hour. But men bow rather than shake hands; do not kiss ladies' fingers; nor cast brotherly arms round each others' shoulders. The touch of the young man's hand on the ticket collector's spine, quietly and gently done, is intentionally improper. The nub of it lies, of course, in the feel of the finger stubs.

The two of us sensitive and high-minded academics feel a bit twitchy. As soon as the attendant comes round, we order large drinks, and chatter with artificial enthusiasm about academic prospects and professorial personalities at Kyoto University.

32

THE YEAR OF THE CAT IN 'HARRY HONKERS'

Hong Kong in the sixties (for a young diplomat) was love at first sight.

The Kowloon ferry and the Cantonese food; the bustle and the bargains; the efficiency and good humour of this hard-working people. I have gone back regularly ever since, on any pretext. I still boast summer suits by Amen Bros and bespoke footwear by Leakyboots of Kowloon (almost, if not quite, their real names – you will know who they are and where to find them).

In the 'eighties there was some sort of muddle in the European Commission in Brussels, and I became a tiny bit Grand. If not quite the King of the (very) Common Market, at least the Sir Humphrey of EU Trade and Aid Policies – what they called the EU Director-General for External Relations. Gazing at myself rapturously in the shaving mirror, I was both moved and impressed. Inevitably, however, after Pride, the Come-Down.

In the Chinese Year of the Cat, en route back to Brussels from Beijing or Borneo or somewhere (no, not Bournemouth – the Tory Party was not in conference and Eurocrats were unwelcome, at any rate as far as Mrs T was concerned), I once again sweep graciously into the crown colony. An accessory aim is to pick up a new lightweight tuxedo. But, first, a lecture to the chamber of commerce; then a trip halfway up the peak, to kiss the feet of H.E. the Governor, the late and much respected Sir Edward Youde.

Alas, the man is a critic of mine of some years standing, and I of him, for arbitrary and trivial reasons which are not in the least to my credit. For example, the previous time I have then seen Teddy was when he was Chief Clerk at the FO. I was on secondment to the Commission and currently half way through a visiting fellowship at St Antony's College, Oxford, reading up about Japan before taking post in Tokyo as the EC Ambassador. In an off-the-record briefing to Australian journalists, I had been less than entirely respectful of Mr Malcolm Fraser, the Australian Prime Minister, who had once chased me around the grand piano in the Residence of his Brussels Ambassador, in a rage about the Common Agricultural Policy. I was shopped. Articles were gleefully published Down Under. The High Commission in London (untypically, but under firm instructions from Canberra) had registered a protest. So it was up to London from Oxford, pronto, for little Leslie, and onto the Chief Clerk's carpet. 'Conduct unbefitting a senior member of the service, which could compromise your future career', Teddy had said, not without satisfaction.

('Nonsense!' snorted my new Director-General in Brussels, Sir Roy Denman, when I subsequently reported back to him that I had been thus rebuked. 'Of course Fraser is a ****. And what the Hell's it got to do with the Chief Clerk anyway? You're *Commission* now, and come under *me*!').

And so it is that, in the Year of the Cat, while the 'lux tux' fits like a glove, and the chamber of commerce plays like a Strad, 'H.E. the Gov.' stitches me up with a diatribe about EU trade protectionism and the evils which it is inflicting on the Crown Colony. I reply that, whatever might be true of the Colony, the Crown is all for my EC Trade Policy, which fully meets the wishes of the Department of Trade and Industry, the entire British Cabinet and both Houses of Parliament, not to speak of every voting citizen of the UK. More follows, ding-dong, in like vein. Practicalities of GATT Multifibre Agreement; scope and limit of EU preferences for developing countries; concept of 'graduation' in international trade theory. After this invigorating but prickly exchange, Teddy (a kind man at heart) takes me out and shows me around his rose garden. Being not only the younger, but also the lesser, man, I cannot refrain from commenting, with solicitude, what a pity it is that his garden is now overlooked by the new Bank of

China skyscraper, thereby discouraging out-of-doors dalliance with any gubernatorial concubines there may be on the premises.

On which happy note of fraternal Diplomatic Service solidarity and intense mutual esteem, we part company. I am off like a shot down the peak to the Mandarin Hotel for shower, shave and shampoo, in preparation for the real highlight of the visit – a private dinner as the guest of an old friend, and fellow gastronome and oenophile, at a Chinese restaurant of his choosing.

My host is a true Nabob, a prince among box wallahs, later to be decorated, quite deservedly, for services to British exports. One of his commercial specialities is flogging Scotch whisky by the firkin to the thirsty nations of the orient. A task one might, at first blink, have thought not entirely suited to a clerk in holy orders and non-stipendiary minister of the Church of England; but one that he nevertheless discharges as conscientiously as he carries out his priestly duties. He being rather High, I sometimes call him 'Father'. But, in what follows, he shall also be referred to, quite rightly, as The Tai-Pan.

'My dear fellow, peace be with you.'

'And also with you, Father.'

'How did it go, dear boy, with the Governor?'

'Alas, I lost my temper and was rude.'

'How many times, my son?'

'Repeatedly.'

'Very well. Time for your penance: The South China Blue Seas Bistro beckons.'

We are off through the trams and rickshaws, over Wanchai and along Causeway Bay, with a swish of air conditioning and a whiff of leather upholstery, the angel on the radiator navigating its way. We begin with a perfectly delicious soup.

'Kidney?' I murmur.

'No, snake', the Tai-Pan whispers, 'It's the season, you know.'

The next course comes in: reassuringly pheasant-like slivers, served in a rich, dark broth. I ply my ivory chopsticks with exhibitionist panache, pausing only to remove unexpectedly sharp little bones and lay them out beside my bowl, puzzled.

'And this delicious dish?'

The Tai-Pan replies, silkily: 'Civet cat.'

I gulp my way gallantly onwards, until I find a lumpy something between my palate and my tongue. I remove this also. It turns out to be a paw – fur, claws, pads and all. Sod it. But Chinese faces are watching. Mustn't let the side down. Better go through the motions. 'Officer Qualities' needed. Take the initiative. I suck the paw dry and fold it reverently in its winding sheet, a red silk handkerchief taken from my breast pocket.

'I shall take it back to 'Brassholes' and give them 'paws' for thought. Ho, ho'.

'Even so, dear boy.'

The banquet moves majestically onwards. Maotai has given way to Margaux by the magnum.

'Tonight', I confide, 'I'll sleep sound in my first class couchette on Cathay Pacific. What a magnificent meal. Don't get the 'penance' thing, though. Take these brochettes. Quite like venison. Didn't know the Chinese had it. Mouflon, perhaps, flown in from the Gulf? Or Muntjak, from the Zoo? Truly mouth-watering, anyway. Pray enlighten me'.

The holy man pauses for reflection; then says:

'I believe he was called 'Rover'.'

To this day, the Good Father, God bless him – now no longer Tai-Pan in Hong Kong but Preacher to Gray's Inn in London – has declined to elucidate.

33

'DEATH SQUAD', IN BELGRADE

'He who dares, wins' is the motto of the Special Air Service. And the last man standing tends to be the first man to the drinks cabinet. But beauty sleep has to go by the board.

In other circumstances, Belgrade, in the month of June, was not too bad a holiday destination. But this was June 1983 and the 'Sixth Ministerial Meeting' of UNCTAD (the United Nations Conference on Trade and Development) was in ample and extended session – these 'meetings' quite often lasted for up to four weeks, to allow for a little leisure on the job. But Belgrade was to prove the most chaotic, non-consensual and bad-tempered international encounter that I have ever attended. Until the very last moment, utter deadlock.

There comes a moment in most of our lives, when 'a man must do what a man must do'. This was one of them. I proposed the setting up of a very small negotiating group of half a dozen key people and nationalities (the US and the EC naturally included) – which I called 'The Death Squad' – with the task of working out a satisfactory outcome, non-stop, night and day, until they dropped.

To this *'Escadron de la Mort'*, as the European Community's front line trade negotiator, I sent one of my most talented and toughest deputies, Roderick Abbott. He was a great GATT expert and an experienced international negotiator, later to become the deputy head of the WTO. Telling him 'Die like a man, with your boots on', I myself sat outside in an armchair, where I could readily be consulted, night and day – except when briefing the representatives of the EC member states on the progress (or lack of it), or lobbying ministers from other countries, or attempting to soothe the increasingly hysterical Chairman of the whole Conference, the Yugoslav Foreign Minister, Lazar Mojsov.

In the final stage, Abbott and I found ourselves negotiating, lobbying, coaxing, wheedling and threatening for three days and two and a bit nights, almost entirely without sleep. Not for the first time – or, indeed, the last time – in my 15 years as an international trade negotiator. Absolutely nothing to be proud of. No way to run a railroad. But sometimes, 'needs must'– and someone has to do it. While gentlemen in England lie abed.

The background was the general drift towards trade protectionism, in the international recession then just past its peak. The West was arguably in part to blame and simply had to give the lead; and, within the Western camp, the European Community was best placed to hold the centre-ground, given its generally good relations with significant parts of the developing world. At the G7 'Summit of Advanced Industrialised Countries' in Williamsburg earlier that very year (after another one of those all-night sessions, but of the 'sherpas', not the principals), the right phrases had been shoved into the final communiqué. Also, a start made, in the Paris-based OECD, with the process of what was called, in the jargon, 'Stand Still and Roll Back', meaning first a freeze on protectionist measures, and then their progressive dismantlement. Not enough and not soon enough, in my view – at the OECD's 'Executive Committee in Special Session', I had quipped that the process looked to me more like 'Roll Still and Stand Back'!

Sadly, meanwhile, the developing countries were in denial. They had got together, at a meeting in Buenos Aires, to construct a rigid and largely unacceptable platform of demands. The West was told that all was black and white. There was no protectionism, economic mismanagement or any other sins of omission or commission in the developing world. What was required was immediate, unrequited and long overdue capitulation by the developed world (assumed to be universally in the wrong, and totally without economic problems of their own). The Latin American debtor and protectionist countries dominated the debate, while more moderate voices from ASEAN, and Europe's associates in Asia, Africa and the Pacific, were lost in the rhetoric and general *'auto-intox'* (as the French put it).

And so, to Belgrade. It quickly became a shambles. Cuba and the 'state-trading' countries of Eastern Europe stirred the pot, calling for 'all-or-nothing', talking about a mass walkout, and vaguely hinting at a radical realignment of the world economy on socialist lines. The initial speeches were oratorical flights of fancy more like those heard in the United Nations General Assembly (on a bad day), than the down-to-earth discourse customary in practical, negotiating fora like the GATT in Geneva. The UNCTAD secretariat serving the Conference was proving useless; the Yugoslav hosts, out of their depth and impotent; the (Bulgarian) Chairman of the UNCTAD Trade Committee (whom I later shoved into the Death Squad, to neutralize him), far from independent. The latter was, incidentally, one Andrei Lukanov, later Minister for Foreign Economic Affairs in Sofia and briefly, in 1990, Bulgaria's last communist Prime Minister. You get my meaning? Unsurprisingly, UNCTAD VI was going to hell in a handcart.

Word soon reached me, in Brussels, of impending disaster. This mattered – not so much for the good name of the UN (which had been marginalised or had made itself look silly before), or for any threat to stable overseas development assistance (we and others like us would continue as donors, whatever UNCTAD thought or did), so much as for the threat of the further and unhelpful politicisation of what were basically trade policy issues, calling for pragmatic, negotiated settlement in the more serious and disciplined structure of the GATT (and I and my fellow conspirators in the External Relations Directorate-General in Brussels were already plotting a further round of liberalisation for world trade). So, the President turned to the Commissioner for overseas development issues, and (more important, because this was where the real issue at Belgrade lay) to the Vice-President responsible for the Community's common commercial policy, the idle Willi Haferkamp. But the latter (see Chapter 28) predictably copped out, hiding his head under the blankets, muttering that he had a party to go to in Nordrhein-Westphalia; that Belgrade was not that important; that in any case it was all insufficiently political and far too technical for him – in his colourful, blue-collar, parlance, a matter more for the departmental *'Scheiss-Experten'*. So I dropped everything, and went out, with a few good men, to handle it all myself.

The ranks somehow rallied. Counter-proposals by 'Group B' (for the non-initiate, the industrialised countries) were tabled; appeals made for moderation and compromise all round (addressed in particular to our friends in the 'Third World'). But the draft 'Ministerial Conclusions' stayed studded with points of difference and disagreement. Indeed, the working text on my arrival in Belgrade was so full of brackets, that you could hardly make sense of it. Chairman Mojsov waved it at me, during my initial courtesy call on him, and denounced it as 'the worst international working document which I have ever seen!' But we took Slivovitz together, and I told him not to worry. We would get there in the end – *'Nemari ništa! Polako pasigurno!'* ('Don't worry – slowly, we'll get there!'). He should relax. I would get a 'Death Squad' going. Later, I was to draft for him, privately, the final compromise, which he tabled in his own name on the penultimate day, and which – with a little further polishing – finally secured general acceptance.

On my triumphant return to Brussels, I was met with a slight and subtle shift in the attitude of my professional collaborators in the Directorate-General. Like the international trade specialists in the DTI in London, nine months previously, on hearing that I was to come back from Tokyo, to take over from the great Sir Roy Denman, the Commission staff were not entirely sure that a gentle and conciliatory diplomat from ('shock-horror') the dreaded Foreign and Commonwealth Office was entirely the best choice for the job.

Of course, from the start, and by definition, I had worked like the clappers, and whizzed around everywhere. Even the French Permanent Representation in Brussels – ever hoping that the Brits would skid on a banana skin – seemed convinced. ('It seems that you read EVERYTHING – and people are calling you *"Le Grand Manie-Tout* [untranslatable – but maybe Finger-in-every-Pie Fred?] *de la DG.'"*) In a spirit of malice spiced with envy, Swiss opposite numbers in Berne spoke of me behind my back as the Commission's 'Director-General of *State*'. But in their flinty hearts, the grizzled veterans of the Commission's DGI had kept their counsel. Until Belgrade. After which, having survived the baptism of fire, I was finally accepted as one of them.

But, back in Belgrade, there was still one thing more to do, before taking the Club Class back to headquarters. Matchsticks propping my eyelids open, in my favourite restaurant on the banks of the Danube, a fish dinner for the team, with Slivovitz as the aperitif, and some dark, red wine (as you will know, the local white wine is too sweet and sticky). We raised glasses to the Death Squad and all those who had stayed awake with her. 'Cheers, Maties!' (Actually, I said it in Serbo-Croat, out of sheer exhaustion: *'U vaše zdravlje!'* But people cottoned on).

34

THE DISCREET CHARM OF THE G7 SUMMITS

In the 1980s, the summits of the Heads of State or Government of the then G7 (today, G8) industrialised countries (the US, Canada, Japan, France, Germany, Italy and the UK, plus the President of the European Commission, plus the occasional slightly awestruck Prime Minister from any smaller EU country which happened to be chairing our Council of Ministers at the time) were not without their discreet, bourgeois charm.

As the senior competent official for EU trade policy in the Commission, I accompanied the Commission President's *chef de cabinet* to the 'sherpa' meetings which prepared each summit – and which were convened all over the place – Hawaii having been I think the furthest from home. At the summit itself, there were side-meetings of foreign ministers and finance ministers, to swell the crowd and add to the fun. But what really mattered were the restricted sessions, confined to the presidents and prime ministers. It was there that the President of the Commission had to speak alone for the entire EC, when it came to international trade, because this was a so-called 'Community Competence'. It made a break from the grunt and grind of the normal negotiating processes which consumed me in Geneva and elsewhere. Also from my unremitting efforts to avert trade wars across the Atlantic. To say nothing of routine Brussels office work and endless huddles with the representatives of the EU member states, to hear their wisdom and nevertheless keep them all in line. And the sherpa meetings were often quite stimulating. But during the summits themselves, the presidents and prime ministers sat alone, save for one *chef de cabinet* or equivalent behind each potentate, to take notes when needed and to seek advice from the rest of us – who otherwise simply lolled around outside the conference chambers enjoying the local hospitality in Colonial Williamsburg, or Ottawa or Venice or wherever.

Sherpa-dom offered a good way of bonding socially with successive Commission presidents. Gaston Thorn, a plucky but endlessly self-interrogatory Luxembourger, I comforted and re-assured – especially when he found himself the periodic target of Mrs Thatcher's handbag. With President Roy Jenkins, there was no self-interrogation and no problem with handbags; but we did talk about wine. At a private supper party in the margin of one summit in Tokyo, I served the boss my very best claret, on which he commented with massive expertise. But he disarmed me with advice that I have always subsequently followed. 'When asked to give an opinion on any claret, Leslie, I recommend taking a good squint at the label first'. At another Tokyo summit, in May 1986, I made even Jacques Delors laugh at my imitation of a female entertainer at a Geisha party. (Delors had what I thought was an exaggerated respect for British mandarins, because of a slight, entirely engaging, personal hang-up. He confessed to me that he had had no university education and thus had not been able to attend the *Ecole Nationale d'Administration*. But he was careful to add – this was, after all, the point of the narrative – that, later on, as French Finance Minister he had naturally given lectures there!)

My fondest recollection, however, is of the London summit in June 1984. Little Gaston Thorn had done well, by standing firm with President Reagan and Prime Minister Nakasone on international trade policy, notwithstanding the misgivings of the German Chancellor, but assisted (uncharacteristically, and for once) by Margaret Thatcher.

Now, it was all over. One by one, the great men were being motored from Lancaster House to the concluding banquet in the City, the President of the Commission going first, being the junior. Demonstrators were out on the streets, and departures to the Mansion House were being phased and delayed. Eventually, I found myself alone in Lancaster House with the US and French Presidents, who had the greatest seniority-in-office. I approached them, to make polite conversation and offer ritual excuses.

Ronald Reagan, however, was too busy enjoying himself with two uniformed female sergeants in the Royal Military Police. He made them seize his arms and pose for a photograph. 'Later on, you will be able to tell your kids that you arrested the President of the United States, ha, ha!'

So I turned to François Mitterand, who showed evident relief when I spoke to him in French. After an exchange of banalities about street demonstrations, on which we were both qualified by vast experience to comment (I, myself, in 1968 in Paris – see chapter 20), we glanced to one side, at Reagan. As Mitterand turned back towards me again, there was a slight shrug of the Presidential shoulders, then a twinkle in the Presidential gaze.

'Il est assez remarquable, ce garçon, n'est-ce pas .... vu son âge,?'

Mitterand, of course, although the elder, was the *real* ladies' man of the two, as he and I both knew, even if Reagan did not.

35

TOP GUN

Sometimes, in Brussels, even the Director-General was on target. Let me expand and justify.

It is the summer of 1984. I am an onlooker at the annual EU rifle competition in Brussels, organised by the European Commission. As some foreign ambassadors and international business personalities are present, and as I am the Director-General for External Relations, I am inveigled into putting in an appearance for protocol reasons rather against my will. I have a hangover from last night's party with the Chinese (too much Maotai); I happen not to like too many big bangs; and I am very much aware that, within the hour, I must grab a suitcase and a bundle of briefs, before flying off from Brussels for trade talks in Tokyo.

For possibly mixed motives (but surely not to take the 'Mickey' out of the DG?), a smiling German official asks me whether I would care to show willing and take part in the final shoot-in. Nodding gloomily, I take the proffered two rifles, fire off the appointed number of rounds at various targets and retreat to the sidelines, where I rejoin a group sipping beer. Apart from me in my pinstripe, almost everyone seems to be exquisitely attired in Loden jackets and knickerbockers. A tape recording of Austrian hunting horns sets the tone, in between the crash of the volleys. I explain apologetically that I have not fired a rifle since a spot of Moufflon hunting with the Qashqai in South Persia, 25 years previously. My interlocutors, sensing that *qui s'excuse s'accuse*, change the subject of conversation politely, away from the immediate proceedings. I start wondering when I can decently escape.

The fact is that my father gave me an air rifle when I was 14; my grandfather, the use of a .22 rifle when I was 16. Pa, himself a rifleman in the First World War, instructed me. I gradually got the hang of it, although without any enormous enthusiasm.

Later, at Aldershot, Company Sergeant-Major Bennett, MM, Coldstream Guards, quite rightly took a dim view of me. I was called dozy, idle, and (not his precise words) unsoldierly; and was twice invited to circumambulate the drill square of Mons Officer Cadet School at the double, holding my Lee Enfield rifle at arm's length, vertically above my head. (We were all wary of Bennett – his Military Medal was rumoured to have been won during the retreat to Dunkirk in 1940; with no officer surviving, the remnants of his platoon were defending a village which was being approached by a Panzer; he grabbed some soup plates, smothered them in mud, laid them out over the main street, and waited for the German tank; when the crew got out to verify the nature of these mines and prepare to shift them, Bennett popped up in a window and shot them all dead).

Eventually, we went out on the firing range, for small arms training. When the targets came back, the 'Cum-Sar-Major' stomped over to me. The last to fire, I for my part was still prone in the firing position in a relaxed fashion, gazing dreamily down the range. He addressed me, furiously, with a purple face. 'Where did you learn to shoot like that, MR (sarcastic over-emphasis) Fielding?' Leaping to my feet, I snapped smartly to attention and barked out a polite 'SIR!' I decide to leave my father and grandfather out of it, and offered an innocent-faced but (to Bennett) thoroughly annoying explanation, about having recently received two days' rifle training at the Royal Regiment of Artillery's basic training camp at Oswestry. CSM Bennett snorted and growled: 'You should be in a proper *soldier's* regiment and wear a proper soldier's *'at'*. (A reference to my floppy dark blue beret and his peaked and gilded Guardsman's cap). All my rifle rounds were bunched in a tight group, three inches across.

But back to Brussels. The Austrian hunting horns are switched off. The babble of German/French/Italian/Dutch/

English and even Irish voices gradually subsides. The judges are conferring, examining my targets. The argument is apparently about whether two of my rounds have gone through the same hole, or I fired one less bullet than I should have done. Not wanting to miss my plane to Tokyo, I am already beginning to shuffle off to the exit. But I am called back, handed an immense silver cup and congratulated on having won that year's competition. And there it stands in my office in the Berlaymont building until the following year, when I compete again. I shoot wide. Out of a diplomatic desire to yield prominence to others? In reality, of course, I am making sure that, in my 54th year, I will not be recalled to the Colours to fight the Taliban or whoever. (I am still, theoretically, a member of the 'Regular Army Reserve of Officers' and have a silver buttonhole badge to prove it.)

I am to shoot a sporting rifle only one more time. We are after elk, in northern Scandinavia. With the exception of the German Ambassador (a veteran of the Eastern Front, naturally, as they all mostly are), the other guns (mostly well-heeled but clueless box wallahs) shoot appallingly. It falls to me to drop other people's limping and mangled targets with a shot through the head or behind-the-shoulder-and-through-the-heart.

Never again. Although I admit that I persisted in the view that my pheasant were so dim-witted that they amply deserved every Left and Right that I could give them.

36

LATIN LOO LOCK-OUT

Having been seated – for the purpose of intimate evacuation – in a Latin American loo, I attempted to exit and wash my hands outside. But, the door would not unlock! Curses!! Then, panic!!!

As I rattled the door knob, memories came back, of those rugby football songs which we Elizabethans sang in the coach home, victorious – as almost always – in our away matches. (In this case, a ditty to do with three old ladies locked in a lavatory; they were there, allegedly, from Monday to Saturday; no one knew they were there).

The panic in my breast arose because this was October not 1950, but 1986, in Punta del Este, Uruguay, within five minutes of the official opening of a ministerial meeting of the World Trade Organisation (then known as the GATT). The purpose was to launch a new round of international negotiations for the further liberalisation and above all expansion of trade, not only in *goods* but also (an innovation of mine, which managed somehow to appeal to both the Americans and the French, normally at opposite ends from each other) in *services*. Master-minded by the European Commission, with the vociferous encouragement of (among others) the US President and the British Prime Minister – Ronald Reagan and Margaret Thatcher – I had made this the corner stone of my command of the common commercial policy of the EC, in my new capacity (chapter 32). So, in October 1986, the stocks were sold; the press was squared; the middleclass was quite prepared.

But, in Punta, the Commissioners from Brussels would surely be tongued-tied and terrified without a 'Yes, Minister' at their elbow. And it was by now four and a half minutes to go to the starting bell in the Conference Room beyond.

As with a drowning man, my mind flashed back. The long preparation for this day. The pessimism and trade protectionism of the international ethos, when I had taken over in Brussels in 1982, in the grip of a world recession. First, 'Stand Still and Roll Back' (i.e. all countries to stop raising new barriers to trade and start dismantling those already erected). Then holding the ring against wreckers and rhetoricians in the United Nations Conference on Trade and Development in 1983 (see chapter 33). Then endeavouring to restrain 'gung-ho' tactics by an over-enthusiastic American government vainly attempting to bulldoze and bully the developing countries. Rather, the latter, in my view, needed to be convinced, brought on side, and generally 'shmoozed'. For the European Community unquestionably held the centre ground, and could, if it chose, play the pivotal North/South role upon which success or failure would depend. With that in view, the Commission had conducted much diplomacy within the EC. Without troubling my President and his Commissioners too much with the detail – i.e. by informing them, without consulting them – I had launched at our twelve member states a series of five interlinked documents of economic reasoning (the so-called 'Alpha-Epsilon Non-Papers') – a professional pleasure to write, but almost a death wish to table. Happily, a solid consensus fairly quickly emerged, within the EC. There followed intensive sessions with the EC's principal Western partners in the so-called 'Executive Committee in Special Session' of the OECD (mercifully, mandarins not ministers), at successive G7 Summits and in the Commission's more informal 'Quadrilaterals' with the US, Japan and Canada. Finally, my principal sidekicks in the Commission and I quartered the globe, rallying support from the 'Third World'. Not least, from those touchy interlocutors, India and Brazil; but also from our loyal ex-colonial territories in Africa, Asia and the Pacific, (ACP), and our partners in the Association of South East Asian Nations (ASEAN).

Thus it was that the circles had been squared and all the ducks lined up. And, finally, the world had come to Punta del Este.

With three minutes now to go, I finally yelled out. *'¡I Ayúdame! Estoy encarcelado en los servicios. Soy un personaje importante. ¡Que me saquen de aqui!'* But no reaction – although I could hear some shuffling outside my cabin. Maybe my Brussels accent had put people off? Despair!

In sad surrender, I gave the lock, this time, a soft and gentle caress. Bingo! The door sprang open. I sallied forth.

At last, Sam had picked up his musket. 'Let battle commence', I muttered to myself. In the event, we fought and won. *Floreat Europa!!*

37

WITCHETTY GRUB SOUP

The witchetty grub is repulsive. I refer to that native of Australia, the small white larva of the ghost moth. Aborigines, in their formerly nomadic existence, wandering over vast and inhospitable terrains, regarded it as a delicacy. While the men hunted ahead of them, the women of the group would gather the grubs on the march – feeding themselves and their babies and gathering more for the communal meal by the camp fire. Yuk!

Flying up to Ayer's Rock (as it was still called) in November 1986 with the Royal Australian Air Force, I knew nothing of the ghost moth, the larva or the end-use. I simply stared in awe through the window at the savagery of the rocky desert landscape beneath me, sweltering in the heat. As so often, beyond the 'black stump' in Oz, I marvelled at the courage and endurance of the first British explorers, map-makers, geologists, telegraphers, railroad engineers and others who ventured into that vast interior from the more readily inhabitable coastline. Eventually, like a vast prehistoric monster, Ayer's Rock itself, black against the khaki coloured plain, reared up ahead of us.

The Australian authorities had been generous. This was my last official visit to the subcontinent, before leaving the Commission. Where would I like to go? What hadn't I seen?? Maybe Alice Springs??? I confess that I already knew Alice – and most other places. But the unknown Ayer's Rock in the centre of the country appealed, the spiritual centre of aboriginal culture – in those days, only just beginning to be opened up for tourists. Carvings and paintings about the beliefs and world picture of Australia's original inhabitants – their 'dream time' – were, within respectful limits, open to outside inspection; the Rock itself, to perilous ascension along guide ropes.

In a way, I thought I had earned this treat. Both instinctively and analytically pro-Australian, I had done my best, from the moment the UK joined the European Community in 1973, to get the latter's relations with Australia on a firm footing.

I had already negotiated a Commercial and Economic Agreement with Canada, at Prime Minister Trudeau's insistent request for what he termed a 'Contractual Link' with Europe; and I thought the Aussies should also get a look-in – albeit more modestly, and in line with our relations with New Zealand, for which I was also responsible.

Not all the EC member states fully shared my enthusiasm, when I tabled a positive policy paper in 1976. Luxembourg had never heard of Australia; France mistrusted it. Also, there were serious trade problems, arising not least from the protectionism of our Common Agricultural Policy which the Australians hated; but also, in other areas, where the Australian footing was less firm, and the boot was arguably on the other foot. And there was another problem. With senior Australian officials – in a reciprocally firm but friendly way – I always had good relations, which respected the art of the possible and gave prominence to the positive. But Australian cabinet ministers – sometimes a wild, ill-informed and bloody-minded breed – were another matter.

Prime Minister Malcolm Fraser received me frostily in his office in Canberra in 1977, when I came to discuss his forthcoming visit to Europe. On his subsequent arrival in Brussels, he clashed with President Jenkins, and chased me round the grand piano in the Australian Ambassador's drawing room (I later got into trouble for inadvertently blabbing about it to the press – see chapter 32), to express his frustration that, Fraser's brazen trumpet blast having sounded, the walls of Jericho had not fallen. It even got rather petty. Roy Jenkins's correct title, under the founding Treaties, was indeed 'President'; orally and in writing Fraser insisted on '*Chairman* Jenkins'. (To be fair, he may have been put up to it by the British Prime Minister, James Callaghan, who disliked Jenkins personally and didn't see why the latter should be a President when the former was merely a Prime Minister).

At that point, after a short sabbatical at Oxford, I disappeared to Tokyo in 1978, to head up the EU Delegation there. But the war sadly continued. By 1984, the Australian Trade Minister (John Dawkins), was speaking of a 'crescendo' of hostility against the Community. The latter, for its part, in so far as it noticed at all, simply shrugged all this off and got on with other business, leaving the Australians frustrated and impotent.

Eventually, the admirable Bob Hawke took a grip as Prime Minister, and there was a return to sanity. Ministerial heads in Canberra were banged together, permitting a long-overdue hatchet-burying and fence-mending. Having come back from Japan in 1982, and picked up with Australia where I had left off, I instructed my team to exercise ingenuity, as well as goodwill. One blow for freedom was, in the world-trade negotiations in the GATT, to secure a relaxation of our restrictions on the import of Australian table wine, to the benefit of the European consumer and my own intense personal satisfaction. (The French, in their complacency – because they assumed that they had nothing to fear from Antipodean competition – accepted my recommendation).

Thus it was that, in November 1986, I brought out a Commission Vice-President and a raft of other senior people to Canberra for 'High-Level Consultations' with the Australian Government, and for the signature of an agreement or two; while the head of the newly established EU Delegation in Canberra, with personal rank of Ambassador, was up-graded by the Australians and accredited to the Prime Minister, as Head of Government, rather than, the year before, merely to the Minister for External Relations.

Hence, Ayer's Rock. Once safely delivered by the RAAF, I climbed up to the top and made a pilgrimage to the Aboriginal sites and carvings. A banquet was then laid on, in the only hotel. I basked in the official attention and admiration – both nevertheless, surely amply justified by my signal services to Euro-Australian relations?

Despite the heat, a hot lentil soup was served in the air-conditioned dining room. I congratulated our host, a top official from Canberra. But I had been bushwhacked.

'Nah, Lezzers, that's not *lentil* soup. Your digger mates thought you'd like some *witchetty grub* soup'.

But, as they say in the Royal Navy, you shouldn't join the 'Andrew', if you can't take a joke.

38

TRADE WAR: EYEBALL-TO-EYEBALL ACROSS THE ATLANTIC

It was one of those blizzards in which New York seems to specialise. In late January 1987, one week before a major trade war was due to begin between the US and the EC, a high-level group from the Commission set out for Washington, in a last ditch effort to avert the storm. They were met by a different kind of storm – one of Mother Nature's. High winds and deep snowdrifts gravely disrupted transatlantic travel and closed airports in New York and Washington. The Agriculture Commissioner never got beyond London. The Vice-President for External Relations found himself diverted to Montreal. The team were scattered quite literally to the winds.

As the man with overall responsibility for the exercise, I had set out one day early, accompanied by Roderick Abbott (the hero of the Belgrade Death Squad – see chapter 33). Despite commandeering Concorde in great haste, we only just made it to New York, before La Guardia closed. Then there was the problem of how to get to Washington. We eventually succeeded, but only after an epic 11-hour journey by coach, Amtrak, Metro, taxi and finally on foot, in conditions of unimaginable disruption, across an ice-bound landscape and through outraged hordes of stranded US citizenry on the verge of civil commotion.

While the crammed and crowded train crept cautiously along, the hours passed by, the blizzards blew and the snow continued to pile up, I repeatedly found myself wondering what the Hell I was doing, and why?

I had always felt at home, I mused, with American people and admired the USA (see e.g. chapters 11 and 16). In the course of my previous career as a British diplomat, I had worked closely on common bilateral causes and Atlantic Alliance affairs with the State Department and (at one remove) with the Department of Defence and the CIA. I had found them fine fellows and sometimes even kindred spirits.

But, since joining the European Commission in Brussels, I had also had to negotiate eyeball-to-eyeball with the office of the US Trade Representatives, (USTR), on sordid trade matters, in a different spirit. They – the successive and often predatory 'Trade Representatives' and their teams of pushy lawyers and hungry economists, most of them looking for lucrative subsequent jobs in the private sector – the Bad Guys in the black hats. Me – the detached, idealistic mandarin with an eye more for political justice and economic common sense them for commercial banditry – the Good Guy in the white hat. And always, behind my US opposite numbers in USTR, up on the Hill, lurked special interest groups, protectionist lobbies and pork-barrel politicians with little notion of and even less heed for international rules, agreed norms and commonly accepted trading practices.

So now, Once-More-Unto-The-Breach in Washington, because the negotiations seemed to me to have reached pretty much the touch-and-go stage.

This trade dispute was about the likely consequences for US exports to Spain and Portugal of the entry of these two countries into the European Community (an entry enthusiastically endorsed on political grounds by White House and State Department). The American trade people argued that it would become more difficult to continue doing business on the same scale, once Spain and Portugal were in the EC camp, guided by Community Preference and more likely to 'buy European' from their new partners, than they had been when they were still outsiders. Worse still, US maize and sorghum exports to Spain would face increased barriers, because of the dreaded Common Agricultural Policy (CAP). We had argued that, on the contrary, life would be at least as good for American exporters, and probably even better, for the fact that Spain and Portugal would be giving up their high past levels of trade protection, to conform with the much more liberal import regime of the European Community and could be expected to enjoy much higher future economic growth.

Not satisfied with this argument, in May 1986 the USTR had taken the preparatory first steps to punish the European Community by the interdiction of $400 million of our exports to the US market, invoking chapter XXIV: 6 of the General Agreement on Tariffs and Trade. On the basis of this contingency planning, the US formally opened compensation negotiations in Geneva with the Community. Their initial demands were unjustifiable and excessive, and my people told them so, saying that if the US proceeded as threatened, the EC would retaliate in equal measure. But, pragmatic as ever and wanting peace in the valley, we also tabled conciliatory, if much more modest, counter-proposals. As the dialogue continued, the gap between the two sides resolutely refused to narrow. And the EC member states continued to stand foursquare behind the Commission – including the British, who agreed that the Americans had little or no case to argue.

The deadline for agreement originally set by the American side had been the end of 1986. But USTR became increasingly apprehensive, wondering whether they had not bitten off more than they could chew. Unable to see an easy way out – 'Peace with Honour', if you will – they postponed the deadline until the end of January 1987, and moderated their demands. But not by enough.

The two sides therefore found themselves in their toughest and most dangerous bilateral confrontation since the notorious 'Chicken War' between the US and the European Community of the Six in the 1960s – before the UK was in the EC. A succession of retaliatory and counter-retaliatory trade sanctions looked as if they were about to be triggered off, which would be disastrous not only for bilateral flows across the Atlantic, but also for the future course of US trade policy (already protectionist enough, by instinct, without an appeal to emotion through xenophobia). To say nothing of the successful pursuit of the new Uruguay Round negotiations for the liberalisation and expansion of world trade, on which the

US and the EC had embarked together, earlier in 1986, in Punta del Este (see chapter 36).

In Brussels, alarm grew, just as it did in the US camp – but fortunately not actual panic, at least at the European end. It was time for me to drop everything else and get personally involved, full-time, as the competent Director-General in Brussels. In close cahoots with my sympathetic French colleague, Guy Legras, the Director-General for Agriculture, I worked out a plan.

The trick was going to be in the timing. Not easy, with three interested Brussels commissioners and a President, plus twelve member state governments, to be put in the picture and kept in line. Not easy, either, given that the Community's institutions always tended to leak like a sieve. If, within the EC, I floated further concessions too soon, the Americans would hear of them, pocket them, and then demand more. If I fleshed out the final form of compromise prematurely, either my side or the other side would poke sticks in its wheels before I could formally roll it out. So Legras and I put our heads together privately and sketched out our ideas (not for circulation in writing or for indiscreet airing in too recognisable a form in international telephone conversations). If the Americans, as I expected, made a final move in our direction, we would respond positively and at once – but with a last trump card up our sleeves. This we could play, at the very last minute, if USTR reached the point of wanting to shake hands on a deal, yet were not quite able to bring themselves and their clients to do so.

In the event, snowbound in Washington, it went like a dream. As earlier agreed, the tariff for the enlarged EC of twelve member states was fixed at the level of the previous EC of ten, for products of significant interest to the US. In addition, where the Americans had earlier demanded deep temporary tariff cuts in the EU to cover 40 American products to the tune of $400 million, they finally accepted shallower cuts for 24 of these products. For maize and sorghum exports to Spain, where the Americans had initially demanded a quota of 4 million tonnes per annum for four years, we reached agreement on 2.7 million tonnes – up from the initial

European offer of 1.6 million. Both sides agreed to a review at the end of four years, to see whether, as the Europeans claimed, the US had had nothing to worry about in the first place. Such was the outline of the final pragmatic compromise. But it was nevertheless not quite enough for the Americans, anxious though they were to settle.

So, the 'Trump Card' came out of my sleeve – a concession on US cereals exports to Portugal over the next four years, in which the 15 per cent market share hitherto reserved for the benefit of other EC country suppliers would be waived. The timing was perfect, the effect dramatic. They grabbed it in both hands. The American Number Two, a trusted acquaintance of mine, greatly relieved, slapped me on the back and said it was a done deal.

I stepped out of the room to make a quiet call to my chum, Brian Crowe, the Minister in the British Embassy (who was naturally in the dark about the trump card, and only in outline aware of the likely shape of the overall deal). He in turn, through secure Embassy channels, informed both London – where Mrs Thatcher was fretful – and the UK Permanent Representation in Brussels – where Sir David Hannay, the Ambassador, was waiting on tenterhooks. (Having loyally backed the Commission throughout the protracted negotiation, he would have had egg on his face, if I had failed to find a way through).

Of course, dots had subsequently to be put on 'i's, 't's crossed, tiny details sorted, with a nip here and a tuck there and a constructive fudge somewhere else. All that, we were able to finalise on the transatlantic telephone with USTR, once back in Brussels, over a period of three days and two nights, carrying our Member States with us – some eager, some reluctant, some just plain confused, but all of them finally on board. It was the 29th of January, 1987.

Accordingly, I felt free to leave the Brussels Commission honourably, later that year ('ride out on a white horse', as David Hannay put it). All my main objectives had been achieved, and a reasonably clear desk left to my successor. Inevitably, fresh troubles with the US began to flag themselves upon the horizon, in the shape of rows over Airbus subsidies and over the community's insistence on hormone-free beef. But these were issues of lesser magnitude, falling within the habitual noise levels. In the words of the famous Norse dictum, 'Let no man call the day good, until it be the eventide'. But it would all be all right.

I have always held the 30th of January in horror – being the anniversary of the decapitation of King Charles I of England, Saint and Martyr, at the hands of the detestable regicide, Oliver Cromwell. But it remains a consolation that the 338th infamous such anniversary was not to become blacker still for a trade war between allies. Nevertheless, as the Duke of Wellington once said in another context, it was 'the nearest run thing you ever saw in your life'.

I still wonder what would have happened if Roderick Abbott and I had followed EC budgetary regulations (strictly enforced at that time – but so what?) and taken a Jumbo, not the Concorde; or if the five star New York blizzard had come 24 hours earlier. It pays to be lucky – and reserve funds can have their uses.

PART THREE: HOMECOMING

39

WELCOME, LORD LES!

'Welcome, Lord Les!'

The Press got hold of it, when I was struggling to launch the 'Uruguay Round' in the GATT (chapter 36). It rumbled on, while I was busy negotiating with Washington to avert a European trade war with the US (chapter 38). In September 1987, I was to shove off to the groves of academe, to become Vice-Chancellor of the University of Sussex.

First, 'Men and Matters' by Quentin Peel in the F.T. ('Fielding for Sussex'); then, the Brighton 'Argus', the Times, T.H.E.S. and Sunday Times; followed by a bright and breezy full-page spread in the Independent ('Slightly eccentric choice by those Sussex shockers').

But quite the best of the lot was the front page of Unionews, the University's student union newspaper. This carried the headline: 'WELCOME, LORD LES! or where will the horses be kept?' Also, a picture of Swanborough Manor – a crumbling pile once gifted to the university by Lady Reading for use as the Vice-Chancellor's official residence, should he so require. The story opened with the words 'Revulsion greeted the announcement of the new head bureaucrat at Sussex University. Mr (naturally) Leslie Fielding is a career diplomat, whose only qualifications are his Oxbridge and public school ties... he has used the Network to obtain the V-Cship and will add additional £n thousands to his annual unearned income'. Worse still, the story went on, the stables at Swanborough were to be recommissioned and the surrounding paddocks allocated to the new V-C's horses, while the house itself, at that time divided into flats, was to be re-converted for single use by the V-C's family – the transient outside visitors to the University currently accommodated there, to be driven out into the snow, babes at breast. All this was a scandal, hooted Unionews, when 'hundreds of polytechnic and university students are forced to live in tents and on the floors of friends' flats'. So 'the plush sweep of the lawn at the Manor will seem all too inviting' for a student sit-in. And so on.

Apparently, the students were restless. And there was certainly more to come.

In the summer term of 1987, before I arrived to take over, student militants occupied the university's administration building – including the V-C's office. They comprehensively trashed the place, and stayed in occupation for the greater part of a week, before a reluctant police force finally agreed to eject them, on health and safety grounds. All that, in protest, not against life at Sussex, but against national policy on higher education and the evils of Thatcherism generally. The stunt was in reality a *coup de main* by the hard left – many of them not even students at the university, but Trots and Marxists, druggies and dropouts from the squats of Brighton, plus a quota from the local Polytechnic.

I had not at that point met my predecessor, the mild-mannered and inoffensive Sir Denys Wilkinson, formerly Professor of Experimental Physics at Oxford. As soon as I could, I hopped across the Channel to convey my personal sympathy, as an act of solidarity. Rising from behind his desk, a tall, thin, slightly harassed man advanced across the new carpet (the previous floor covering had been soiled by the sit-in people). He shook hands with a wan smile and the words 'Brave man!'

Not long after that, Lord Briggs (the V-C before Wilkinson) had me up to lunch at Worcester College, Oxford, to tell me where the bodies were buried; and Lord Attenborough (the Pro-Chancellor – he later took over from the Duke of Richmond as Chancellor) likewise, at Simpson's-in-the-Strand.

There was plenty to get stuck into when I settled down to work – research priorities to be re-ordered; problems with maths, physics and law to be sorted; fifty redundant members of the academic staff (approaching one tenth of the whole) to be weeded out and sent on their way with rather meagre compensation money from H.M. Treasury; governance to be rationalised and reformed, from top to bottom. Beginning at the top. The V-C could not continue to be a railwayman living in a signal box in which the levers of power were connected nowhere and to nothing: he had not only to reign, but also to rule, as some sort of 'Chief Executive' of the kind recommended in the recent Jarratt Report.

But, first, there was that little problem with the 'Yoof', or at least their professed leaders. I thought it best to take the bull by the horns, to avoid seeming too much of a pussy cat, even if I was much more on their side than they were (at least initially) on mine.

I began by calling in the editor of Unionews and his colleagues and calmly taking them through the purely factual errors in 'Welcome, Lord Les'. I was not a Toff, to the Manor Born, but a scholarship boy from an inner London family down on their luck. I had not used the 'Network' (whatever that was) to get the job at Sussex – indeed, I had had a comfortable Oxbridge Headship of House offered me, as well as glamorous and lucrative international appointments, all of which I had turned down in order to come to Sussex. Nor had I come for the money (which was peanuts anyway, in the wider world from which I came). Indeed, I had asked that one quarter of the salary offered should be assigned not to me but to student welfare; while a percentage of the remaining salary went to the university's Nelson Mandela Fund, to assist student victims of apartheid in South Africa. As to politics, I was not a Tory or indeed any sort of Party Political Animal – adding that, if they and their activists had seen as much as I had of politicians, at close quarters, round the globe, they would think twice about simplistic and sloganised student political allegiances. It was true that my wife and I did occasionally ride horses – but so did Mongolian tribesmen and Gauchos in Argentina; and, anyway I was no John Peel nor John Wayne cowboy myself (see chapter 3). It was not true that I was a stranger to universities and higher education generally – I had undergone seven academic years of undergraduate, post-graduate and vocational education and training, at home and abroad; had lectured on international relations at the LSE and elsewhere; and was married to an historian who had taken her first degree and doctorate at Birmingham, and subsequently taught at Cambridge, Leeds and Oxford, in that order. Far from intending to lead a 'Baronial' life at Swanborough – a dank and crumbling pile, a good deal less grand than my wife's family home in Shropshire, which at least had an indoor swimming pool and a small Ball Room (although, at Dickie Attenborough's suggestion, I didn't tell them that), I intended to open the place up to members of the University and also looked forward to offering hospitality there not only to the Teachers' Union but also (shock, horror) the officers of the *Student Union!* I was not a tiny bit scared of a student sit-in – I had met much more serious mob tactics in the Middle East and South East Asia (see chapters 6 and 11). If they intimidated my wife and children or damaged university property, I would meet them with the full force of the law – and see the student perpetrators in court. By the same token, I would also take action against any further libel of me in their miserable magazine – not, in that context, by legal action, but simply by withdrawing the university's (and the British taxpayers') subsidy from Unionews and spending it on something more worthwhile, in under-developed countries.

Slightly to my surprise, they made no attempt to justify the offending editorial. I then gave them a drink.

I followed this up with a series of contacts, on friendlier and more constructive lines, with the president of the Student Union and his senior colleagues. This was not easy. They had a real problem with their own extremist 'entryists' – people who took over the microphone *manu militari* at union meetings; and who were, at that period, insisting that they should accompany the (elected) officers of the union to any meetings with Authority, in order to check that a tough enough line was being taken and in order to launch their own hard left harangue at the V-C.

In the event, it all worked out OK. Students generally – although I had to work at it, over five years – were ultimately the least of my problems.

As to the leaders of the Union, we arranged to meet discretely, just as I had done with the Cambodian Prime Minister and other senior figures in Phnom Penh in 1965 (see chapter 12). Later, they became bolder and more confident – making a dramatic entrance, at my invitation and for all to see, at the first ever university Garden Party, which I held at Swanborough Manor later in my first year. We became, cautiously, and with natural caveats, almost partners; and each president, a friendly personal acquaintance. I introduced them to newcomers at Freshers Week each year, urging all new students to support the union and turn out in large numbers to elect its officers, to protect democratic pluralism. I listened to the Union's grievances and acted on them when they were justified and within the means available to me. When there was a spate of late-night 'queer bashing' by the Rugger Club or whoever, I marked my disapproval by walking the campus at midnight with the president and his deputies (plus a couple of beefy security guards, should physical intervention be necessary). When British Rail threatened to discontinue their late-night service from Falmer to Brighton, because of alleged hooliganism by students returning to their digs down-town, I rode the tracks myself, with the Union, to establish the facts, before making my representations to the rail managers (whom I strongly suspected of concocting a calumny to justify a cost-cutting exercise). When the union floated with me the idea of a formal Summer Ball, with compulsory evening dress, I advanced them an interest-free loan and told them to get on with it (which they did very efficiently and with prompt repayment).

More daring yet, when things had settled down further, I decided to set up an Officer Training Corps. Discussing the idea with the student leaders, I got some good advice. They were not worried by the (by then much diminished) mad Maoists; but advised against the Army (which could be portrayed by the hard left as always shooting Irish patriots and the like) and the Air Force (always liable to be bombing babies in the Third World). The thing to go for, they said, was the Navy (which neither shot nor bombed anyone but was a dab hand at hurricane relief and similar socialist activities). So

I persuaded the Senior Service to give us an URNU (University Royal Naval Unit) and a smart, grey, sea-going warship. She was a great success, with a long student waiting list – women as well as men (the uniform was flattering).

For the rank and file of students, my wife and I hosted, six or eight times a year, a simple buffet supper (curry, ice-cream and Sussex-brewed real ale), for cross-sections from all intellectual disciplines and fields of study. The object was for them to meet the V-C and chat with him about campus life. Their tutors were included in the party, for the on-the-spot discussion of any complaints. Once again, and on each and every occasion the Union officials came along, too, at my insistence.

The final blow for freedom was to enlist the Union's cooperation, over an initiative that I wished to take with Westminster. This was an invitation from me to the Minister of Education (then the sympathetic Kenneth Baker, whom I had got to know while chairing a government committee for the re-writing of the National Curriculum for Geography in primary and secondary schools). He was to visit the university, see what we were up to, discuss what problems we faced and – finally – to walk the campus and browse in the University Library (just him and me – no security). When Ted Heath had come to Sussex, some years before, someone had flung a pot of red paint at him. My academic advisors were nervous. But I went ahead. In the event, Kenneth Baker and I met with no resistance, other than a tiny group of token protestors, outside Sussex House, posing no threat to anyone, and whom we simply sidestepped. At the end of a full day, he departed in peace, Sussex prestige enhanced and his understanding of academe, down on the ranch, suitably amplified.

I should have mentioned that, within a week or two of my arrival, Unionews began to carry a slightly teasing, but personally sympathetic, strip cartoon, featuring 'Lord Les' (re-christened 'Sir Lord Les' after the New Year's Honours List came out). It was their gesture of atonement.

In my farewell address to the University Court in 1992, I took care to mention by name each of the presidents of the

Student Union I had known, with an expression of my thanks. Wherever they now are, I send them Sally's and my best wishes.

40

THE HAIRY HANDS

Let me begin by explaining to civilised sceptics that odd things can and do happen, not only East but West of Suez; not only to the North of Kathmandu but occasionally also to the North of the English Channel. Take the West Country as an example.

There is something about the wilder parts of Devon and Cornwall that makes them different from the rest of England. Something untamed and primitive, beneath the external appearances of peaceful green fields, plentiful cream teas and potent rough ciders.

Especially on and around Bodmin Moor (where I recommend a sprig of garlic in the buttonhole and a crucifix in the breast pocket) and the inner wilderness of Dartmoor. Geologically, the substrata are immeasurably old. Prehistorically, cavemen came early to the thin-soiled uplands, to clear the scrub and scratch a living. Ethnologically, there remains today, among some of the locals, an element of the squat, dark and pointy-headed proto-Celt of pre-Roman times. Also, the occasional hint of in-breeding. (I once overheard, at Hatherleigh Sheep Fair, one shepherd say to his neighbour: 'Of course, Mum and Dad was brother and sister, like…', to which the interlocutor nodded and said, 'Aar', with unfeigned indifference).

The Christian civilisation of the centuries may seem to command, but does not in practice always control. The square granite towers of hundreds of parish churches keep watch over a landscape which slumbers with earlier memories and which dreams of the dark.

Nevertheless, *'vive la différence'*. I have always loved the region, despite the 'The Hairy Hands'; and (before I get to the latter), despite two other strange experiences which may help to set the scene and encourage the reader not to be too dismissive, but to suspend his disbelief, at least for the duration of my narrative.

One summer day in 1975, I purchase an Old Vicarage in the badlands to the north of Dartmoor – twisty, single-track roads; contorted folds of poor, bethistled pasture; scrubby, windswept woodlands. My hamlet has no shop, no pub; but the house enjoys a clear view of the Tors. The place, say my detractors, is a mere toy, a detested 'holiday home'. To me, however, it is a place of refuge from jet-setting and slick city life, the wrangling and hysteria of all-night negotiating sessions at international meetings – and the awed silence of crowds, when announcing their outcomes. A sort of shooting lodge, to fill with friends. The immediate locals are friendly, too. But, when I enter training as a Lay Reader, to save the Norman Parish Church from Episcopal accountants and axemen, the arrival of a 'Preacher' attracts the attention of a coven across the hills. Animal entrails start to appear on the doorstep; cabalistic signs are daubed in blood on windowpanes. Mis-shapen rag dolls congregate in the shrubbery; a manikin, with pins protruding from rude places, is propped up on a stick outside my study window. Discreetly, I ask around. No immediate joy; but a few oblique and embarrassed looks. And then it all stops, as abruptly as it started. Metaphorically, I shrug and pop another bottle of Bolly, leaving the diocesan exorcist un-summoned. The Rector, from two Parishes away, a jolly former Veterinary Surgeon, wisely persuades me to sweep it all under the carpet.

On another day, one year before, when still house hunting, I am less phlegmatic and do actually do a runner. A farmhouse is for sale; has been for some time; is now unoccupied. I grab the particulars and go for a gander. It turns out to be an ancient, timber framed building; pretty enough, but a touch too small, with too many dilapidated outbuildings – and too tucked away up the chine. Not a soul is in sight.

I complete my inspection and start to move down the track to my car. But there is a footfall. Out of nowhere pops an elderly rustic, his green eyes flecked with brown, like a deep dewpond. I make the first move.

'Good Evening. How do you do? You must be the owner?'

He replies: 'That oi *were*, Young Master.'

'You have already sold, then?'

'Nooo. But I bain't here no longer, zee?'

'No. So I observe. You must be sorry to have left such a nice place.'

'Aar, very sorry.'

'Moved to somewhere nearby?'

'Near enough, Zir. More like six foot.'

'Ah, jolly good.'

'Kind of you to zay zo, I'm sure, but 'tis under the ground, look.'

'Ah, become a Troglodyte then? Gone to earth, sort of thing…? (Nervously). Ha, Ha.'

'Wull, thing is, oi be dead now, Zir, zo oi don' need un no more.'

'My dear chap. Frightfully sorry to hear that. How terrible.'

I look at my watch and mutter about being late for my next appointment.

'Aar, turrible it *were*. 'Twas the milk lorry, early in the morning, a year or two back. Misty-like. Us'n dun see un. Then, Bang! Oi were dead. Zo oi 'ad to zell up.'

I begin to walk briskly on, feeling for the car keys.

'Us'n show you round the back, Zir. Oi can show ee *sum'n special!*'

I am off, in a puff of high octane from my V8 engine.

So now I come to the so-called 'Hairy Hands'. To cut a long story short, it was an odd business in the 'sixties. It all began to happen high up on Bodmin Moor. A friend's father, a retired senior naval officer, happened to be a Cornish JP. Cases were coming up before the bench, of cars running right off the road. Usually after midnight. No other vehicles involved. No mechanical failures. No pubs for miles. Nothing else for miles either. Hard for the police to get things straight. Drivers, found gibbering and deathly white, claimed that they suddenly felt presence of great evil. Steering wheel seized by hairy hands, right in front of their very eyes.

I hear about all this, while a houseguest in a late medieval, mullion-windowed, Devon manor house, from a table companion, the magistrate's son, himself a respected solicitor and a model of sobriety. After dinner, the Squire and I decide to check it out alone. The Squire map-reads; brave idiot, I drive. The magistrate's son, for his part, not only refuses to accompany us, but also implores us earnestly not to go. We get there just before one in the morning. It is a God-forsaken spot, the night as black as the Ace of Spades. 'This is the stretch', says the map-reader. I check my rear view mirrors, half expecting to see something horrendous; lock the doors; and move to full alert, chest tightened with nerves. Suddenly, it seems icy cold. The navigation lights dim and flicker. The tyres start growling. The driving wheel trembles. But no 'Hairy Hands'. So, we head back across the Cornish border to Devon and our four-poster beds. As I drive, I pat my breast pocket and glance in the driver's mirror to admire my buttonhole. The garlic sprig becomes me.

There is something about the wild West Country. I love it still. But, in later years, once married, I concluded, sadly, that we had to move. Just couldn't keep the Nannies. Not that we are entirely out of the wood here in the Welsh Marches, where one other Knight and I take it in turns (he on the even days, I on the odd days) to hold the Ludlow Gap for the Queen. It is not in all respects the sinecure you might assume. According to the Hereford Times, there have been frequent sightings of a supernatural black panther. And then there's 'Up The Goggin'.

The locals are pretty cagey. But I recently overheard something in Welsh, in the snug bar of a pub in Powys. *'Cyrn Brawdychu'*, they whispered, shuddering. Not easy to translate. The nearest I can get to it is the 'Horrible Horns'. I wondered whether I should chip in, and tell them about Bodmin's *'Dwylaw Dafadennog'*, but thought the better of it. No point in upsetting people, needlessly.

Not when there's trouble enough, anyway.

41

THE ‘QUADRUPLE NEGATIVE’

When assailed by house builders, children’s problems, a falling stock market, or a plummeting pound, I find that sometimes only the Scottish Highlands and Islands will do. A fine refuge, also, from foreign tongues (apart from the Gaelic, second nature to a loyal Campbell of Cawdor, on his mother’s side, like me – the so-called ScotNats can’t speak a word of it). And, indeed, a fine refuge from Professional Diplomacy and Foreign Parts generally. So, my wife and I are seated at table, at a posh hotel in the Summer Isles, beyond Easter Ross. Gratifyingly gastronomic. Beautifully bibulous. We have earlier walked the hill. Now, we are at rest. Kilt smoothed out and Sporran comfortably akimbo, slaking my thirst, I count my blessings and dismiss my dilemmas.

But, at the next table, there is a highbrow group, donnish and discursive. The grey-haired and exceptionally distinguished gentleman who resembles the Regius Professor of Comparative Semantics at the University of Sussex, suddenly raises his voice in evident intellectual ecstasy, exclaiming the words *‘The Quadruple Negative!’* The remainder of his companions evince both respect and recognition. His ‘street cred’ is established, not only with them, but also with me.

But a raw nerve has been touched. My semantic synapses begin to spark. From which linguistic discourse does a ‘Quadruple Negative’ spring to mind? I search, feverishly, in the alas now all too depleted folds of my cerebral cortex. Mentally, I ransack grammar books long sinced placed in guest bedrooms (to impress, enlighten and attract dust). I interrogate all the idioms I can summon. The Arabic quadriliteral paradigms immediately spring to mind, and their

Hebrew and Akkadian predecessors. No go. Perhaps the Ugaritic or the Old Sogdian? Not obvious. Cambodian? No way. Japanese? But the Japanese don't like saying 'No', anyway. Mandarin or Cantonese? Not. Swahili or South Pacific Pidgin? I don't think so.

A quick slug of The Malt, to boost the brain-batteries. Then, I turn to my wife, formerly an Oxford Medievalist Don, and no slouch with the Anglo-Saxon. 'Quadruple Negatives' in Beowulf? In Ethelred's Charters?? Not really. It appears that the negative particle in Anglo-Saxon is prefixed, in a negative sentence, to every finite verb and, in addition, to every word which may have a contracted negative form. Yet these are not truly 'Quadruple Negatives', but rather alliterative and partly redundant iterations. (Is the gentle reader still with me?)

Another Malt, and I rise to my feet, move unsteadily across to The Table of The Dons, and introduce myself, modestly, and without any hint of pomposity or self-importance i.e. probably as something like Lieutenant, Acting Captain, Dr Sir Leslie Fielding, RA (TA) Ret'd, Cavaliere Grand'Ufficiale dell'Ordine Equestre di Sant'Agata della Repubblica di San Marino (see next chapter), Silver Medallist in Ballroom Dancing and Latin American Rhythm, and former Patrol Leader of Peewits in the First East Barnet Scout Troop. I then enquire, reverentially, as to the etymological origins of the – to me – unknown 'Quadruple Negative'.

'How kind of you to ask. Easy, really. This is my father'. (How do you do? – Lieutenant, Acting Captain, Dr Sir Leslie, etc…). 'I was reminding him how, when I was five, I directed a withering comment at a young lady, of similar age, as an indictment of her ignorance of ornithological matters. What I said to her was: "You don't know nothing, don't you not?"!'

I withdraw, linguistically relieved, feeling still able to hold my corner at the Members' Table at the Travellers Club in London. My interlocutor, a Consultant Otolaryngologist at Manchester, clearly knows what he is talking about. And, I, as an amateur Orientalist, am in the clear.

Phew! Sometimes, only the Scottish Highlands will do. Even an Englishman (on his father's side) knows that.

42

STARS OF CHIVALRY

'Men', repeatedly affirmed the late Dragoon Colonel who featured in chapter 23, '… Men are led by baubles'. Naturally, Charles had a number of them himself, from the Suez Campaign medal to a military OBE for bravery in Ulster. In evening dress, with the miniatures on his lapel, he looked distinguished. Discreetly distinguished. But nevertheless unquestionably *distinguished.*

Bare-chested myself, for most of my life, I was unavoidably in the shade. In the 1970s and '80s, my former colleagues in the Diplomatic Service were advancing from Companion ('Call Me God') to Knight Commander ('Kindly Call Me God') to Knight Grand Cross ('God Calls Me God') in the Most Distinguished Order of St Michael and St George, while modest and self-effacing little me simply slaved away unrecognised in the Berlaymont Boiler Room in Brussels, a mere international civil servant. Possibly even some sort of 'jumpship', Euro-Federalist, 'low-life', to boot – busy trying to snatch sovereignty from Britannia and transfer it to Europa!

Today, I wouldn't give it a thought. Decorations for senior civil servants are being diverted to athletes, pop stars and inner city headmasters. In the Diplomatic Service, the Gs have had to make do with Ks (if they are lucky); the former Ks have been lucky to receive Cs (even if complaining of 'Knight Starvation'); while the rest have remained unlucky and ungazetted. But it was not thus, in the late 20th century, when being unrecognised meant that something had gone wrong. So I avoided, whenever possible, all social occasions which called for 'Evening Dress *and Decorations*'.

Not that there had not been some stray straws in the wind. As I was close to being posted away from Phnom Penh, a figure at the Court of the Cambodian Head of State sounded me out on my willingness and ability to receive the *Ordre Royal du Cambodge*, in the rank of *Commandeur*. I intimated that, while quite willing, I was unfortunately unable – the edict of Elizabeth the First being very much in force for British career diplomats. ('My dogs shall wear no other collar than mine'). As to my own Sovereign, I was to learn, a few months later, after arrival in Paris, that I had been put up, by the FO, for an Honour in recognition of services supposedly beyond the normal call of duty. I was deeply touched. But, alas, the Rt Hon. Harold Wilson, PC, OBE promptly changed the rules; any civil servant likely to receive a higher award, later, was in principle not to be given a lower award, earlier. Wilson had – understandably – a horror of a Sir Frederick Fishface KCB, CMG, OBE, MVO, TD. A pity, that, because I had already bought the miniature at Spink, to see whether it suited my complexion. But it was not to be wasted – I passed it on, years later, to a chum who had really earned it.

The breakthrough came, as so often in life, with the Most Serene Republic of San Marino. As Director-General for External Relations in Brussels, I had some notional responsibilities for the European Community's relations with that Republic, although in practice I was never made aware of them in any concrete form. Until, that is, the Captains Regent paid a courtesy visit to the European Commission. I was there and then presented with a red leather box, containing the *Ordine Equestre di Sant'Agata*. I was petrified. Too late to refuse. Couldn't send it back through the post (bad service from Brussels to San Marino, too, by the way). But H.M. the Q. might well be unamused, if She were ever to hear about it. Conclusion: don't tell anyone. Until today, that is.

Then the rules changed. It was all on account of Lord Carrington, then the outgoing Secretary-General of NATO. Peter already had plenty of 'bling' – not least his MC with the Grenadier Guards in 1944. But simply every member country in the North Atlantic Alliance that did that sort of thing (not, of course, America, having improvidently surrendered its colonial status, under George III) insisted in wanting to pin a star on his Lordship's breast – to his entire personal embarrassment, it deserves to be said in his defence. So the new rule of thumb was laid down that senior international functionaries owning primary allegiance to the Queen of Great Britain and Northern Ireland might exceptionally be permitted to receive foreign decorations – on their retirement – provided that they did not actually wear them, or at least not unless in the presence of the Foreign Head of State concerned, on a formal occasion. And it so happened that L.Fielding Esquire was leaving Brussels at about the same time as Lord Carrington.

This gave the EFTA countries their chance – or at any rate those of them who were about to enter the European Community. Iceland, Switzerland and Norway did not come into the act – the first two had always turned their face against membership; the latter had decided against it in a popular referendum (to the chagrin of their senior officials and most of their cabinet ministers; and to my own regret, because they would have been good Europeans and a breath of fresh air in Brussels). Of the remainder, the Swedes gave me a box of chocolates; the Austrians, the Order of Merit; and the Finns one of their decorations named after English pubs (in my case the very posh 'White Rose' – lesser mortals were given the 'Red Lion'). Unsolicited, unexpected, undeserved, but fun nevertheless (especially the chocolates).

There was, of course, a serious motivation for these kindnesses. When I had taken over as Director-General five years previously, I had made it my business to visit all six EFTA capitals at intervals, because they were our close partners and I wished them well in their relations with us. For four of them, the relationship involved lengthy and detailed negotiations with the Commission on the conditions of their entry into the European Community, should their constitutional ratification procedures subsequently confirm the move. The technical talks were carried on by others in my sprawling department. I, for my part, saw it as my job to talk to the EFTA governments about macro-economic and political matters in which the EC was heavily involved (including G7 Summits and trade strategy in the GATT), so that I could take their views into account in what I was doing;

and so that they would be fully up to speed with us once they came in. Austria, I already knew quite well (family and business connections, on my wife's and my family sides, going back – in my own case – to the 19th century). But Scandinavia was unfamiliar territory, apart from the experience of three days spent in Oslo in the early '60s to attend a NATO Ministerial Meeting. I did, in fact, learn a great deal from my talks with all the EFTAs, and trust that I was not too didactic or imperial in my turn (although they found it unusual, in Stockholm, to be lectured to rather than to lecture – it must have been hard to know which party was more 'goody-two-shoes', at times). And our exchanges were liberally lubricated. After one working lunch with the Finns at their Brussels Embassy, my loyal German chauffeur delivered me back to the office with unambiguous words of advice to my Queen Bee PA, the late Susan Besford (FO-trained; with a cheerful temperament; but never disposed to take any nonsense from anyone, including me). Besford and chauffeur accordingly arranged me on my sofa, locked the two doors (an extra door had been added, because Susan's penetrating voice sometimes interrupted my meditations), disconnected all telephone lines, and refused any of my staff access to their Director-General until it was time for the evening whisky soda.

But I must move on. In the autumn of 1997, still a humble Esquire, 24 years on from leaving the Diplomatic Service, I was at work at my desk at the University of Sussex. The telephone buzzed. An important person was on the line, who wanted to know whether Mrs Thatcher might put my name forward to the Monarch for a KCMG (as mentioned above, sometimes rudely deciphered as 'Kindly Call Me God'). Gulp. S-stutter. Thinks: *Domine, non sum dignus.* But 'Thank you and... er… yes please'.

So, then there were *four* stars, instead of three. In later years, Michael and George were to receive – and still do receive – a regular airing at formal occasions – Lord Mayor's Banquets and the rest. But the other three stayed locked away in the safe. I felt sorry for them, as they must have been so lonely. Occasionally, I took them out and pinned all four stars on the left breast of my tailcoat – there was only just room, without them clinking against each other in a vulgar fashion – and always with M and G at the top, naturally. But when would I ever meet the Presidents of Austria and Finland and the Captains Regent of San Marino, on one single occasion?

Finally, I threw discretion and good taste to the wind. In 2004, in the capacity of Patron of the Society of King Charles the Martyr, I was invited by the Duke of St Albans to be Guest of Honour and speaker at the annual Banquet of the Royal Stewart Society in London. White Tie and Decorations. Bags of continental ex-Royals, Archduchesses and the rest, to be present in full fig; together with assorted Prelates in full canonicals (Roman, Uniate, Orthodox and Anglo-Catholic). As this delightfully old world and slightly pompous evening was to take place in the Library of the Travellers Club in Pall Mall, where I am a member, I would, I reasoned, be *chez moi*, on a purely private occasion. So the safe was opened, the nappy pins inserted, the four stars each securely put in place, the collar badge of the KCMG fixed just below my white tie, and the long, red ribbon and medallion of the Blessed Charles added, for final effect. While friends in the Club who saw me ascend the Grand Staircase thus attired and embellished, stared in disbelief, Royal Stewarts at the Banquet found absolutely nothing out of the ordinary and everything went off smoothly.

To round off my speech, I sang – as one does, these days, on such occasions – a Jamaican 'Gangster Rap' Song of my own composition. At a signal from me, footmen distributed copies among the guests, so that the company might sing the responses to my versicles, as in Church. (I am glad to say that all present complied, Majesties and Graces, Eminences, Beatitudes, Excellencies, Lords and Ladies included). The opening verses went something like this:

> 'Dook, it's awesomely great, to be here tonight; and
> support a cause dat sure is right.

[Gentlemen : UGH!]

'So here Ah am, in White Tie and Tails – dey don't
have none of this, down in Wales!
And Ah got plenty of de-cor-ations; from all de European nations,
Dis one here is de 'White Rose of Finland' – had to
de-clare dat, to de Revenue, Inland.
Dat one here's from San Marino – when dey give me
dat, we sure had a Beano!
Austria, also, was reel kind to me – got two of dem
medals, as you can see.

[Ladies: WOW!]

'But only ONE count in de Travellers Club, only one
get free drinks in de Pub.
Yeah, Ah happen to be a 'KCMG'! (Noblesse
Oblige', so Ah's waiving my fee).
Proud to be a Knight of Queen Elizabeth de Second.
Ah came a-runnin', man, when she beckoned!

[Ladies and Gentlemen: YEAH!]

So, as the Colonel indicated, baubles do have their place.

PART FOUR: TO BE SERIOUS

43

ARE DIPLOMATS IMMORAL?

Ethics and diplomacy, morality and foreign policy; are *diplomats* immoral? 'Of course they are!' I hear you cry. 'A bunch of creeps and crooks – almost as bad as politicians', is perhaps the popular prejudice.

In the famous quip of the Elizabethan Provost of Eton and sometime overseas envoy, Sir Henry Wootton, a diplomat is an honest man sent abroad to lie for the good of his country. Is it not so that, under the doctrine of *raison d'état*, the diplomat cannot be bound in public affairs by the same morality he will respect in private life? Count Cavour once said: 'If we did for ourselves what we do for our country, what rogues we should be'. Then there is that famous dictum of Karl von Clausewitz: 'War is the continuation of politics by other means'. If so, perhaps diplomacy is the continuation of war by other means? Beneath their smooth exteriors and behind their often bland public utterances, might the true game of diplomats be ruled by an unprincipled and duplicitous ruthlessness?

To be sure, the real world has never been a cosy place, a Victorian Sunday school, an embodiment of the Queensberry Rules at work. Thomas Hobbes, in Leviathan, saw the life of man, when it lacked central government, as 'solitary, poor, nasty, brutish and short'. As to international society as he then experienced it, Hobbes wrote that

> '...kings and persons of sovereign authority, because of their independence, are in continual jealousies and in the state and posture of gladiators, having their weapons pointing and their eyes fixed on one another—that is, their forts, garrisons and guns upon

> the frontiers of their kingdoms, and continual spies on their neighbours, which is a posture of war.'

And indeed it is to some extent true, even today, that while the primitive condition of fear and insecurity for the individual has long been remedied by the institution of state government, at least in the Western democracies, nevertheless, where international affairs are concerned, a suggestion – perhaps more than a suggestion – of that primitive condition, that fear and insecurity, can still subsist. Sovereign states tend to collude and contend, seeking to maximise their power, promote their national interest and strive contentiously to uphold their national security.

Something of the kind has certainly been the human predicament for as far back as we can see.

Egypt in the third millennium BC, under the fifth to the tenth Pharaonic Dynasties, struggled unsuccessfully with rapacious neighbours and domestic instability. Even the Greek city-states of the classical period, though enlightened in many respects, nevertheless in their relations with each other pursued policies of almost undiluted self-interest. Thucydides recorded their intrigues and conflicts in his History of the Peloponnesian War – caused, he wrote, by the growth of Athenian power and the fear that this aroused in Sparta. He recorded an Athenian orator as reminding his listeners that they lived in a world where the strong did what they had the power to do, and the weak accepted what they had to accept. In the end, the Periclean Age self-destructed. Philip II of Macedon and Alexander the Great did for the city-state democracies, inaugurating military dictatorship at home, and offering the excitements and distractions of imperialism overseas. Things were not so very different in other parts of the world. In China, in the 'Warring States' period of the 5th to the 3rd centuries BC, before a single dynasty (the Qin) forcibly united the country, the individual mini-kingdoms jostled and fought, allied and betrayed, in brutal and cynical fashion.

The concept of *Realpolitik* was to put into stunning effect in the Western Europe of the so-called 'Enlightenment' – in the 17th century machinations of Cardinal Richelieu; the stratagems of Frederick the Great and Bismarck in the 18th and 19th centuries; the brutish violence of the 20th century nationalist and ideological dictators, Mussolini, Hitler, Stalin and Mao Tse-tung; the genocide of Pol Pot; the 21st century Al Qaeda phenomenon.

But diplomacy – as opposed to politics – is not in itself a moral desert. At its best, it is about charm, not coercion; persuasion, not deception; about building where possible on trust and on common interests, rather than on mendacity and egotism. Like DNA, it has the structure of a double helix. People readily discern an ever-resilient strand of self-interest. Intertwined with that is, however, an idealist second strand of ancient derivation, which these days, may be increasing in strength. A sense of the primacy of justice has arisen; the belief that there is some over-arching standard beyond the national interest, by which diplomacy must be judged.

This instinct has a long history, rooted in religion and in ancient notions of natural law.

In the case of the ancient Greeks, despite their sometimes appalling behaviour in practice, there was also in theory the aspiration to common political institutions, the Amphictyonic Council and the Olympic Games. An example often quoted is the rejection of Themistocles' advice, following the Persian retreat, that the Athenians should set fire to the fleet of their Greek allies, then conveniently in harbour close at hand, and so ensure lasting Athenian ascendancy. The suggestion was rejected as being, 'exceedingly advantageous and exceedingly dishonourable'.

In post-classical times, in medieval Christendom, before the emergence of the nation state, certain moral and religious restraints bound civilisation together. In the medieval world, feudal oaths and allegiances were taken seriously; careful thought was given to what constituted a 'Just War'; the temporalities of a Europe of Dynasties were overseen by a Church that supported, where it could, a stable European political order.

When that medieval European order passed away and growing nationalism and state power took the centre stage, modern diplomacy came into being. Initially to push that power to the hilt; but also, where necessary, to soften the crunch and seek solutions – ending, for example, the Thirty Years War in 1648.

There are more modern instances: in the 19th century, the suppression of the slave trade; after 1945, British decolonisation. They were both morally driven. British support, in recent years, for the enlargement of the EU to Central and Eastern Europe also had a component of altruism. In American foreign policy, US diplomacy has rarely been free from a strong ethical impulse – amounting, at times, to something like a moral crusade. Presidents Woodrow Wilson and Jimmy Carter were examples. (The Nixon-Kissinger period was perhaps an uncharacteristic interlude, in which realism and power play were naked and less ashamed).

A word here about individual freedom of conscience. The modern British diplomat is a public servant – albeit of a superior kind, at least in his own estimation, and carrying a Commission for the Queen. If he has a sympathy for one British political party rather than another (as he is entitled to, in a free society), he keeps it to himself and loyally serves the elected Government of the day. He is also bound by the Official Secrets Act. But he is not obliged to help carry through a major foreign policy with which he profoundly disagrees on moral grounds. He can advise against it. If overruled, he may ask to be assigned to other duties. In an extreme scenario, he can resign, in which case the only basic requirement is that he should do so discreetly. If he wants to kick up a fuss, he must first go into politics. While still a member of the Diplomatic Service, and always in a situation of crisis, he must not betray the trust vested in him, or in effect blackmail the government of the day, by public disclosure of dissent or by the overnight withdrawal of expertise and manpower. Diplomacy, as conducted by professionals, is not a 'Kiss-and-Tell' calling.

I myself occasionally had doubts about certain British policies of the day, including two or three with which I was directly involved; but these were doubts as to the judgments made and the outcomes to be expected – in a word, doubts about credibility and effectiveness – not reservations of a primarily moral character.

The Suez crisis might have been different, to those working behind the scenes. The adventure must have seemed a muddled, ill-prepared, perilous and at times duplicitous undertaking, conducted incompetently by a sick Prime Minister who brushed aside awkward but honest diplomatic, financial and even military advice, and went behind the backs of some of the political colleagues and professional advisors who disagreed with him. If I had been in the Foreign Office with direct responsibility for Suez, I might well have considered resigning my commission, once the immediate business in hand was over, as much on the grounds of the damage done to British national interests throughout the Middle East, as over the associated loss of life and the apparent breach of international law. As it was, no direct crisis of moral conscience ever came my way, nor (as far as I know) that of any of my immediate contemporaries.

To return to the central theme, conscience does constrain the exercise of power; realism is sometimes tempered by idealism; morality can set limits to the reach of *raison d'état*.

In tomorrow's world, I grant that we could all recidivate. Let us not be Utopian. The past 50 years could be seen, in retrospect, as an Antonine era for Britain, of peace and prosperity. Few thinking people doubt that there will be massive world changes – even upheavals – before the new century is out. Not only today's severe economic recession (possibly even tomorrow's world slump), but also scientific accidents, nuclear and biological terrorism, fundamentalist religious fanaticism, water wars, population explosions, disorder generated by climate change, even social damage caused by the more malign forces of IT and economic globalisation – any combination of these could upset the apple cart, and sweep us back, if not to outright barbarism, then to Realpolitik with a vengeance.

But, as things are now, we still have diplomatic options. There are particular reasons why this is so, in today's world. They relate to the development of regional institutions, and the obligations and restraints which they impose on their members. (See also the next chapter on 'The New Multilateralism').

We have, first, the development of treaties, conventions and practices which set limits to anarchy and help the growth of international norms. I think of the United Nations Security Council, the International Court of Justice, the Declaration of Human Rights. The United Nations has set up war crimes tribunals, to deal with those implicated in genocide.

Regional institutions have been developed, such as the British Commonwealth, the European Union, the Council of Europe, each with its corpus of rules, orientations and ideals. International relations generally are increasingly rule-based; our memberships of NATO or the OECD or the WTO carry obligations, as well as conferring privileges and rights. In such bodies, the participating countries hold each other, as it were, morally hostage; and a new multilateral diplomacy is called for, which might have seemed odd to Metternich, but which has stood the test of effectiveness in the modern world.

The EU is of particular significance in this context. The original European Community was not primarily driven, as is sometimes claimed, by fear of communism and by cold war considerations. It had a more positive motivation – the determination that Europe had to be so re-constructed as to eliminate permanently the national rivalries which had culminated in the two world wars. In that sense, it was an ethical enterprise, in which national sovereignty and national interest would be tempered, reconciled and even fused, to the common economic advantage. Whichever side you take in the current argument, as to whether the Union should be more 'inter-governmental' or more 'federal', with a greater or lesser role for the central institutions of Europe's Commission, Parliament, and Court of Justice, the EU represents a huge success story of a moral nature, through a new style of international discourse quite unknown at the Congress of Vienna in 1814/15, or even anticipated by the Versailles Conference in 1919.

The naked abuse of national sovereign power in international diplomacy is also constrained these days, not only by alliances and treaties, but also by public opinion.

Up to and even beyond the Napoleonic Wars, very few Europeans concerned themselves directly with foreign affairs; it was the preserve of Princes and a small aristocratic body of ministers, envoys and diplomatists who probably had more in common with their foreign counterparts than with their own ill-informed and impassive co-nationals back home. The English public, as a rule, were indifferent. To be sure, young gentlemen of good family, accompanied by their chaplains and tutors, dragomans and domestics, embarked on the Grand Tour. The Duchess of Richmond even gave a Ball in Brussels (and was gravely inconvenienced by it falling, unforgivably, on the eve of the Battle of Waterloo – but what else could one expect of that vulgar little Corsican, Mr Bonaparte?). Jane Austen's novels, and Parson Woodford's diaries, record an English social scene that appears largely indifferent to the clash of continental armies and oblivious to the knavish tricks of foreigners.

Today, however, we live in a global political village as well as in a global economy. A flagrantly amoral, Machiavellian, diplomacy would not be practicable, even if there were ministers and ambassadors irresponsible enough to try to apply it. In contemporary western society, everyone has views on foreign policy; far from being a closed preserve, it has become, like our views on education and our notions of the shortcomings of the young, a public park where anyone is free to kick a ball about. In this country, not only learned institutions like the RIIA and the IISS, but also party-political and private 'think tanks' abound, second-guessing the professionals.

The media, too! There has been an enormous increase in the power of the press. I am not greatly enamoured of the simplified world of the sound-bite, and the short attention span of the TV screen; the know-all assurance of the teenage scribblers on the broadsheets and the bar-stool bragadaccio of interviewers on the 'Today' programme. They are also highly derivative and dependent on others. I was once mildly amused, but also somewhat outraged, by a journalist who spent long hours being briefed by me in a foreign country with which he was unfamiliar, only to offer the opinion, having returned home and published his articles to wide acclaim, that newsmen had made embassies redundant.

But I concede that these people can have their value – as, famously, did US television cameramen, press commentators and news agency reporters (to my direct experience and awed admiration) during the Vietnam War.

Yet if media men are necessary, they are not sufficient. They offer only episodic, not continuous, coverage of people, places and events. Their modish opinions and smart chatter cut little mustard, when applied to the sheer complexity of many world issues. The global waters are all too often opaque, even muddy. There is the old diplomatic joke: to every entangled and obscure international issue, there is always one answer that is simple, lucid and logical – but it is always wrong. As Henry Kissinger points out, in his massive book on 'Diplomacy', foreign policy has long been, and will continue to remain, a complex blend of the idealistic and the hard-nosed.

I would add to this that a degree of inconsistency is probably inevitable.

A basic principle of the UN Charter is non-interference within the domestic jurisdiction of sovereign states but without prejudice to enforcement measures dealing with threats to the peace and acts of aggression. In the Suez crisis and in Vietnam, the UK and the US respectively are now judged to have acted immorally; in Iraq (and Yugoslavia?), morally but mistakenly. In Iran, we and the Americans intervened to secure the overthrow of Mossadeq and to assist the late Shah back onto the Peacock Throne in the 1950s; but stood to one side, in the 1970s, in the commotion at the end of the Shah's reign.

It was in the name of self-determination that Hitler roused the Sudetens and achieved the dismantling of Czechoslovakia. The so-called right of national self-determination was also seized upon as a slogan of peoples seeking to cast off the chains of colonialism. Yet in 1945, the Western borders of Poland were settled not by self-determination but by ethnic cleansing. (The US, the UK and France accepted this injustice in order to avoid armed conflict with Stalin's Soviet Union).

Perspectives can change; possibilities do not remain the same; principles cannot always be put into practice.

Thus the Kurds and Armenians were once thought worthy of self-determination, when Russia, Turkey and Persia were weak; unworthy, later, when Western strategic interests had shifted – all of which may have been inevitable, but was (and is) certainly sad. The Armenians of Eastern Anatolia were massacred or forcibly deported by the Ottoman Government in 1915; perhaps as many as two million died and only one million survived. In the course of the First World War, there was nothing we could do about it. In the Treaty of Sèvres in 1920, the victorious allies recognised a United Armenia as a sovereign republic. Yet in practice they subsequently allowed the country to be partitioned between Turkey and the Soviet Union. Self-determination was not worth another war. Also in the Treaty of Sèvres, the Kurds, too, were given undertakings, as a nation, by the allies; undertakings which had to be withdrawn three years later, in the Treaty of Lausanne. It was not that the allied powers had suddenly become cynical. Between the two Treaties, the Turks had reformed and reasserted themselves under Ataturk and thereby changed the balance of power. There was no appetite in Britain or anywhere else to confront a new Turkey on behalf of distant Kurds. The need to prioritise peace over justice seemed inescapable.

Something similar happened at the end of the Second World War. Churchill refused, at the Tehran Conference in 1943, Joseph Stalin's request that 50,000 German officers should be executed at the end of the war. But in order to avert a conflict with the USSR, the Western allies later felt obliged, at the Yalta Conference in 1945, to go along with the repatriation of 70,000 Cossack, Serb and Croat prisoners, some of whom were without any great political motivation but had ended the war wearing the wrong uniform. They were put to death.

Today, our own and other Western governments react to human rights abuses in one way in a small country like Sierra Leone, and in another way towards the giant power and the immense potential export market that is China. This is probably realistic. We do our best to act responsibly over arms sales, to ensure that British-made weapons will be deployed for self-defence and deterrence, rather than internal coercion or external aggression; but, as the second largest arms exporter after the US, we also have to look to jobs and industries at home. This is probably realistic. It is not, however, consistent, let alone watertight. The equipment with which we supplied Indonesia was possibly used, some of it, against the vast majority voting for independence in Indonesian-occupied East Timor, with whom we were furthermore politically in sympathy.

Where there are conflicting objectives and ill-defined lines of moral demarcation, the fact is that British diplomacy, and that of other well-meaning democracies, has to deal with the world as it is, pragmatically, and with as much moral decency, but as much realism, as we can muster. The logic, such as it is, will often be 'fuzzy'.

The best criterion by which to judge whether a foreign policy is worthwhile – whether it is moral – is that of results. Motives are secondary, in this context. The Grand Duchy of Luxembourg, aware of its insignificance, can, if it chooses, as it usually does, merely confine itself to posture. Italian foreign policy, when vacuous and vacillating, has sometimes been dismissed as a *Diplomazia di Presenza*: a mere bystander's diplomacy. That will not do for Britain.

Certainly, the UK carries a significantly reduced relative international clout into the 21st century. We vie with France for the fourth largest GNP in the world. But any bar chart will show how far we fall behind the US and Japan; and, how close at our heels follow the other aspirants and 'uppers-and-comers'. Our admirable but always under-recruited and often over-stretched and ill-equipped armed forces are now much too small for purpose. Our productivity gap with the French and Germans remains substantial and our income per head is one of the lowest of the advanced industrialised countries. We possess a marginal national currency the international parities of which go up and down like a yo-yo. There can therefore be no place in our diplomacy for illusion, nostalgia, or comforting visions of our own superiority and the weakness of foreigners.

Despite these handicaps, we are nevertheless still (just) a medium-sized power, with informed opinions on some, if not all, world issues, and a modest but effective potential to project influence. Rightly, in my view, we still aspire to be taken seriously. But it is not enough to look beautiful in the changing room mirror, before the match: the aim is to go out and get the ball into the net, against often determined opposition. Size may not matter; competence and success do. So the effectiveness of British diplomacy, like its morality, is up to us: to the resolve of our political leaders and the skill our professionals.

Let me conclude as follows. War is the failure of diplomacy. The basic role of a diplomat in international affairs is to implement foreign policy by peaceful means. He should, to carry conviction, be frank and straightforward; where he is obliged to be 'economical with the truth', he must at least avoid downright lies. He needs to strike a balance between a healthy respect for power and an appropriate acknowledgement of principle; he has to be both a realist and a moralist, weaving those two distinct traditions in international relations together; he must be ready to listen perceptively and talk straight, to enemies and friends alike. Ethics are important. But what is crucial is realism and *savoir faire*. Perhaps also, oddly enough, modesty and self-criticism.

To use a metaphor inspired by CAMRA (the Campaign for Real Ale), beneath the froth of party politics in this country, the basic brew is a good one. If we think of British ministers, we may charitably assume that, of whatever political colour, they and their advisers are men of moderate virtue, who serve the UK, but also seek a better world. They want peace rather than war, stability rather than instability, democracy rather than tyranny, international prosperity rather than poverty, free trade rather than protectionism. They want these things, not necessarily because they are themselves particularly virtuous men, but because anything else would be contrary to Britain's national interests as a small, densely populated island crucially dependent on free international commerce and a world as far as possible at peace. In other words, they seek a broadly moral foreign policy for that most enduring of reasons, enlightened self-interest.

So, back to the initial question: Are diplomats immoral? Many people take them to be so; but this is unjust. In their private lives, diplomats may well be. In their professional careers, never – or, hardly ever.

But, as I just implied, it is important that diplomats should be intellectually modest and self-critical men and women, as well as moral ones. My own experience is that things go wrong more often through human frailty and error, than through failed diabolical conspiracies; through idiocy, more often than through immorality; through lack of insight, imagination and expertise, rather than through too much of those three.

44

ARE DIPLOMATS REALLY NECESSARY? THE NEW MULTILATERALISM

Diplomacy is essential, today as always. But its practitioners must be ready to learn new tricks in an old game. Multilateralism is now with us, and calls for considerable skill; it makes diplomats more necessary than ever.

What stands out a mile, to readers of Ernest Satow, Harold Nicolson and the memoirs of an earlier age, is the extent and complexity of the change which diplomacy has undergone over the past fifty years.

Embassies have proliferated in number, as newly independent countries have established their overseas representation, while international and regional organisations have burgeoned. The work of an embassy has extended from the political and consular to the cultural and commercial. New issues, such as protection of the environment and post cold war peacekeeping, have been added to the diplomatic agenda. Improvements in communication and facility of contact have brought greatly increased ministerial travel, and instant and constant consultation between ministry and embassy. The diplomat's past quasi-monopoly of knowledge about previously arcane foreign places and peoples has been challenged by the growing expertise of media men, academics and the staffs of chambers of commerce and of non-governmental organisations, as well as other government departments and ministries back home.

Multilateral diplomacy, in particular, has become a mega-phenomenon, demanding new knowledge and often novel techniques. This is, of course, attributable to the development of the institutions referred to in the previous chapter: the

United Nations; other international bodies such as the GATT/WTO, and OECD; and the evermore comprehensive structures of the G8. Also the rise to international pre-eminence of the European Union (which not only has a raft of ministerial councils and important official committees in Brussels, but now also supports well over a hundred EU diplomatic missions of its own around the globe). Also the growth of regional structures elsewhere, such as NAFTA, LAFTA, ASEAN, APEC, ASEM, OPEC, GCC and the rest, each with its internal co-ordinating mechanisms and external patterns of international contact.

In consequence, diplomacy has become more challenging. Certainly, the multilateral diplomat must be an eclectic, a polymath, a team-worker. He must be not only intellectually resilient but also even physically vigorous (see below). Above all, he must be open to new concepts, eager to acquire new knowledge and adept at facing new players both in government and in the private sector.

My own views on multilateral matters are much coloured by my fifteen years with the EC (now the EU). They required familiarity, internally, both with the bureaucratic jungle paths of the European Commission, and with the layout and habits of the EU member states' various tribal Indabas (the 113 Committee, the Coreper, the Council of Ministers, the European Parliament). Externally, these years demanded knowledge not only of the EC's principal trading partners individually, but also of the collective working of UNCTAD, the GATT CG18, the Executive Committee in Special Session of the OECD and the 'sherpa' structures supporting the regular G7 – now G8 – Economic Summits.

Multilateral economic diplomacy of this kind is more focused and more specialised than bilateral political diplomacy. It is politics in the shape of economics – and the politics is as much in the narrow detail as in the broad proposition. It demands more actual negotiation, and probably also a greater bargaining and deal-brokering skill, than is normally expected of a quiet bilateral diplomatic chancery. Oratory and polemic, of the kind sometimes associated with the UN General Assembly, solve no problems and offer no escape. Indeed, other than in marginal institutions such as UNESCO and the calmer reaches of the Council of Europe, there is really nowhere to hide. The individual has to be psychologically and intellectually strong enough to know and be known in depth. The number of peer players is restricted; they are captives of each other; today's opponent is tomorrow's accomplice; networking is of the essence, in both attack and defence.

In terms of human beings, the diplomatic requirement is for men and women with a particularly high IQ. Fluency in the main international languages is a must, often of a higher order than that demanded in bilateral posts, in which quite a lot of a diplomat's time is spent within his own embassy. Also indispensable – at any rate in internationally integrated bureaucracies such as the UN Secretariat and the EU institutions – is the ability to operate in a state of semi-perpetual 'culture shock', in close daily working relationships with colleagues from many different backgrounds, driven by different priorities and animated by different assumptions.

There is a place in multilateralism for diplomatic generalists; but only provided they are ready to devote themselves initially night and day to the acquisition of specialist knowledge (as I myself was compelled to do). It helps to have an inter-disciplinary approach and collectivist instincts – diplomats work best in these environments in small teams that share their expertise and insights. Notwithstanding the obvious constraints in handling what are apparently technical matters, imagination and lateral thinking often prove priceless. So does the creativity required to manipulate a shifting pattern of complicities and alliances. Even physical stamina can be important. At the launching of the Uruguay Round in Punta del Este as the EU front-line negotiator (see chapter 36), I worked all through the final night until the following afternoon. At a difficult UNCTAD ministerial meeting in Belgrade (chapter 33), my EC negotiating team and I worked for three full days and over two nights with a total of no more than four hours sleep. This requires good health, strict short-term abstinence from rich food and alcohol, and an iron will; without them, the strongest negotiating position and the most cogent argument can cease to be unassailable.

I will not conceal that, in my experience of diplomacy, I found bilateralism the more agreeable, but multilateralism the more demanding. But one should not exalt the multilateral, nor exult in its elitist astringency. The multilateralist can become addicted, and give way to the temptation of a busy but bogus self-importance. In reality, the true dimension of much multilateral diplomacy is more that of the goldfish bowl than of the globe. Its practitioners can become remote from outside realities and out of touch with the public which they are in theory supposed to serve. Today's EU, for example, has to some extent become the victim of 'regulatory capture' by a restricted circle of assorted Euro-mafiosi (politicians, diplomats and administrators). How else should the famous 'Maastricht Treaty' have become such a byword for professional opacity and public unease? The 'Lisbon Treaty' is no better. There is still scope for old-fashioned political diplomacy and much demand for cultivation of soundly based bilateral understandings between independent sovereign States.

Looking to the future, I would expect diplomacy in the coming decade to continue to be marked by:

- The intensification of inter-state co-operation, at least in political and economic affairs and in defence, if not in the commercial field (where individual countries are still as much competitors as collaborators).
- To that end, the future development of IT, including the widespread application of videoconferencing and other forms of instant communication and data processing. This should be seen as potentially an enhancement, not a hobbling, of the diplomat's scope for action in the field. He may be more closely overseen from his capital, yet he may in return have greater opportunity to influence headquarters – just as more frequent ministerial travel should mean that the ambassador gets more of a chance to nobble his master, the politician, at close quarters. But this

advantage will disappear if the ambassador is kept in the waiting room and embassies get by-passed by ministerial cronies. (Whichever way the cookie crumbles, ministers and top officials in different countries will increasingly deal direct with their opposite numbers, as I did myself).

- A further blurring of the distinction between bureaucrats and diplomats or between 'Home Civil Servants' and 'Foreign Service Officers' – a process already quite far advanced in Whitehall. In an interdependent world, in conditions of 'globalisation', water-tight compartments make less and less sense, whether within a national bureaucracy or between nation states or within international frameworks.
- A moderate further growth of multilateral at the expense of bilateral diplomacy (although multilateral Parkinsonism and personnel proliferation could eventually germinate the seed of its own destruction – diplomats are already sufficiently misunderstood and mistrusted by democratic tax payers).
- The continuation, nevertheless, of bilateral diplomacy as the basic professional instrument, in the way that the infantry remains the military *sine qua non*, whatever the sophistication of armour, artillery, air power and the rest. Multilateral diplomats in a serious national foreign service will not be fully effective if they are not willing to work hand in glove with their colleagues in bilateral posts. The latter can offer the multilateralists a depository of expertise on a given country, a source of analysis of that country's intentions, and a means of discreet bilateral lobbying in favour of multilateral objectives.
- Training and retraining, in new skills and subject matters, as the constant future requirement to be laid upon the diplomatic profession, as it already is for most other professions, from banking to marketing and manufacture – and even in some respects the law. (Our own Diplomatic Service, in particular, has long been good at this).

- The crucial importance of quality in the selection of diplomats, if they are to be cost-effective in working conditions of increasing exigency. This is above all true for small countries, whose interests are so often overlooked or trampled under foot; but which can grasp more for themselves at the margin than the big countries can, if their diplomatic *Apparat*, though small in number, is qualitatively a strong one. (This applies particularly in multilateral fora, where smaller countries already have an inbuilt relative advantage, which can be exploited to great effect by skilled and determined diplomatic operators who have a keen sense of priorities. The classical illustration is that of the Grand Duchy, whose influence within the EC/EU is greatly in excess of what it would be if Luxembourg stood alone).

In short, diplomacy these days, far from being unnecessary, is increasingly indispensable. It has no fully effective substitute.

In the multilateral equation, media men have their place and value, but – as noted in the previous chapter – we should not expect too much of them.

Business expertise and acumen, too, will continue to deserve respect. But multi-millionaires and tycoons are usually opinionated and sometimes mistaken. As a resident Head of Mission in Tokyo with some experience of the post, I recall listening, en route from the airport to his hotel, to a lengthy but flawed exposition of what made Japan tick, delivered by a top French 'box wallah' on his first ever visit to the country.

Then there are the academics, of which I am still in a sense one. A serious scholar usually likes to listen to a competent and knowledgeable diplomatist; and I have always encouraged the latter to do the same to the former. There is, however, a real difference between the two – the diplomatic operator being 'positive' where the academic analyst tends to be more 'normative'. International relations theory, in particular, where it can be understood at all by the non-specialist, has sadly proved of little or no application in the real world.

Meanwhile, diplomacy, while indispensable, must be vigorously self-critical. Diplomats may be necessary to keep the world turning, but they are more prone than most to narcissism and complacency, and at times even arrogance. Just occasionally, they can even stop listening. I recommend to all of them – especially to the multilateralists – a prudent measure of modesty and self-criticism. Yet I hope I have made it plain that, if they did not exist, diplomats would have to be invented. As long as they move with the times, continue to be diligent, and are wary of what they cost the public purse, the world will do well to continue to afford them – and will in any case be unable to do without them.

45

HUBRIS, COMPLACENCY AND MISPLACED NATIONALISM

If Sir Roy Denman was the outstanding Director-General in Brussels (chapter 29), the hero of my generation as Permanent Under-Secretary of State in the Foreign and Commonwealth Office was Sir Michael Palliser.

After Wellington and Oxford, and an interval at the sharp end in Western Europe with the Guards Armed Division, speaking flawless French (and married to the daughter of a distinguished post-war Belgian Prime Minister), Palliser was among the first in the Foreign Office to recognise the importance of Europe. A founder member of the Planning Staff (chapter 24) and an influential Private Secretary at No. 10, he was appointed to the crucial position of Minister (i.e. second-in-command) in the Paris Embassy, in support of Prime Minister Harold Wilson's brilliant political appointee as Ambassador, Lord Soames. Michael Palliser smoothed the passage of British entry into the European Community and subsequently became our Permanent Representative with the EC in Brussels, before his final appointment back in London as Head of the Diplomatic Service.

His colleagues admired Palliser and liked him, not least for his unfailing personal courtesy (not Denman's strongest suit) and his widely remarked willingness somehow to find time to help everyone where he could. It was therefore natural, for as many of us as could make it, to crowd into the 'Reflections Lecture' which he gave to The Pilgrims in London in March 2006, in which he looked back on a lifetime spent at the centre of things.

The following extract speaks for itself – and expresses the convictions of both his generation and mine:

'In the changed, ever more globalised world of the post-cold war era, the notion of a Britain outside the EU, acting independently and on its own, attractive to some of our compatriots, in reality seems ever more fanciful. Equally, a much larger and more diverse EU, including this country, has to achieve a greater degree of political and economic integration if it is both to compete and also to co-operate not just with the countries of the American continent but also with the huge, rising Asian powers, China and India, to say nothing of Japan, still the world's second largest economy. I have long been an internationalist not a nationalist. That does not mean any lack of affection or respect for my own country. I have spent 40 years of my life (whether as a soldier or a diplomat), trying to defend it and doing my best to advance its interests. But it does mean recognising that my country is no longer dominant in the way it was in the 19th century nor even the imperial power it still was in the first half of the 20th century. Two world wars settled that; but some people in Britain don't seem to have realised the fact. There is still a degree of complacent jingoism, which disguises itself as patriotism, in parts of British society, which makes more difficult the conduct of a foreign policy that really reflects British interests…

I leave you with this final thought. This is a great country and I am proud to have served it. But as a nation, we need to avoid hubris, complacency and misplaced nationalism. We shall do best by Britain in the 21st century, if we work as closely as we can with others, in Europe and across the Atlantic, and do not cherish the illusion that in the new and changing world of the 21st century, we can or should contemplate going it alone. That way lies only further decline.'

Complacency

In agreement with the foregoing, I would add the following.

It ought to be axiomatic that the purpose of this country's foreign policy, in the last analysis, should be to serve the national interest; that the policy should be pursued within the national means of what is now no more than one of many medium-sized countries in a multi-polar and complex world; and that the policy should take into account how that outside world actually is, not merely how we would like it to be. Realism, practicality and professional expertise are as essential in international diplomacy as in a scientific laboratory or an accountancy back office.

Alas, in recent years, following the close of the cold war epoch, and with the shift in the centre of gravity away from King Charles' Street to Downing Street, British foreign policy has sometimes given the impression of having lost the plot, through amateurism and unreality. The 'normative' – occasionally even the slightly messianic – has too often overridden the 'positive' and practical, in politico-military analysis and policy formation.

In all this, the convictions of shifting Republican coteries surrounding The White House have carried more weight with no. 10 than the cool and detached assessments of British professionals. We have certainly come a long way from the time when a Labour Prime Minister, as Sir Michael Palliser put it to the Pilgrims, managed 'against difficult odds to preserve the Anglo-American relationship, despite also resisting sustained American pressure to commit British troops to the Vietnam War and incurring the fury of President Johnson in the process'.

In those days, if no longer always today, the British still believed themselves entitled to their own assessments; to think themselves, as I have written elsewhere (in *Before the Killing Fields*), 'Allies, not Helots – Free Yeomen, not Yes Men'. The sad fact is that, in more recent times, and perhaps without our political leaders even realising it, we have gone along with a US inspired Western policy towards Russia and her neighbours that has been rather less than shrewd and far-sighted; towards Iraq, that was deeply flawed and poorly executed; towards Afghanistan, today, that is local reality-lite and ‘crusader’-heavy.

46

AND ONE MORE THING

Let me put the question of international ethics, raised in the previous chapters, in a different way.

You may not know it, but beekeepers commonly talk to their bees – it is the lore of the countryside to do so – about things that matter to the local community. One of the things that ought to matter in diplomacy is a fitting concern for those around us. Since 'The Fall', individual humans have not been too good at it. Nor have nations, for that matter. Hence the need for a diplomacy that is moral – or, at least, is not immoral.

To ring the changes on sermonising from an Anglican pulpit, I once wrote a purely secular morality tale in the form of an (unpublished) novel, called 'The Bees'. It was arguably not The Top Novel of the Modern Era; but it will serve now, to round off the above reflections on the ethics of diplomacy.

Five trendy people are having a holiday together in a villa near St Tropez. All begins well, but comes apart later. The soldier, unsuccessful in courtship, volunteers for Afghanistan. The hedge fund manager gets himself drowned – or drowns himself, deliberately. The amateur entomologist and his bluestocking partner decide to cut the cackle and get married – although the word on the street, later on, is that it doesn't work. The 'celebrity' heroine, who is also the narrator, pushes off for a while to a commune of women, where she is assigned to work with the beehives.

Here is her 'take' on it all, at the end of the book. She is walking through an apple orchard, carrying a swarm of bees; and, of course, talking to them.

'We humans are like you bees, in some ways. The five of us at Les Greniers were distinctly bee-like. We were a kind of élite: capable, industrious, busy with our achievements. Also we were utterly determined in the pursuit of our ends, in doing the things that we wanted to do or felt we had to do. We took our pleasures seriously and thought we were 'worth it': taking what we had appetite for and discarding what seemed superfluous. We did not question our place in the world: we laid claim to it with complete confidence. Yet we did possess a sense of something beyond ourselves, a sense of group, of fitting into the world about us. And inwardly and secretly I believe we each felt, whatever we might reason or openly declare to the contrary, that we shared in a mystery: that we possessed souls, or were part of the spirit of the created world, or were somehow linked to, even were a small integral part of, the whole of nature.
By the pool that day at Les Greniers, talking about you bees, one of the clever clogs among us produced the 'Georgics' and read out a passage. Later, I got him to write a translation out for me. It went like this:

"Wise men have said that bees share in the divine understanding and have in them something of the spirit of the universe. For God pervades and is present in all things: throughout all the lands of the earth and the expanses of the sea and out into the further depths of space. Flocks and herds, man and beasts, all when they are born derive their tenuous lives from him. And later it is to him that all creatures do return; all that die are restored to him. Death has no dwelling place; rather, they take wing among the stars and rise up into highest heaven."

These words are beautiful. But also terrible. The five of us were unquestionably guilty of failure. Failed fully to grow up into the creatures we were intended to be. We lacked, when it came to the test, not talent nor industry nor achievement, but any very obvious or deep-seated sense of what it was to be someone else. Ultimately, each of us was living simply within his or her own skin. So, we were less than the bees that flew about us.'

Me, Leslie Fielding, I reckon that diplomats (or, for that matter, City people) should read their Virgil more than they do. Or take up apiculture as a hobby (it only hurts to begin with – even if the bankers deserve it!).

PART FIVE: IN CONCLUSION

47

EPILOGUE

In my last year at Cambridge, sitting quietly in the College library, I finally made up my mind. An academic career would take several more years to get off the ground. The little family business was on the edge of bankruptcy. My tentative vocation as an Anglican priest and perhaps as a Religious had imploded, in a spiritual and psychological crisis comparable to, but fortunately much less intense than, that experienced by Karen Armstrong. It was time to leave academe and indeed England and to make a fresh start.

It was certainly time to travel to the Ends of the Earth, to escape what I had been and to discover what I should now become. And remember that, fifty to sixty years ago, in the austerity of the immediate post-war period, overseas travel was a rare privilege for the few, not – as today – the resort of the many. When I flew to Tehran in 1957, I had never travelled by air before, nor ever been further east than Rome.

By happy outcome of a series of examinations and interviews, I joined the Foreign Office in 1956. There, I was to find myself a round peg in a round hole. There were of course processes of adjustment – some of them laborious and painful – and difficulties and even dangers along the road. But almost all the time I was as happy as a sandboy.

Leaving the FO for 'Brassholes' in 1973 seemed the right way to go at the time. I saw our national future as an integral part of Europe rather than as an ex-Imperial offshore island. It was also hard to resist when Christopher Soames and David Hannay beckoned – and Ted Heath and Denis Greenhill prodded. But, sad to say, I confess that I hated the European Commission to begin with. This was mistaken of me and even perhaps a tiny bit babyish too, because initially I had more to learn than to impart and it was hard and humiliating work. In the event, I ended up with a deep respect for the Commission – or at least for its external affairs side. And I began enjoying myself fully as much as I had done in 'The Office'.

Deciding to quit the Commission was difficult, therefore. People seemed to want me to stay on – possibly, if I wanted the job, as Secretary General of the European Commission (the position eventually taken by David Williamson, a well qualified candidate from the Cabinet Office); or, after another couple of years, as the successor to Roy Denman as the EC Ambassador in Washington. At the same time, and as an alternative, I was invited to think about putting my hat in the ring to succeed Arthur Dunkel, as Director-General of the GATT – I was well-known and reasonably well liked in Geneva and it was arguably time for someone from a Member State of the European Community to take the helm there (as Peter Sutherland and Pascal Lamy, both ex-Commission, were eventually to do).

But none of this appealed. My wife, an Oxford don before marriage and still engaged in writing and research in medieval history, wanted us to return to England after the nine years we had spent together in Tokyo and Brussels. We had the children to think of (their schools, but also their cultural identities). I myself felt that I had probably had enough of abroad, after 24 years of it – and of spending half my days, latterly, on aeroplanes and half my nights arguing and negotiating.

So it was back to 'Blighty'. But what to do? Certainly not the City – and I eventually contented myself with only a couple of non-executive industrial directorships, just to keep me in gloves and scent. Not disappearance to our house in Shropshire – I was still too young (only 55) for total immersal in 'Country Life'. Maybe something academic, my wife suggested? But not, I thought, a Head of House at Oxbridge (though first one, and then another, came calling), because there would not be enough to do and the transition from jet set Eurocracy too abrupt. So, out of the blue, I replied to an advertisement for Sussex; and managed to make it, from their final shortlist.

But the challenge (not to say the shock) of re-entry into the UK in a vice-chancellorial capacity was considerable; and I cannot claim that I did not subsequently wonder whether I had done the right thing. I certainly needed every diplomatic resource I could muster. There was the 'Yoof' problem; but also, difficulties with the dons. Sussex was (as it still is) a remarkable institution of higher education; but, in 1987, the 'vibes' were not too good where collegiality and common purpose were concerned. Because, to some extent, the place had lost its way.

The first and foremost of the new, so-called 'plate glass', universities of the early 1960s, endowed with a splendid new campus designed for it by Basil Spence, headed by the charismatic figures of first Lord Fulton, and then of Lord Briggs, designing a 'new map of learning' developed by bright young academics fleeing the stultifying conservatism of Oxford (Sussex in the sixties was known as 'Balliol by the Sea'), and enjoying the ample state funding of yesteryear, life for the much envied and eulogized University of Sussex had flowed along like a song.

But then, times began to change. The bright young things grew old; some of the best of them moved on; other new universities – rivals, as well as copies, of Sussex – sprang up like mushrooms; the Treasury started to turn the funding taps and demand economies and newfangled efficiencies. Things began to slide downhill. Yet there persisted, in a few areas on campus, traces of a collectivist instinct worthy of a Stalinist tank factory; a deep mistrust of the capitalist model, and of all Conservative governments, where education was concerned. The 'avatars of the status quo', as I later called them, joined the Marxists and Anarchists in the refrain 'we've been robbed'. They called for a return to what they saw as their former freedoms, in the form of feed-on-demand public funding, without public accountability. The necessity to make changes in order to survive in a changed, less clement environment was not readily accepted in some quarters. So, by the early to mid-1980s, running the place, for my immediate predecessor, must have been like wading through a sea of treacle; any notion of top-down reform, anathema.

Time, therefore, for an outsider and a new broom. Time for Fielding. Time, even, for 'kick-ass' – although I did not fully realise it, on first appointment.

I gave it my best shot; located and empowered, within the university, well-disposed academics willing to help secure a change of course; called in top class people from outside, where necessary, to advise; mobilised the excellent but under-used and even partly ostracised corps of administrators; introduced new concepts and mechanisms of governance (delegating authority where it was safe to do so, but never without accountability and oversight); turned the finances round; recruited extra lecturers for an enlarged student body and an expanded research programme; founded two new postgraduate institutes (medical research and contemporary European studies) and erected various new buildings – mostly good quality student accommodation on campus; developed cooperation with the (in part, very good) local Polytechnic; explored academic synergies with other universities in the South East.

Just for the fun of it, I gave honorary Doctorates to, among many other national heroes and celebrities, my friend Terry Waite; my former Ambassadress Mary Soames, the Sussex alumnus Thabo M'Beki, later President of South Africa (but maybe Sussex should keep quiet about the latter!) and the splendid Soviet dissident academician Andrei Sakharov. I also attended - and where necessary and unavoidable, even spoke at - the regular national meetings of the 'Committee of Vice-Chancellors and Principals' – invariably well chaired by competent and shrewd leaders; but, collectively, an underwhelming, institution. Its membership fell into three categories of roughly equal size: those who would probably have been almost equally successful in another career; those who made one wonder why they had been appointed vice-chancellors at all; and finally those who were essentially preparatory school headmasters. My ambition, naturally, was to escape from the second category, to join the third!

Having got almost everything sorted, in just under four years – albeit with indispensable back-up from the late Tony

Trafford, an innovatory, national-rank, medical consultant and Tory politician, who chaired the mostly lay University Council; and with the affectionate patrician support of the philanthropic Charles March, later Duke of Richmond, our Chancellor – I surprised myself and left the University after five years, despite having been cordially invited to stay a full ten-year course.

Why? I now regret my decision – I should have seen everything through to its ultimate end, to ensure no unravelling; and led the institution upward and onward. Building on our strong school of biological science and the new medical research institute, I should have liked to have set up a full-blown medical school, in concert with the major hospitals in the area (something that my successors in office eventually managed to pull off). And I had other agendas, among them more quality time on fund-raising. Also, now that my face fitted there, a higher profile nationally, on the dreaded Vice-Chancellors' Committee.

But, there were family reasons. The children needed different schools, in other parts of England. As her health was not of the strongest, my wife wanted to return home to Shropshire, while she could still enjoy life in the dark-panelled manor house which had been her parents home. I really had done all I had been first called upon to do. And I had become just a tiny bit bored. To quell my doubts, I reasoned that it was time to pick up the priesthood thing again – if only as a rural lay reader in the diocese of Hereford. To say nothing of getting in some good shooting – not an activity either possible or desirable, at Sussex.

So it was a case of home is the sailor, home from the sea and the hunter home from the hill. My wife and I kissed everyone goodbye and left Swanborough Manor forever. It was nevertheless Hilaire Belloc who wrote:

'When I am working in the Midlands
That are sodden and unkind ......
The great hills of the South Country
Come back into my mind'.

Whatever may be true of the Midlands, the Marches, at least, are mostly not sodden, and only rarely unkind. But I confess that the South Country does come back to mind; and I do go back regularly to the University of Sussex. Although neither yet a rich man nor one grown old, I bear in mind Belloc's memorable conclusion:

'If I ever become a rich man,
Or if ever I grow to be old,
I will build a house with deep thatch
To shelter me from the cold,
And there shall the Sussex songs be sung
And the story of Sussex told.
I will hold my house in the high wood
Within a walk of the sea,
And the men that were boys when I was a boy
Shall sit and drink with me'.

48

ENVOY: SWORD PLAY IN SHERINGHAM

Goodbyes are difficult. It is hard not to feel a lump in the throat. Because, as John Donne famously put it, each one of us is 'involved in Mankind'.

Even the Passing Out Parade at Mons Officer Cadet School, in Aldershot, on 24 April 1952, was quite a wrench. Of course, one wanted to be commissioned and to move on to regimental duties as a subaltern. But Mons had been my home for a tough and intensive four months, and I had made friends there. A particularly weepy-wunnerful moment was registered as follows, in the 'Detail of Parade', which I still have in my possession:

> 'The Passing Out Troops [of Officer Cadets from artillery, cavalry and tank regiments] march off in Slow Time to the tune of 'Auld Lang Syne' [Band of the 14/20th Hussars] while the remainder present arms.'

The Adjutant (Captain N. Webb-Bowen, Welsh Guards) rode his white horse after us, up the steps and away.

Death, in its way, can be easier, because of its physical finality. Ernest Hemingway conveys this, in 'For Whom The Bell Tolls'. His Robert Jordan, who is immobilised by injury, and who has no hope of surviving as his enemies approach, says splendidly to Maria:

> 'Thou wilt go now, rabbit. But I go with thee. As long as there is one of us, there is both of us. Do you understand? What I do now, I do alone… If thou

> goest, then I go, too. Do you not see how it is? Whichever one there is, is both'.

It can be worse when life continues, and normality returns – when a man finds himself sundered from the one he loves. I think of Anthony Hope's 'The Prisoner of Zenda', when Rudolf Rassendyll, the English hero, takes his departure from Ruritania and Queen Flavia. Rudolf is seen off at the station by his comrades-in-arms, Colonel Sapt and Fritz von Tarlenheim.

> 'I [Rudolf] stood with my two friends, and waited till the train came up to us. Then we shook hands again, saying nothing; and both this time – and, indeed, from old Sapt it seemed strange – bared their heads, and so stood still till the train bore me away from their sight'.

More moving yet, Christopher Robin's farewell to his Bear, at the conclusion of A.A. Milne's 'The House At Pooh Corner'. Christopher is growing up, and must leave children's things behind.

> 'Still with his eyes on the world, Christopher Robin put out a hand and felt for Pooh's paw.
> "Pooh", said Christopher Robin, earnestly, "if I – if I'm not quite –" . He stopped and tried again – "Pooh, whatever happens, you will understand, won't you?"

And so it was, when I came to the very end of my farewell speech to the University Court at Sussex, I could not quite finish the words of Hilaire Belloc, about 'the men who were boys when I was a boy'. But then, I'm neither Robert Jordan, nor Rudolf Rassendyll, nor even Christopher Robin. At times, I am only an apprehensive small bear who has lost his way. I suspect this is probably true of most of us, if we are honest. (Indeed, at the heart of even the most 'macho' alpha-male, there can lie, curled up tightly, what Robert Burns once famously addressed as a "wee, sleekit, cow'rin, tim'rous beastie").

But no more tears. I will end with a different Adieu, of an undignified and discreditable character.

It took place at my final summer firing camp, in Norfolk, with a Territorial Army artillery regiment that was about to be axed. The regular Adjutant wanted to spend more time with the guns and the gunnery, and less in the office; so they made me (who had forgotten much of the technicalities of my TA trade while reading medieval history at Cambridge) Acting Adjutant. As well as manning the telephones in the regimental office behind the lines, I decided to swot up on my sword drill. We always had one around gathering dust somewhere, of correct regimental pattern. But it was rarely if ever seen on parade. I intended to change that, and leave with a flourish. I summoned up memories of Webb-Bowen, the aforesaid Adjutant at Aldershot in 1952.

At the final review and march-past, the regiment was drawn up in three ranks, line abreast on the grass field assigned to the parade. Wearing my best barathea service dress, a leather scabbard clipped to my highly polished Sam Browne belt, I marched up, in front of 500 men, and came to a halt in the centre, stamping my feet smartly, in the manner enjoined by Company Sergeant-Major Bennett MM (chapter 35). I then called the regiment to attention and saluted, sweeping the glittering sword up and then down, elegantly and slowly, in the approved style.

For some reason, I slightly lost control and sliced up a molehill just in front of me, in a puff of dust. There were audible intakes of breath and one suppressed guffaw from the Territorials immediately behind me. But the inspecting Brigadier was glaring angrily at a low-flying aircraft at that moment; while our Colonel – an industrial tycoon when not playing at soldiers – wore pebbly glasses anyway and was very short-sighted. As for the other officers in the regiment, they were staring rigidly ahead, in front of their own troops and batteries. 'Fine bearing on parade, Fielding. Jolly good show!' the Commanding Officer said to me, in the officers mess, afterwards. None of the other officers said anything.

Cor, Blimey. At the end of the, like, day - better be born lucky than rich, Guv. Innit? Whatever! Say no more - nudge, nudge, wink, wink. Take care. Mud in your eye. Down the hatch. Toodle-oo; Cheerio; Goodbyee!

APPENDICES

BACKGROUND READING

Despite episodic weedings, there remain four thousand or so books on my shelves at home, of which over half are devoted to politics and international affairs. To assist the general reader (rather than professionals and academic experts), I have arbitrarily picked out just a few, for those who might be interested, as background reading to the diplomatic incidents and encounters described in this volume.

The Governance of Britain Today

Dennis Kavanagh and Anthony Seldon: *The Powers Behind the Prime Minister*, 1999
Onora O'Neill: *A Question of Trust*, 2002
Nicholas Faith: *A Very Different Country*, 2003
David Marquand: *Decline of the Public*, 2004
W.G. Runciman (Ed.): *Hutton and Butler: Lifting the Lid on the Workings of Power*, 2004
Philip Stephens: *Tony Blair*, 2004
Christopher Foster: *British Government in Crisis*, 2005
Peter Oborne: *The Triumph of the Political Class*, 2007
Anthony Seldon: *Blair's Britain 1997-2007*, 2007

Intelligence and Security

Christopher M. Andrew: *Secret Service*, 1985
Stella Rimington: *Open Secret*, 2001
Percy Cradock: *Know Your Enemy: How the Joint Intelligence Committee Saw the World*, 2002

Iran

William Shawcross: *The Shah's Last Ride*, 1989

Christopher de Bellaigue: *In the Rose Garden of the Martyrs*, 2004
Vesta Sarkhosh Curtis and Sheila Canby: *The British Museum Persian Love Poetry*, 2005

Cambodia
William Shawcross: *Sideshow*, 1979
Leslie Fielding: *Before the Killing Fields: Witness to Cambodia and the Vietnam War*, 2008
Milton Osborne: *Phnom Penh*, 2008

China
Sir Percy Cradock: *Experiences of China*, 1994
Jung Chang and Jon Halliday: *Mao*, 2005
George Walden: *China: A Wolf in the World?*, 2008

France
J.R. Tournoux: *La Tragédie du Général*, 1967
Pierre Rouanet: *Pompidou*, 1969
Jean Lacouture: *De Gaulle: Le Souverain*, 1986

UK/US Relationship
John Dickie: *Special No More*, 1994
Christopher Meyer: *DC Confidential*, 2005
Chris Patten: *Cousins and Strangers*, 2005

Japan
Herman Kahn and Thomas Pepper: *The Japanese Challenge*, 1979
Ezra F Vogel: *Japan as Number One*, 1979
Hugh Cortazzi: *The Japanese Achievement*, 1990

European Commission
Roy Jenkins: *European Diary, 1977-1981,* 1989
Charles Grant: *Delors*, 1994
Sir Christopher Audland: *Right Place, Right Time*, 2004

Britain and Europe
Sir Percy Cradock: *In Pursuit of British Interests*, 1997

Background Reading

Hugo Young: *This Blessed Plot*, 1998
Sir Roy Denman: *The Mandarin's Tale*, 2002
Stephen Wall: *A Stranger in Europe*, 2008

Diplomatic Life
Donald Maitland: *Diverse Times, Sundry Places*, 1996; *The Running Tide*, 2000
Rodric Braithwaite: *Across the Moscow River*, 2002
Chris Patten: *Not Quite the Diplomat*, 2005
Brigid Keenan: *Diplomatic Baggage*, 2005
John Leahy: *A Life of Spice*, 2006
Rory Stewart: *Occupational Hazards*, 2006
Hilary Synnott: *Bad Days in Basra*, 2008

The Way the World is Now...
Robert Cooper: *The Breaking of Nations*, 2003
Martin Rees: *Our Final Century*, 2003
Sir Nicholas Stern: *The Economics of Climate Change*, 2007
Philip Bobbitt: *Terror and Consent*, 2008
David Hannay: *The New World Disorder: The UN after the Cold War*, 2008

...And the Way the Foreign Office is Today
David Owen writes about the 'ever-growing dominance of No. 10', in his contribution to *British Diplomacy: Foreign Secretaries Reflect*, 2007. I have given my own view, in the Epilogue to 'Before the Killing Fields'. Significantly, chapter 7 of Peter Oborne's *The Triumph of the Political Class* (see above) is entitled *The Fall of the Foreign Office and the Rise of MI6*. On the latter, it is noticeable that a senior diplomat no longer chairs the Joint Intelligence Committee, as of right. On the former, a senior former colleague has commented privately to me as follows: 'Alas, it's not just a matter of retirees complaining that things aren't what they were. There has been a significant decline in available resources while, at the same time, activity in 'services' such as consular and immigration work has increased enormously, as have the burdens of accountability and Freedom of Information. This has taken its toll on political analysis and expertise'. Perhaps

Mr David Cameron will redress the balance and restore morale? If Bobbitt, Cooper and Hannay are halfway right, there is no time to lose.

THREE DOCUMENTS FROM INSIDE 'EUROPE'

A: THE COMMISSION EXCORIATED

During my *first months* in 'Brassholes', I was appalled – and homesick for the FO and the Diplomatic Service. *Later*, I came to realise that I had been wrong, at least as far as External Relations and 'The Big Red One' (DGI) were concerned; and that I had a steep learning curve ahead of me. But *then*, I was still a square British peg in a Continental round hole.

A senior ex-FCO colleague in the Commission (Sir Christopher Audland, then the Assistant Secretary General) was collating and analysing our first impressions, now that we were insiders. So I took up my pen, dipped it in acid, and wrote as follows, on a 'UK-Eyes-Only' basis. It was 29 May 1973, two months into the job.

'First Impressions of the European Commission

Following our recent discussion, you asked me to set down on paper my initial impressions of the way the Commission works, with particular reference to what is wrong and might be put right. I have not fully got my measure of the Commission's operations and what follows is tentative and incomplete.

General

In general, I have found the Commission a good deal less impressive, seen from the inside, than when observed distantly over the last ten years from the outside. Its good external reputation has perhaps been built upon its pivotal position and the dedication and brilliance of individual operators. Its weakness seems to me to be lack of coordination and teamwork, inefficient working methods (including a poor archival system), and an uneven personnel.

Coordination and Teamwork

Lateral communication between Directorates-General does not seem to be frequent enough or easy enough to arrange. The traditional alternatives are either written communications between Directors General; or haphazard, 'old boy net', contact between friends and co-nationals. In my own sphere, there seems to be a wall of silence between DG I (external relations) and DG VI (agriculture). A certain mutual independence also seems the usual form between Directorates in a single Directorate-General. The classical bureaucratic operation is vertical and frequently takes the form of the personal 'quick trick' or the 'bounce'.

I should like to expound on the 'quick trick', which illustrates pretty well everything that I think is inadequate about the working methods of the Commission. A gifted individual seizes a major question in which he is interested and which falls to some degree within his technical responsibilities. With the possible aid of juniors and friends, he assembles all the information available, absorbs it, hits upon a line of action and then puts it straight up. He does not consult other interested Directorates or DGs. He may even find some pretext for skipping a link in his own hierarchy (e.g. cutting out his Director-General; addressing himself direct to his Commissioner's cabinet, etc.). Other officials with contributions to make or competences to defend who have not been consulted learn about it too late to do anything; or, if alerted soon enough, put up their own vertical comments. Everything then lands on the lap of the Commissioners. If the 'quick trick' is really quick enough and tricky enough, it tends to come off, even if the weight of global argument, or the thrust of existing policies, go against it. The 'bounce' is the large-scale version of the 'quick trick' – one DG will launch a proposal at the Commission at short notice and without prior consultation with other DGs.

Inefficient Working Methods

The system of handling papers is, I suspect, in need of reform. Written procedures are rigid and formal. Questions which could well be dealt with at Head of Division level are far too often submitted for signature and approval to Directors-General. (The latter's desks are consequently often too cluttered up). There is inadequate use of the draft: papers are put up, in fact, in final form. This inevitably discourages drafting changes and tends to be incompatible with lateral consultation.

The archival system is, by Whitehall standards, grossly inadequate. In essence, working papers tend to be kept together by individual officials, who often regard these papers as their personal property and guard them jealously from the eyes of rivals and dissidents. A central registry seems to exist in a given Directorate-General, but not to have much of an operational role. I suspect the contents of most of these registries are slim. Thus there is no single comprehensive and accessible official file on a given question; if you want to brief yourself, you have to make do with inherited bits and pieces and such other documentation as can be secured by personal entreaty.

Personnel

This is the thorniest long-term problem and is, I suspect, standard form in most international organisations. Commission officials seem to me to be essentially a collection of individuals rather than members of a real service. There is much idealism; but no unifying bureaucratic tradition. The quality of officials varies much more widely than in Whitehall. Personal rivalries and the general attitude of suspicion towards colleagues seem to me, as a newcomer, to be more marked than in any other working context I have known. The efforts of the individual to shine *coûte que coûte* are sometimes pathetically noticeable. The situation is not eased by the fact that promotion is slow and sometimes has to be rigged to permit the maintenance of overall balance between nationalities. To make matters worse, it is apparently difficult to re-train, warn, discipline, move or pension off officials whose performance is inadequate. The confidential report system does not work – everyone seems to get a good chit, irrespective of his performance.

Some Suggestions

There is little to be done about personnel since, even if personnel policies are improved (which I do not doubt they will be), we shall still be left with the fact that a coherent European Civil Service will take decades to build up. In the meantime, it can only be an uneasy amalgam of national tradition. (I sometimes think that the present Commission embodies the worst practices of the six founding Member States of the EC).

Some effort could, however, usefully be made to improve working methods. Possibilities are: ……. (etc, etc, etc).

B: THE COMMISSION EXHORTED

An early difficulty encountered in Brussels in 1973 was over the drafting of papers. My continental subordinates were brilliant at crafting legal documents, regulations, formal decisions for submission to the Council of Ministers. They could also write learned, technical analyses of issues and problems. And they could conduct international negotiations like crazy, all day and all night. But they did not habitually write anything which could be easily grasped by Top People – for example, for information or decision by their Commissioners (the equivalent of Ministers in Whitehall). They seemed to expect Commissioners' cabinets (private offices) to do the necessary assimilation and explaining – which either imposed a strain on the cabinet, or alternatively gave it too much discretion and power of decision.

I found that this did not in practice affect institutional efficiency – the Commission simply worked on different lines from the FO. But I did, at the outset, complain; and attempted some reform. This is what, in June 1973, I gave my staff – who were either bemused or suspicious. They then carried on much as before.

'Preparation of Documents'

> The following are some reflections on the preparation of high-level documents in my Directorate. I have no rigid requirements: every case can be treated on its merits. But the ideal is worth stating.
>
> (a) Briefs for Vice-President Sir Christopher Soames in preparation for visitors

A brief of this kind should normally be divided into:

(i) Talking Points
(ii) Background.

At (i), we should try to set out, succinctly, a handful of points for Sir Christopher to make, expressed in language that Sir Christopher might be expected to use. If appropriate, these can be subdivided into 'Points to Make' (Sir Christopher to take the initiative) and 'Defensive points' (for Sir Christopher to use only if the interlocutor raises the matter). The golden rule in preparing such drafts, is: 'Put yourself mentally in Sir Christopher's place and put down what he should say at the meeting'.

At (ii), we should give the minimum necessary elaboration of the subject. Details can be relegated to annexes. The golden rule here is: 'Distinguish between what Sir Christopher needs, and does not need, to know'. He is usually busier than we are.

The Talking Points at (i) should never be longer than one side of paper. The Background at (ii) should, if humanly possible, also not exceed one side of paper.

(b) Formal Memoranda

When my Directorate submits a formal memorandum to a Director-General, or prepares a draft memorandum for a Director to submit to Sir Christopher Soames, it is often useful to adopt a lay-out like this:

(i) a very brief statement of the problem
(ii) background (preferably, but not necessarily, in an annex)
(iii) supporting argument

(iv) recommendations.

Naturally, this order can be re-arranged – e.g. the sequence (i) (iv) (iii) and (ii) is equally valid.

(c) Short Notes

Short explanatory notes for Sir Christopher's Cabinet, a Director General or myself can, of course, be entirely informal and do not need to be broken down in the systematic fashion suggested at (b). These are not 'high-level documents' in the sense intended in my introductory paragraph.

Please ensure that all your officials, however junior, understand the need to impose clarity and a sense of proportion upon their written work; and to avoid too much undigested and/or academic technicality. I repeat that there is no rigid presentational requirement and that all cases need to be treated on their merits.

Here are (fictitious) specimens of (a) and (b) above, by way of illustration.

Leslie Fielding
21 June, 1973

[Specimen (a): Brief for a Visitor]

Note for Vice-President John Brown

Subject: Visit of Bongolian Minister

Mr N'Mngö (pronounced 'Non'), the Bongolian Minister of Industry, Finance and Social Harmony, is to call on the Commission at 11pm on 31 December. This will be his first visit to Brussels. The following notes may be of use to the Commissioner.

Points to make

(a) We in the Commission have much welcomed the closer ties that Bongolia has developed with the Community over the past 2 years.
(b) Mr N'Mngö's visit is particularly timely in relation to the present phase in the Haïti Convention negotiation. Does he think that the Bongolian Tribal Council will soon ratify the agreement reached ad referendum last month? We are sorry to hear that Mr O'wy (pronounced 'Oui'), is unwell.
(c) Assuming ratification of the Agreement, the practical application of the Community's proposed new levy system to Bongolian bone-meal exports may give rise to technical difficulties: but the essential thing is to give the Agreement a trial run for at least a year.

Defensive Points

(d) The Commission's heavy programme still makes it difficult to fix an exact date for our President's visit to Bongolia-ville. We are sorry to have to say no to Mr N'Mngö.
(e) We hope to make early proposals to Bongolia on the gold discount rate for the floating Bong. Like

Bongolia, the Community is determined to respect the snake, if at all possible.

<u>Background</u>

(i) The rate for the Bong is wrong. The Bongolian currency is still well outside the internal snake. But it is now at least inside the external snake (last week 1 Bong = 0,003 EUC: see statistics at Annex A for more details). This is a step in the right direction, which we must welcome.

(ii) There has been a drop this year in the quality of Bongolian crushed bone-meal; the existing variable levy has therefore been adjusted downward by 2 EUC. This is a technical problem in which the Commissioner need not involve himself.

(iii) The outbreak of cannibalism in the outer islands last year, and the recent disappearance without trace of two A 6 officials on leave in Bongolia-ville (there may be a link here with (ii) above), rule out a visit from the Commission President for the time being.

(iv) The members of the Bongolian Tribal Council were released from house-arrest last week; no date has, however, been fixed for their next official meeting, and their Chairman, Mr O'Wy, (the President of the People's Bank) is reported to have snake-bite. This could imperil the new agreement and we must re-act appropriately.

(v) The text of the EEC/Bongolia agreement under the Haïti Convention, still ad referendum, is at Annex B. (Paragraph XCIV 13 (a) (ii) – (xi) covers the new levy arrangements).

Giuseppe Verdi; Director-General

[Specimen (b): Memorandum]

Submission to the Director-General

Subject: Ruritanian Decorations

The Problem

We must decide whether to recommend to the Commission that Mr Dupont may accept a Decoration from the Emperor of Ruritania.

Background

1. Mr Dupont, formerly of DG LXIX, was the principal negotiator of the agreement on Rhinoceros Horn Products concluded with Ruritania last June. We have heard privately from the Ruritanian Chargé d'Affaires that the Emperor would like, in recognition of this agreement, to confer on Mr Dupont the Order of Chastity Fourth Class, with Clasp. Before doing so, however, His Imperial Majesty (H.I.M.) would wish to know whether the European Commission might see objection.
2. Bestowal of decorations in these circumstances is a well-established practice, and there is no known instance of the Commission having withheld permission. (See historical annex.)
3. The Rhinoceros Horn Products Agreement is, however, unpopular in some sectors of Community public opinion, led notably by the Wildlife Protection lobby in Uccle and the Anti-Aphrodisiac League in Naples. A hostile demonstration following the signature of the Agreement resulted in damage to the Berlaymont building; a counter-demonstration in the Ruritanian capital ended in an orgy in front of the Community's local office.

4. Mr Dupont is moreover now Secretary General of the Commission's Family Planning Programme.

Argument

1. To refuse permission would give great offence to H.I.M. personally (he is Grand Chancellor of the Order of Chastity, jointly with his seventh concubine). This could adversely affect the Community's agricultural trade with Ruritania, the quotas for which are determined by the Imperial Concubines' Committee on Swaps (see statistical annex: one Rhinoceros Horn at present equals 100 long tons of butter-oil).
2. To grant permission would be to diminish Mr Dupont's personal credibility in the forthcoming worldwide 'Gild the pill' negotiations in Tahiti. If the decoration were conferred before the European Parliament adjourned for the summer recess on 2 February, the Commission would be exposed to severe criticism in the Chamber.
3. The balance of advantage accordingly lies in giving permission; but in such a way as to minimise embarrassment in Brussels.

Recommendation

It is therefore recommended that:

(a) Our Representative in Ruritania should explore with H.I.M. the possibility of raising the rank of the decoration from Fourth Class with clasp to First Class with fig leaf (to meet the 'Gild the Pill' requirement, and to appease the Anti-Aphrodisiac League);

(b) The ceremony should take place after 2 February, privately and away from Brussels (the Commission's Paris Office, Rue Chabanais, has appropriate facilities);

If (a) and (b) are agreed in principle, the Commission should be advised to give their formal assent to the award.

H. Schmidt
(Director of Protocol)

C: THE COMMISSION EXTOLLED

In July 1987, in my fifteenth year with the Eurocracy, I was preparing to say goodbye. They had been good years, with great people, on gutsy international business. And I had had to eat my own hat, in revoking my own initial criticism of how the Commission worked.

For my last five years, in charge of the EC's external relations across the board, I had taken a leaf from the book of the then current practice of the Permanent Under-Secretary in the FCO in London, by writing a monthly personal letter to the Heads of the Commission's 'Delegations' or diplomatic missions around the world, to tell them what had really been going on, back at headquarters. I sent copies to my four Deputies and ten Directors (the DUSs and AUSs, in the old Whitehall terminology – today's Whitehall 'Director-General' is the equivalent of only a Deputy Director-General in the Commission); but the letters were, as a point of principle, not shown to Commissioners. These were the private thoughts of a professional, for fellow professionals. The first draft, each month, was done by my Private Secretary (Eric Hayes, a bright Magdalen man), after oral discussion between us. The final version was, however, very much me!

So, here are extracts from my last letter, signed off in July 1987:

> 'This is my final personal monthly letter as your Director-General, before I leave in 10 days' time for a different world, and for my third career, at the University of Sussex. So, I have given the letter a more general and reflective character, as befits a 'Valedictory'. When I arrived in the Commission at the beginning of 1973, on UK entry, I brought with me 17 years of professional experience in the UK

Diplomatic Service. But, on arrival in the Berlaymont, I knew by definition almost nothing about in-house EC matters; and not a great deal about economics. (My student days had been spent, in the then not un-typical English way, studying
medieval and ancient history; and scrutinising the Persian mystic poets in the original tongue.) To be truthful, I later completed a correspondence course in economics; spent three months at a business school in France; and was put through a gruelling four-month course by the Treasury just before coming to Brussels. But all that gave me no more than the ability to conduct a conversation with a real economist! Thus, I was initially the victim of what I believe is called 'culture shock'. So my early apprenticeship years here were a vivid learning experience; just as my more operational, subsequent, years were never to know a dull moment.

Personal Retrospect on Five years as Director-General

Looking back over the past five years, one tends to think first of the frequent tough times.

There has been the steady run of 'close shaves' and 'macho' confrontations in EC/US relations, beginning with steel and the gas pipeline problem in the autumn of 1982 and extending through citrus and EU enlargement to the as yet finally unresolved pasta dispute. I still marvel at the time and energy that EC/US's relations have consumed, at the expense of other things. Perpetual crisis management can be a drag, even if one is as personally committed as I am to good Transatlantic relations. Then, too, there has been the endless struggle with Japan over burden-sharing and reciprocal market access. And I recall the UNCTAD VI nightmare in Belgrade in June 1983 – chaotic, confusing and shot through with North-South mistrust. I will not forget, either, the great GATT battles, from that of the bitter and uncreative Ministerial of 1982 (thoroughly messed up by the Americans and by certain Third World rhetoricians and ideologists; but enlivened by the Quixoticism of M. Jobert; and dignified by a remarkable farewell feat of arms by Sir Roy Denman in the thick of the Geneva fray) to the final victory of commonsense, and Community diplomacy, at the Punta del Este Ministerial last autumn. Let me not fail also to mention the struggle to get from the Council and the Parliament additional resources, more political initiative and imagination, with which to develop the Community's relations with others than the super powers – for instance with Turkey, Yugoslavia and India, and with neglected partners in Latin America and the Gulf; or to do something concrete for the refugees in their camps in Palestine and on the Thai/Cambodian frontier, or for the victims of natural catastrophes whenever the need arose.

But there have been easier times also. To cite a few examples among the many, our relations with ASEAN continue to run quite smoothly. So too have our relations with the EFTAs, collectively our biggest trade partners, and on the whole a very agreeable and like-minded set of people. Our ties with China have developed successfully, to the point that a Delegation of the Commission will be opening in Beijing in December. Closer home, the Community role in the OECD and at Western Economic Summits (at both of which, in the Executive Committee in Special Services and among the Sherpas, I myself have been regularly the EC mouthpiece on matters of Community Competence) is now, in its different and more modest way, as fully accepted as our active negotiating role in the GATT.

In both good times and bad, while ranging the world scene far and wide, the Director-General has always had to have an eye to his base camp and an ear for noises off. Confident and cordial relations with

Member States are naturally essential. Their officials and diplomats are our colleagues – and often also our personal friends; while I have sometimes had to goad and to argue, it has never been my practice to treat them as if they were representatives of some foreign power. Then developments on the home front, within the Community, were and remain of vital indirect importance for the conduct of the Community's external relations. The failure of Summit after Summit to get to grips with budgetary burden-sharing and with agricultural reform were to cast a pall over external relations fully as palpable as e.g. such obvious spasms and contortions as the illegal French import levies on Japanese videotape recorders, in the autumn of 1982; or as the dither and indecision about commercial defence and the 'New Instrument'; or as the row over the Greek Balance of Payments crisis in 1983. The doldrums and drawn-out agonies of the negotiations for Spanish and Portuguese entry cast their own shadow over the 1980s. On the other hand, the renewed EC economic vigour and intra-Community dynamism of present times – the settlement of old quarrels and the move to the 'European Single Market' of 1992 – are reinvigorating our approach to external issues.

For sheer purgatory, I would cite the burden of laborious and frequently pettifogging personnel and administration work which falls to every head of a large department in Berlaymont. This is still in my view the weak spot of the Commission...

But 'begone dull care'! For sheer fun, I look back upon the glamour of President Thorn's official visit to Delhi, with a supporting cast of Bengal Lancers; upon colonial Williamsburg, with assorted G7 Heads of State and Government; upon the Tiananmen, during the 35th Anniversary celebration of the People's Republic, occupied by two million Chinese servicemen, dancers, firework artificers and simple citizens; upon Ayers Rock in the sweltering central Australian desert, with the local aborigines...

A Source of Satisfaction: The New Round Initiative

One particular source of personal satisfaction for me has been – quite unexpectedly – the GATT (of which I confess that I had had only limited operational experience, before becoming Director-General). I am thinking in particular of the protracted process of leading the Community from agnosticism to active commitment, in the matter of a New Round of trade liberalisation, The GATT team and I had to establish credibility and create momentum by committing the Community, in successive meetings of the CG18, [the restricted informal consultations group in Geneva] to some form of roll-back (we succeeded, with QR packages and tariff accelerations). We had to lay out for our Member States in the 113 Committee [the senior body of trade policy officials from Member State Capitals, which 'advises' the Commission on the conduct of the EU's 'Common Commercial Policy', meeting in Brussels] the analytical basis for a New Round – in the famous five 'Alpha-Epsilon Non-Papers'. These last were an intellectual pleasure to write; but we had to stick our necks out in writing them. And we had to fight off continued efforts by the US and others to force the Community to run before it could walk (including having to frustrate Ronald Reagan and his sympathisers at the London Western Economic Summit). It fell to Vice-President Willy De Clerq and to me to steer respectively the Council and the 113, in a marathon session on 12 March 1985, through at times heated discussions, to a carefully qualified but meaningful commitment of principle. That was then only the beginning. Next came, on the one side, our infinite labours to rally doubtful or hostile developing countries (with my team and I quartering the Third

World); and, on the other side, our constant effort to dissuade the US from too extreme and intolerant a GATT crusade for the New Round. In one damned Quadrilateral after another [an informal grouping of the European Commission, the US, Canada and Japan, to consult on economic issues] we hammered home our message – I think especially of the Sintra Quadrilateral last September, where the US became quite *intraitable*, denouncing us for laying the foundation of a workman-like bargain on services with the Third World very close to that which Clayton Yeutter was himself to grasp thankfully a few days later at Punta del Este. All that finally paid off, in the triumph of constructive compromise at Punta del Este, with the Community playing the pivotal North/South role upon which success or failure depended.

I look back on the whole process with pride; because what we did served not only our enlightened self-interest as Europeans, but also the wider interests of an expanding world economy, and with it the deeper needs of the developing countries. It still seems to me probable that, if the Community had never come into being, and Europe's wisdom and weight in Geneva were still divided amount twelve purely national delegations, the GATT would have collapsed for lack of centripetence and cement, and protectionism would be running amok throughout the world.

Towards A European Foreign Service?

I will mention one other personal satisfaction, the origin of which goes back, however, some dozen years. I refer to the steady growth of professionalism in our external, diplomatic Delegations. It does, indeed, take time to acquire expertise and to create a tradition. When I first started work in the Berlaymont, one of the responsibilities of my Directorate –

specially given me by Christopher Soames and my then Director-General, Edmond Wellenstein – was policy governing external offices. There were then in fact few such offices, and there was almost no policy… overseas posts were not fully in the Brussels picture... coordination between press and information people seconded from DG X and diplomats sent out from DG I was defective… traditional diplomatic procedures rarely observed...

Looking back, it is clear that the external representation of the Community has come a long way since the first enlargement, not only quantitatively but also qualitatively. We now unquestionably have the makings of a professional foreign service for Community matters, and one in which my two Commissioners can justly take growing satisfaction.

The Future

Over the next five years, much can be expected to stay the same: continued crisis-management requirements with the US; continued pressure and persuasion to get Japan to open up and behave responsibly; continued hard-grinding negotiations in the GATT (including the on-going saga of textiles, as well as New Round stuff); continued economic and commercial consolidation with EFTA and the Mediterranean partners; continued efforts to secure closer relations with the Gulf; continued endeavours to expand and improve our DGI overseas development assistance activities in the countries for which we have responsibility (already a budget of 700 million ECUs a year); continued expansion and professionalisation of our external diplomatic network; continued battles with the Council over budgets, in alliance with the European Parliament; and so forth and so on.

But there will be some new and potentially exciting external developments too: among them, the slow unfolding of a more substantive relationship with Latin America (itself a process initiated, before Spanish and Portuguese adhesion, by the Commission's paper to the General Affairs Council in August 1984); the steadily strengthening position of the Community in the UN; the cautious opening up of our relations with the Comecon countries; the start of an EC policy on debt; the development of new EC competences outside the straight commercial policy context (monetary, environmental, financial, etc) and their incorporation within, or harnessing to, a coherent EC external policy; the late but not for that the less sweet fruits of Political Cooperation in the form of some kind of genuine European foreign policy.

We shall have to take care for the further viability and development of the EC/US/Japan triangle. We will want to keep an eagle eye fixed on certain up and coming bilateral partners (China and Russia, of course; but also, India and Brazil, and also Korea). We will need to give special succour to the key multilateral institutions, especially the GATT, which is shifting like sand under our feet. (Will the US stop the bus and get off? What effect will China's re-entry have; and could the GATT survive Soviet membership, even of the Gorbachev type?)

And there will be two major factors that will affect decisively the framework within which we operate, over which DGI has no control at all. The first will be the continued growth (or the progressive collapse) of the world economy; the second, the degree of success (or failure) of the internal drive to the Great Market – with all that both imply for future Community strength and cohesion.

It adds up to quite a challenge for all of you, for my two Commissioners and for my still unannounced successor.

The Coldstream Guards of the Commission

DGI works. Indeed, a senior Director-General from the Council of Ministers recently described ours as *'la Direction Générale la plus prestigieuse de la Commission européenne'*. I am glad to have served with DGI for over 14 years in both Brussels and (after an eight-month sabbatical at Oxford) in Tokyo; and to have had the pleasure of heading the Directorate-General for the past 5 years. It is a professional body, not only at home, but increasingly overseas also; and presided over by two first-class political professionals in Vice-President Willy De Clercq and Commissioner Claude Cheysson. Our best, these days, is fully as good as what we usually meet among the Member States, who I think give us peer approval. So DGI has some claim to be *'Nulli Secundus'* in the Commission.

Last Words on Riding Off Into the Sunset

There is always liable to be something slightly ludicrous about last words or final gestures. Like the terminal utterances of Socrates or Rabelais or Goethe. Or as when, at the end of some Western movie, the lone cowboy swings into the saddle and rides off into the sunset – only to fall off, necessitating an expensive retake (it is said to have happened once, to a well-known actor). Nevertheless, I feel moved to write the following last words.

When I vault lightly into the saddle of my battered family Volvo, and zoom up the Rue de la Loi and out onto the Zeebrugge road at the end of this month, I shall wave a cheerful farewell to the formal minuets of the COREPER; and the rustic charms of the 113 Committee; and the challenge of non-stop jet-setting round the world; and the adrenalin of rough and tumble, all-night negotiating sessions; and the gastronomic delights of the Villa Lorraine; and the tinsel crown of petty privilege and empty acclaim. And I admit I can do without working steadily round the clock, year in year out, without seeing very much of my wife and children, or opening a book, or saying my prayers properly. But I shall miss and remember the men and women of the Directorate-General whom I have been lucky enough to know and serve with – past and present, the living and the departed. My best wishes for your future careers. My blessing on you and your families. Goodbye – and thank you.'

On that note, I handed over to my two (later, even three) successors – the Big Red One being judged too large and too important for a single Director-General to head up any longer.